Development of
of
Dyslexia and other SpLDs

'*Development of Dyslexia and other SpLDs* is an excellent read. From a personal perspective, it provided important context to my experience as someone with dyspraxia; I found it fascinating to learn about both the commonalities and variability associated with SpLD. Stacey and Fowler's work is thorough and well evidenced, yet they manage to maintain a remarkable levity in their writing. Some of the anecdotes had me laughing out loud! I would recommend this book to teachers, parents and anyone else who is interested in understanding SpLD.' – ***Archie F. A. Bott, DPhil in Atomic and Laser Physics, University of Oxford, and former SpLD student of Ginny Stacey***

Development of Dyslexia and other SpLDs is about the persistence of dyslexia and specific learning difficulties (SpLDs) into adulthood. It pulls together experiences of many dyslexic/ SpLD people.

The book is written with non-linear readers in mind: those who need to move about a book picking up ideas that are currently relevant to them; a style that suits many dyslexic/ SpLD readers.

The book gives a framework for understanding the wide-ranging experiences of dyslexic/ SpLD adults. With the greater understanding, there should be better help for:

- adults who still have no strategies for dealing with dyslexic/ SpLD problems
- children who have some skills but not at the level of their overall intelligence
- young children who show the first signs of difficulties
- dyslexic/ SpLD children in mainstream schools.

A new paradigm is proposed whereby all teaching programmes utilise each learner's learning strengths - catering for dyslexic and SpLD adults and children involves vital teaching and learning approaches that are good practice for all.

With the right teaching, 'at risk' children
can avoid many of the problems of dyslexia/ SpLD.

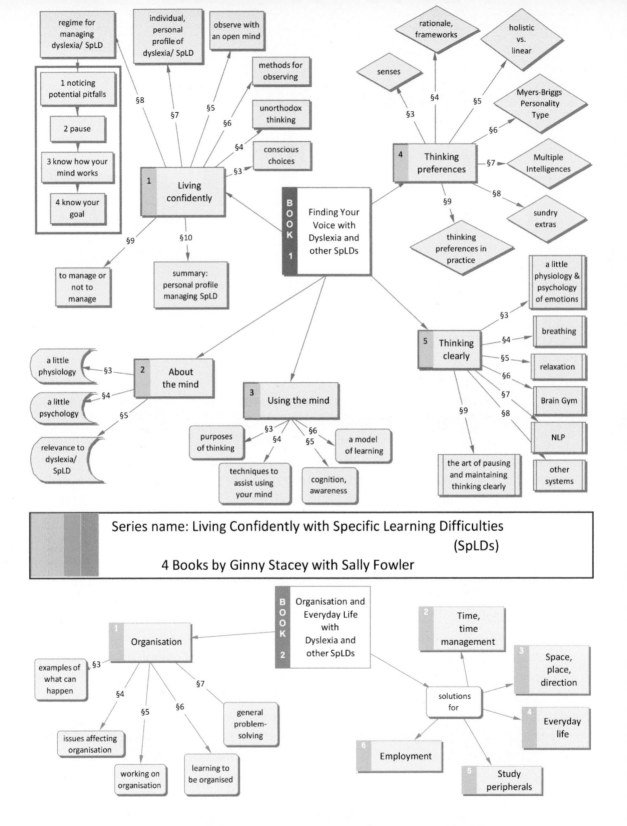

Book 1: Finding Your Voice with Dyslexia and other SpLDs

regime for managing dyslexia/ SpLD

individual, personal profile of dyslexia/ SpLD

observe with an open mind

1 noticing potential pitfalls

2 pause

3 know how your mind works

4 know your goal

methods for observing

unorthodox thinking

conscious choices

§8 §7 §5 §6 §4 §3

1 Living confidently

§9 §10

to manage or not to manage

summary: personal profile managing SpLD

B O O K 1 Finding Your Voice with Dyslexia and other SpLDs

rationale, frameworks

senses

holistic vs. linear

Myers-Briggs Personality Type

Multiple Intelligences

sundry extras

§3 §4 §5 §6 §7 §8 §9

4 Thinking preferences

thinking preferences in practice

a little physiology & psychology of emotions

breathing

relaxation

Brain Gym

NLP

other systems

§3 §4 §5 §6 §7 §8 §9

5 Thinking clearly

the art of pausing and maintaining thinking clearly

a little physiology

a little psychology

relevance to dyslexia/ SpLD

§3 §4 §5

2 About the mind

3 Using the mind

purposes of thinking

§3 §4 §6 §5

a model of learning

techniques to assist using your mind

cognition, awareness

Series name: Living Confidently with Specific Learning Difficulties (SpLDs)

4 Books by Ginny Stacey with Sally Fowler

Book 2: Organisation and Everyday Life with Dyslexia and other SpLDs

1 Organisation

examples of what can happen

§3 §4 §5 §6 §7

issues affecting organisation

working on organisation

learning to be organised

general problem-solving

B O O K 2 Organisation and Everyday Life with Dyslexia and other SpLDs

2 Time, time management

3 Space, place, direction

solutions for

4 Everyday life

6 Employment

5 Study peripherals

Different, larger maps of each book: Book 1: p 25; Book 2: p 27

Contents p xv   Where to start p viii

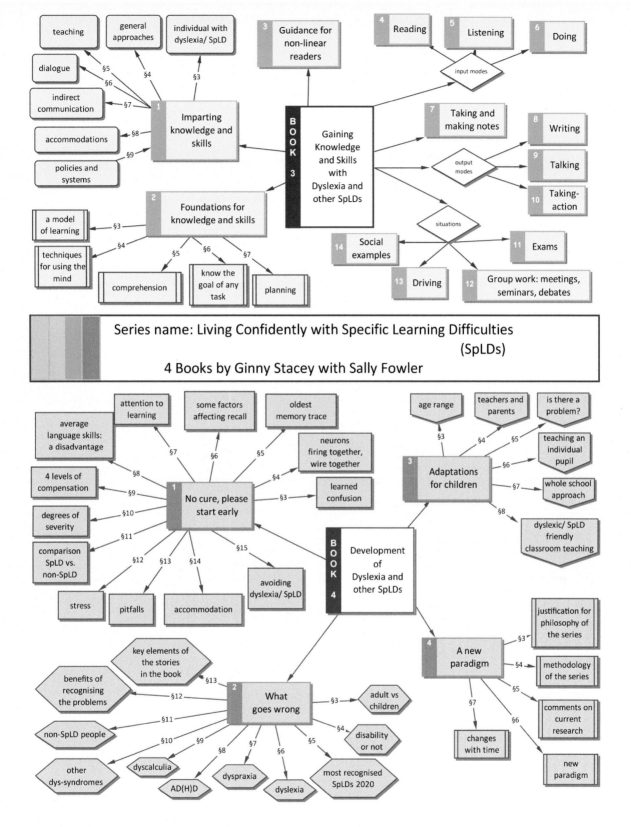

Series name: Living Confidently with Specific Learning Difficulties (SpLDs)

4 Books by Ginny Stacey with Sally Fowler

BOOK 3 — Gaining Knowledge and Skills with Dyslexia and other SpLDs

1. Imparting knowledge and skills
   - teaching §5
   - general approaches §4
   - individual with dyslexia/ SpLD §3
   - dialogue §6
   - indirect communication §7
   - accommodations §8
   - policies and systems §9
2. Foundations for knowledge and skills
   - a model of learning §3
   - techniques for using the mind §4
   - comprehension §5
   - know the goal of any task §6
   - planning §7
3. Guidance for non-linear readers
   - input modes: 4 Reading, 5 Listening, 6 Doing
   - output modes: 7 Taking and making notes, 8 Writing, 9 Talking, 10 Taking-action
   - situations: 14 Social examples, 11 Exams, 13 Driving, 12 Group work: meetings, seminars, debates

BOOK 4 — Development of Dyslexia and other SpLDs

1. No cure, please start early
   - attention to learning §7
   - some factors affecting recall §6
   - oldest memory trace §5
   - neurons firing together, wire together §4
   - learned confusion §3
   - average language skills: a disadvantage §8
   - 4 levels of compensation §9
   - degrees of severity §10
   - comparison SpLD vs. non-SpLD §11
   - stress §12
   - pitfalls §13
   - accommodation §14
   - avoiding dyslexia/ SpLD §15
2. What goes wrong
   - key elements of the stories in the book §13
   - benefits of recognising the problems §12
   - non-SpLD people §11
   - other dys-syndromes §10
   - dyscalculia §9
   - AD(H)D §8
   - dyspraxia §7
   - dyslexia §6
   - most recognised SpLDs 2020 §5
   - disability or not §4
   - adult vs children §3
3. Adaptations for children
   - age range §3
   - teachers and parents §4
   - is there a problem? §5
   - teaching an individual pupil §6
   - whole school approach §7
   - dyslexic/ SpLD friendly classroom teaching §8
4. A new paradigm
   - justification for philosophy of the series §3
   - methodology of the series §4
   - comments on current research §5
   - new paradigm §6
   - changes with time §7

Different, larger maps of each book: Book 3: p 29; Book 4: p 31

Contents p xv   Where to start p viii

First published 2020
by Routledge
2 Park Square, Milton Park, Abingdon, Oxon OX14 4RN

and by Routledge
52 Vanderbilt Avenue, New York, NY 10017

Routledge is an imprint of the Taylor & Francis Group, an informa business

British Library Cataloguing-in-Publication Data
A catalogue record for this book is available from the British Library

Library of Congress Cataloging-in-Publication Data
A catalog record has been requested for this book

ISBN: 978-1-138-20780-6 (hbk)
ISBN: 978-1-138-20781-3 (pbk)
ISBN: 978-1-315-46109-0 (ebk)

Typeset in Calibri
by Ginny Stacey

Publisher's Note
This book has been prepared from camera-ready copy provided by the author.

Visit the companion website www.routledge.com/cw/stacey

Development of Dyslexia and other SpLDs

The cover image represents changing:
'That's the way the cookie crumbles.'
into
'It's a piece of cake.'

Ginny Stacey
with Sally Fowler

Routledge
Taylor & Francis Group

LONDON AND NEW YORK

'This book is a treasure trove containing wisdom, based on personal experience of Stacey's many years work with people who have dyslexia and supported by relevant and current research. She acknowledges that people with dyslexia come in many varieties and she helps them and their tutors uncover the complexities of their learning systems through effective listening, questioning and suggestions of accommodations that might help. The layout of the book invites interaction and reflection to enhance learning and has excellent visuals to suit the dyslexic mind. A book to dip into, essential for tutors and people with dyslexia alike.' – *Bernadette McLean, Independent Dyslexia Consultant, Former Principal of Helen Arkell Dyslexia Centre*

'This is an insightful and accessible read filled with useful information and practical strategies to support individuals. It is supported by reference to research and evidence, along with reflections from the authors' own experiences, that come together to provide a very helpful resource. The contents have been broken down into key areas meaning this book can be dipped into for particular issues or used in its entirety. A useful publication for those with an interest in Dyslexia and SpLDs be they a parent, teacher or other support provider.' – *Helen Boden, CEO British Dyslexia Association*

'This book will be invaluable for assessors and teachers wishing to broaden and enhance their understanding of dyslexia and other Specific Learning Difficulties. Stacey and Fowler bring insights from their own and their students' individual experience of dyslexia/SpLD, together with research and theory, to examine the many different impacts and pitfalls of dyslexia. All of us who work in this field will benefit from Stacey's new paradigm for a positive, holistic approach to SpLDs.' – *Alex Brown, Specialist SpLD Support Tutor and Dyslexia Assessor, Member of Oxford SpLD Tutor Group*

Ginny Stacey did not realise she was dyslexic until her mid-20s. The challenge of learning to play classical guitar helped her to understand how her dyslexic mind works. Committed to helping other dyslexics achieve their potential, she developed a range of highly effective techniques for supporting dyslexic students in studying all subjects and coping with life in general. The techniques are widely used in universities and colleges. She has become a nationally-recognised expert in the field.

Sally Fowler stepped into the dyslexic world in her late 40s. It was a revelation to see the impacts of her dyslexia clearly. She became an approved teacher for the British Dyslexia Association with an M.A. in special education. She taught dyslexics, both children in schools and students at university. In Oxford, she met Ginny Stacey: the collaboration of two dyslexic minds has brought a wealth of experience to the *Living Confidently with Specific Learning Difficulties* series.

<u>Dedication</u>

Dear fellow dyslexics,

The laughter we've shared tells me I'm on the right lines with my understanding of dyslexia. So do:

- the tears some of you have shed as you tell me your story and you know I hear
- the courage you've shown as you reveal your vulnerable side
- the joy you've known as you find ways to take charge of your dyslexia and run with it, not against it.

I hope this book will help many others to find their way through the trials and tribulations of dyslexia/ SpLD so that they can come out the other side to enjoy some of the good parts of being dyslexic/ SpLD.

SpLD = Specific Learning Difficulty

dyslexia
dyspraxia
AD(H)D
dyscalculia

see Ⓖ p 301 for descriptions

Where to start:

- ## Linear readers, who like to read straight through:

In *USEFUL PREFACE*:

➤ Read *THIS BOOK: DEVELOPMENT OF DYSLEXIA AND OTHER SPLDS*.

➤ *THE SERIES: LIVING CONFIDENTLY WITH SPECIFIC LEARNING DIFFICULTIES (SPLDS)*, unless you have read another book of this series.

➤ Read sections marked with this book's icon.

Then read from Chapter 1.

- ## Non-linear readers, who prefer to move around a book:

A) Read the boxes in the *USEFUL PREFACE*
B) Choose one of these 5 suggestions:

1   Read the coloured boxes throughout the book and see what takes your interest.
2   Use the *INDEX* to find topics that interest you.
3   Use *DIPPING-IN TO TRY OUT IDEAS*, §1, in each chapter to find the most important topics.
4   Randomly move through the book to find what takes your interest.
5   Use the *EXERCISE: INITIAL PURPOSE FOR READING* to create your own list of what you want to read first.

THIS BOOK: DEVELOPMENT OF DYSLEXIA AND OTHER SPLDS: p 20

THE SERIES: LIVING CONFIDENTLY WITH SPECIFIC LEARNING DIFFICULTIES (SPLDS): p 23

USEFUL PREFACE: p 0

EXERCISE: INITIAL PURPOSE FOR READING: p 14

Tip: Reading Styles

It is useful to think about how you read.
See *DIFFERENT WAYS TO READ*: p 10

§ = subsection

ⓖ = *GLOSSARY*

@ = Companion website
www.routledge.com/cw/stacey

Tip: This is a book to dip into. Solid reading is not necessary.

About the coloured boxes

Meaning of Box Colours

There are coloured boxes throughout the book:

orange for stories	orange for insights .
green for exercises	*e.g.* light blue for examples .
purple for tips	chapter purple for key points and summaries .
	dark blue for text and diagrams .

Contents of boxes:

> story: a narrative
> insight: story with added information; or an important point
> tip: contains a suggestion to help you make progress
> example: usually more general than a story; sometimes directly expanding
> on some part of the preceding text
> exercise: instructions to try out some idea(s)

Flow of boxes

The boxes are part of the text. They are often split across pages.

Tip: Finding Information

The *INDEX* is organised alphabetically, with some particularly useful groups of entries listed at the beginning.

The Glossary Ⓖ has all the acronyms and symbols, as well as explanations of words and phrases. Page numbers are given for the relevant sections.

Summary of the chapters

Chapter 1 No Cure, Please Start Early

This chapter uses ideas from physiology and psychology to discuss ways in which dyslexia/ SpLD do not go away after someone has learnt correct skills or knowledge. Times when the effects of dyslexia/ SpLD becoming problematic are regarded as pitfalls, opportunities for error. The chapter looks at ways to deal with pitfalls and to reduce the stress they cause. The underlying theme is that there is no cure for dyslexia/ SpLD but that by appropriate, early learning many of the problems of dyslexia/ SpLD can be avoided.

Chapter 2 What Goes Wrong

This chapter discusses the observed behaviours that come from the four most recognised SpLDs. It compares the experiences of adults and children. It looks at: disability issues; the variety of experiences of different people with SpLDs; the different experiences of non-SpLD people. It discusses the benefits of recognising the problems so that something can be done to alleviate them. It ends with a list of all the stories in the book, grouped according to the key element in the each story.

Chapter 3 Adaptations for Children

Many of the ideas in the series are relevant to younger children and to teenagers and adults who are still learning the basic skills of language and numeracy. This chapter discusses the ideas in terms of 1) deciding whether a dyslexic/ SpLD problem exists for a child; 2) teaching an individual pupil; and 3) catering for dyslexic/ SpLD children within classroom teaching. Underlying principles are that dealing with any problems while they are small, keeps them in check; that most of the necessary teaching is good for all pupils; that it is much better for the teacher; and that it minimises the resources used solely for dyslexic/ SpLD children.

Chapter 4   A New Paradigm

The aim of the chapter is to relate the ideas in this series to recent research into dyslexia/ SpLD and show how they could add a new dimension. The chapter starts with a story illustrating misinterpretation of results of psychological testing when the thinking processes used are ignored. It gives the reasons for the philosophy of this series and summarises the methodology of the series. It discusses a literature survey which investigated the use of 5 topics in research papers; the themes were: cognitive profiles, skills, confidence, overlap of SpLDs and model for SpLD. This chapter is also relevant to the assessment process.

A new paradigm emerged from the literature survey. In this paradigm, individual experiences and differences are an important component and averaging over these differences is avoided. The new paradigm is looking for a process of discovering how people think well and how they make progress rather than focusing on what goes wrong.

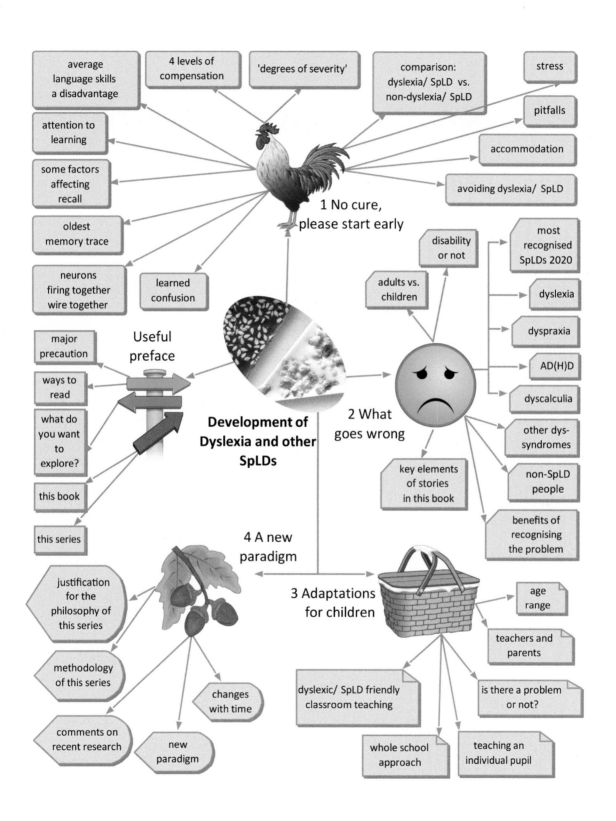

average language skills a disadvantage

4 levels of compensation

'degrees of severity'

comparison: dyslexia/ SpLD vs. non-dyslexia/ SpLD

stress

attention to learning

pitfalls

accommodation

some factors affecting recall

avoiding dyslexia/ SpLD

oldest memory trace

1 No cure, please start early

disability or not

most recognised SpLDs 2020

neurons firing together wire together

learned confusion

adults vs. children

dyslexia

major precaution

Useful preface

dyspraxia

ways to read

AD(H)D

what do you want to explore?

dyscalculia

Development of Dyslexia and other SpLDs

2 What goes wrong

other dys-syndromes

this book

key elements of stories in this book

non-SpLD people

this series

benefits of recognising the problem

4 A new paradigm

justification for the philosophy of this series

3 Adaptations for children

age range

teachers and parents

methodology of this series

changes with time

dyslexic/ SpLD friendly classroom teaching

is there a problem or not?

comments on recent research

new paradigm

whole school approach

teaching an individual pupil

Acknowledgements

These books are the result of working with many, many dyslexia/ SpLD people since 1991. They have told me their stories; they have explored new ways of doing things; they have passed on the solutions they have found. I have worked with a few people with other disabilities or none. It has been a great adventure learning from them all.

I've also had conversations with many other people, sometimes deliberately, sometimes by chance – like a 20 minute conversation with a fellow passenger on a train. The books have benefitted from the ideas generated by the conversations.

My grateful thanks go to all these people.

I'd also like to thank colleagues in The Oxford SpLD Tutor Group, those at The University of Oxford and Oxford Brookes University for formal and informal exchange of ideas and experience. The network of support that we have between colleagues allows us to provide a high quality of support to the people we work with.

Several friends and colleagues have proof-read chapters for me in the final stages. Their comments have been very useful in clarifying the expression of my ideas. Sometimes their comments have re-enforced my view that the experience of dyslexia/ SpLD is foreign to the non-dyslexic/ SpLD world. If my expression occasionally seems strange to you, please wonder whether I'm saying something about dyslexia/ SpLD that is hard for a non-dyslexic/ SpLD person to understand since their minds simply don't give them the same experience.

I'm especially indebted to David Bullock who made 3 structures to lift my laptop, extended monitor, mouse and keyboard so that I worked standing and kept my brain's arousal system alert. Without these structures I would have struggled against the way words and my dyslexia send me to sleep. The final stages of preparing these books would have been months of awful struggle instead of the excitement I experienced.

I'd like to thank my family for their patience during the writing of these books. My husband deserves special mention for his encouragement, patience and his shed, which was my writing shed for many years.

Routledge and Taylor & Francis have been very patient with the time taken to convert the original single book into four standalone books. My commissioning editor, Lucy Kennedy, the assistant editors, Molly Selby and Alex Howard, and the production team leader, Siân Cahill have all done their best to understand and accommodate the unorthodox needs of dyslexic/ SpLD readers and my needs as a dyslexic author. My thanks to everyone who has been involved with this project.

I'd like to thank Carl Wenczek, of Born Digital Ltd., for tuition and much advice on dealing with my illustrations. I couldn't have managed all the visual components and figures without his guidance.

I have been extremely fortunate to benefit from Mike Standing's experience as a retired production manager of a printing company. He came and guided me through many details of the printing process as I undertook author typesetting of these books. Without his input, the typesetting process would have been a horrible struggle.

And finally, my thanks go to Sally Fowler who has accompanied me throughout the writing of the series. When I've been daunted or hit a blank patch, Sally's encouragement and enthusiasm have carried me through. Without Sally's belief in this work, the project would not have been finished.

Illustrations

Illustration acknowledgements and key to symbols

❖   Complete figures created using Inspiration® 9, a product of Inspiration Software®, Inc.
✍   Photos or drawings created by Ginny Stacey.
O   Material by Routledge/ Taylor & Francis.
⚑   Other figures whose sources are acknowledged in the text.

Throughout the book

❖   Mind maps for *USEFUL PREFACE* and all the chapters
O   The icons for the series, books and chapters were created by Routledge/ Taylor & Francis and inserted into the mind maps or other diagrams as appropriate

Front Matter

❖   The series mind map inside the cover
❖   The book mind map

Useful Preface

❖   1   Mind map of book 1
❖   2   Mind map of book 2
❖   3   Mind map of book 3
❖   4   Mind map of book 4
❖   5   Living Confidently with Specific Learning Difficulties (SpLDs)

Contents

 Useful Preface   This is worth reading

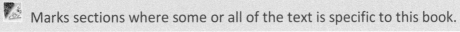 Marks sections where some or all of the text is specific to this book.

Chapter 1   No Cure, Please Start Early

Chapter 2   What Goes Wrong

Chapter 3   Adaptations for Children

Chapter 4   New Paradigm

 Appendix 1 Resources

Contents 252

Appendix 2 Individual, Personal Profile of Dyslexia/ SpLD and Regime for Managing Dyslexia/ SpLD

Appendix 3 Key Concepts

continued on next page

Appendix 3 Key Concepts (continued)

Glossary

Contents 300

List of Templates on the Website

Index

Useful Preface
This is worth reading

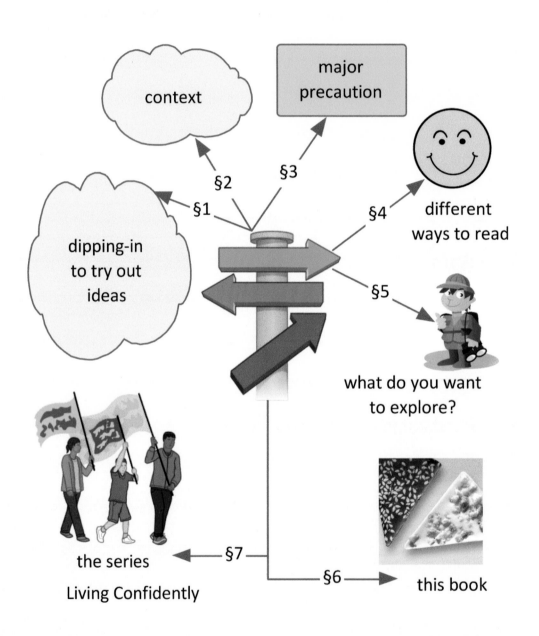

Contents

(G) p 301: SpLD: specific learning difficulty of which dyslexia is the best known and most widely researched

---

Insight: What to expect from this book

Understanding of the persistence and variability of dyslexia/ SpLD.

Some insights into the different dyslexic/ SpLD experiences of adulthood and childhood.

Recognition that early intervention is effective for teachers and parents, the individual person, and society as a whole: that a new paradigm can be to the benefit of all.

Use of pronouns in this book

The books in this series are conversations. I don't know whether you, the reader, are dyslexic/ SpLD or not. For the sake of consistency, I am writing as if you are helping someone else. The usual question arises of what pronoun to use for the person you are helping; he, she, they and all the relevant variations (3rd person pronouns).

Dyslexic/ SpLD people are all very different. To refer to the whole group often doesn't fit reality. Sometimes, I need to refer to a single person, who may not be the person you are helping. Once it was thought there were 4 male dyslexics for every 1 female, but that ratio has not stood the test of time and a significant number of female dyslexc/ SpLDs have been identified.

My decisions for the 3rd person pronouns are:

- to avoid combinations such as he/ she
- to be consistent about the gender within one chapter
- to alternate genders (he and she) between chapters
- to use the plural (they) when appropriate.

Some of the boxes are addressed specifically to dyslexic/ SpLD people; it's the only way they make sense. They are marked with the peach bar in the left hand margin. This information is also in the glossary, Ⓖ.

Ⓖ p 300

Useful preface summary

This preface is similar in the four books.

The book icon shows the sections that are particular to this book. The left margin blue line shows the length of these sections.

§1, *Dipping-in to Try Out Ideas,* suggests a quick way through.

§2, *Context,* shows my positive approach to dyslexia/ SpLD.

§3, *Major Precaution,* is about avoiding an increase in the effects of anyone's dyslexia/ SpLD.

§4, *Different Ways to Read,* is a first look at some of the issues with reading and will help you to read in different ways.

§5, *What Do You Want to Explore,* will help you decide how you want the book to help you.

§6, *This Book: Development of Dyslexia and other SpLDs,* sets the scene for this book.

§7, *The Series: Living Confidently with Specific Learning Difficulties,* gives a broad brush synopsis of the four books with details of the aims, outcomes and benefits.

Templates on the website

A1   *Jotting Down as You Scan*

A2   *Bookmark – Purpose*

A4   *Jotting Down as You Read*

A5   *Collecting Ideas that Interest You*

B1   *Collecting Ideas that Relate to You* (specially for readers who are themselves dyslexic/ SpLD)

Templates
@
COMPANION WEBSITE

Appendix 1 Resources

Collecting Information Together has ideas to help you be systematic about the way you gather information together.

Collecting Information Together: p 254

1   Dipping-in to try out ideas

Read *Insight box: What to Expect From This Book,* above.

Read *§3, Major Precaution.*

Ask your students to do the *Exercise: Avoid More Problems When Learning New Skills.* Discuss their responses with them.

Read the 3 boxes in *§2, Context.*

Scan *§4, Different Ways to Read,* then do the *Exercise: Reading Styles, §4.1.*

Read *§4.2, Something Goes Wrong with Reading.*

Read *Tip: Know Your Reason for Reading, §5.*

Do the *Exercise: Initial Purpose for Reading* in *§5.1.*

§3: p 8
Exercise: Avoid More Problems ... p 9

§2: p 4

§4: p 10
§4.1: p 12

§4.2: p 12

§5: p 14
§5.1: p 14

2 Context

Story: Two dyslexic sailors

Scene: sailing on a yacht belonging to John. I had to learn the sequence for turning on the engine safely.

"I just can't do it that way! I know how my mind works. I've been teaching in the field for ages. You've got to listen to me! Let me ask my questions. Let me understand. Then I will be able to do it."

The frustration of being faced with another dyslexic person who WILL NOT LISTEN!

Both of us are fairly stubborn because we've individually worked out what we need to do to succeed and we're both teachers in different fields. We just don't happen to have the same thinking preferences.

In this situation, I'm slightly at a disadvantage because I'm the novice in John's field and there's no way either of us want me to go into my professional role to analyse his strategies.

We simply both want me to learn to switch the engine on.

If I hadn't found my voice, there was no way I could find my way through my friend's view of how to learn (but see *MARGIN NOTE*).

MARGIN NOTE: I appreciated John's approach when he used it to help me up and down a 604m climb beside a Norwegian fjord.

As we learn we change the workings of our minds. There are changes at the neuron level of the brain. Efficient learning results in good neural networks. The following analogy helps you to think about neural networks.

Ⓖ p 303: neural networks

Insight: Park paths and pruning neurons

Ⓖ p 303:
pruning, neuron

If a park has no fences round it, people will walk across in many different directions.

If a park has 2 gates on opposite sides of the park, people will walk across in a straight line between the gates. A definite path will show where the grass is worn away.

If the park has several gates either side, there will be a series of paths linking the various gates.

When a baby is born, the brain is like the unfenced park: few routes have been established through the brain to respond to the world around.

As a result of good learning, definite neuronal networks become established with use; this is the result of neuronal pruning. The single path is the analogy for non-dyslexia/ SpLD.

Neuronal pruning: Kolb (1995)

The park with several gates either side and many paths linking them is the analogy for dyslexia/ SpLD.

The philosophy of this series

The philosophy of this series of books is that we, dyslexic/ SpLD people, can work out how our minds work, we can direct our thinking so that it is as effective as possible and we can enjoy contributing to the situations that we find ourselves in (see *MARGIN NOTE*).

MARGIN NOTE: As so often, this is good practice for everyone, but VITAL for dyslexic/ SpLDs.

We then have ownership of our thinking and actions. We can achieve to the level of our individual potential. We can confidently take our place alongside everyone else in the situations in which we find ourselves. We know how to *MANAGE*

OUR DYSLEXIA/ SPLD. We can co-operate with others to minimise the effects of our dyslexia/ SpLD on our own lives and on the lives of those who live, work or engage in action with us.

REGIME FOR MANAGING DYSLEXIA/ SPLD:
p 268

Dyslexia/ SpLD is not seen as a static phenomenon, like short-sightedness that only slowly changes with time. Dyslexia/ SpLD is seen as a collection of chaotic[1] neural networks that can exist alongside more useful networks.

Once the chaotic neural networks have established, dyslexia/ SpLD has developed. The chaotic neural networks are not destroyed when the more useful networks are established; they can lie dormant for a significant amount of time; they can be triggered into use in different ways. However well you manage it, you are always at risk of being as thoroughly dyslexic/ SpLD as ever.

The collection of chaotic neural networks will vary from person to person, even with the same dyslexia/ SpLD label.

Ⓖ p 303:
neural networks

Underlying the networks is a constitutional level of difference, which, when ignored, leads to the establishment of the chaotic neural networks. The constitutional level of difference is the permanent part of dyslexia/ SpLD. The chaotic neural networks are the source of the observed, problematic behaviours.

A child born with the differences at the constitutional level is 'at risk' of dyslexia/ SpLD. When recognised early in the development of learned networks, the constitutional differences do not have to lead to chaotic neural networks, though it may be impossible to prevent all of them. The unorthodox thinking processes that many successful dyslexic/ SpLDs enjoy will still develop, since they

---

[1]Chaos theory: when asked to spell a word, many dyslexic people have a collection of possibilities, for example sense, sens, cens, sns, scens. Each of these possibilities is the product of neural networks that connect the prompt to spell the word to the action of spelling it. By practice of the 'correct spelling', these alternative spellings are expected to be reduced (pruned) to only one, resulting in a stable neural network to achieve the correct spelling. That dyslexics continue throughout life with the variable spelling, shows this pruning isn't working for them and the implied collection of neural networks behind the variations is what I mean by 'chaotic neural networks'. The idea comes from my understanding of chaos theory (Gleick, 1997).

Ⓖ p 303: chaos theory

are needed very early in learning to prevent establishment of the chaotic neural networks.

John is typical of many successful dyslexic/ SpLDs who have got through life without any special attention. They may have used:

John is in *Two Dyslexic Sailors:* p 4

> hard work
>
> sheer determination (John: bloody-mindedness)
>
> winging it
>
> the gift of the gab
>
> secretaries, parents, spouse or partner, children, friends
>
> one or two teachers with just the right approach
>
> pot luck
>
> apprenticeships, or other routes to the top from the shop floor, etc.
>
> 'other' (always a necessary option; it's listed in the *Index*).

Whatever the route, they succeeded and they don't see what all the fuss is about now. They are the lucky ones; they made it to success. Many of their contemporaries didn't achieve very much; they can be dissatisfied with life and what they contribute.

Dyslexia/ SpLD, education and beyond

The educational system used to have elements that suited dyslexic/ SpLDs better than current systems do, and it was possible to get promotion without having to produce certificates that showed what qualifications you had.
There are changes afoot, but not ones that look likely to take us back to a regime that will suit most dyslexic/ SpLDs.

Society, workplace practices and education may change to be more sympathetic to dyslexic/ SpLD people (and to those with other disabilities); assistive technology allows access to modern communication systems; but without finding her own voice a dyslexic/ SpLD person isn't fully the person she could be; in using that voice to communicate with others she needs listeners who can hear what she is saying: these last two objectives are the main aims of this series.

Proverb: 'Give a man a fish and you feed him for a day; teach a man to fish and you feed him for a lifetime.'

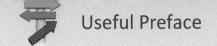

3 Major precaution

Protection from further dyslexic/ SpLD problems is an important aspect of managing dyslexia/ SpLD.

Insight: Anything 'new' needs care

Your student needs to be very careful in the initial stages of a subject, or situation, even before she starts to make sense of it. She can too easily create an unhelpful memory that interrupts her thinking for a very long time.

Example: A problem created at an initial stage

After some 20 years of playing the guitar, my sight reading is still impaired by an early mistake.

One note (B on the treble clef) is an open string for a beginner, i.e. no left hand finger is needed to play it. In musical notation, this note is a blob with a line through it (it is the middle line of the treble clef).

'Blob on a line' equated to 'finger on a string' when I first met it, and it still does. I still have to work really hard to remember the note is an open string; I have to work hard to stop myself putting a finger on a string.

I didn't know then how to manage my dyslexia. Now I know that I have to be careful, particularly at the beginning of something new.

**Exercise for student: Avoid more problems
when learning new skills[2]**

- What were the skills you learnt most recently?
- How did you learn them?
- What task was involved?
- How important are the skills to you?
- What made them easy to learn?
- What was hard about learning them?
- How easily have you been able to adapt the skills to other uses?

Reflection question: Is it a good idea to try out something new on tasks that are really important to you?

- It is OK if you can easily make changes to the way you do something later.

- It is not OK if you find the first way you tackle something leaves a strong impression.

- If this is your experience, try out new systems or skills on tasks that you don't mind about too much but that you are quite interested in.

- It is not OK if you are likely to think: "Can I trust this new approach? Will it muck up this task or topic?" Doubt like this will not allow you to explore the new approach freely.

- If in any doubt, use a task or topic that doesn't matter too much first; struggling with dyslexic/ SpLD tangles is such a pain, it's worth avoiding new problems.

- You won't give a new skill or system a fair trial, if you are worried about it or the task.

This green colour is recommended for colour blind people on the website of Okabe and Ito (Accessed 29 Jan 2017)

---

[2] The way many dyslexic/ SpLD people have to pay attention to learning may mean first learning makes more of an impression than it does for other learners.

4 Different ways to read

You may be dyslexic/ SpLD and not like reading, many don't.
Do take notice of the message in *SOMETHING GOES WRONG WITH READING:* the author's style can cause problems.

SOMETHING GOES WRONG WITH READING: p 12

> ### Tip: Margin
>
> You can use the right-hand margin to jot down your ideas as you scan or read the book.
>
> I have used it for cross-referencing and for references to help you find these when you want them.

The books in this series are written with several different styles of reading in mind.

You need to decide what your style of reading should be; do *EXERCISE: READING STYLE*. You may find a new style that suits you. Different styles might suit you at different times or for different purposes.

MARGIN NOTE: the different ways of reading relate to *THINKING PREFERENCES:* p 290 and in *INDEX*

EXERCISE: READING STYLE: p 12

	The reading style is in green; the writing styles in this book are in blue.
Linear readers	People who read easily, starting at the beginning of a book.
	The books are written with a flow of information that can be read from beginning to end.
Spatial readers	People who would read best by moving about a book, finding the most relevant parts first.
	Each chapter starts with a *DIPPING-IN* section that helps the reader choose the best way to dip-in.
Framework readers	People who need an overview to be able to understand. Some people's brains don't retain information unless they have thought about the framework, or schema, that holds it all together.

Ⓖ p 303: framework schema

Framework readers continued	The *PHILOSOPHY OF THIS SERIES* is one framework of the series.	*PHILOSOPHY OF THIS SERIES:* p 5

Each chapter has a contents list and a mind map at the beginning to help people understand the author's overview.

RATIONALE, OR FRAMEWORK outlines the importance of establishing a schema.

RATIONALE OR FRAMEWORK: p 291

Sense-oriented readers

Some people's understanding is dependent on the sense(s) they use. They may not use the senses equally. Vision, sound and the kinaesthetic sense are the most commonly used ones in education. People vary: of these three senses, sometimes one or another is very much more used, or one may be decidedly less used than the other two. Smell and taste are also senses and may need to be considered.

Senses:
visual,
verbal (oral/aural)
kinaesthetic

Ⓖ p 303:
kinaesthetic
MARGIN NOTE: The kinaesthetic sense uses body perception and physical movement to good effect

1) Visually: different layouts are used to indicate different types of information. For example: exercises for the reader are in green boxes. Cartoons and figures are used.

visual
p 290 and in *INDEX*

2) Orally/aurally: the language is direct, not complicated, but elegant (at least that is the intention).

verbal (oral/aural)
p 290 and in *INDEX*

3) Kinaesthetic: there are exercises for the reader which should engage the kinaesthetic sense; as should the anecdotes about the actions of others.

kinaesthetic: p
p 290 and in *INDEX*

Interest-oriented readers

Some people use their strongest interests in order to understand; they cannot retain information if these interests are not actively engaged.

1) Some ideas about innate interests are listed in *MOTIVATION* in terms of Myers-Briggs Personality Type and Multiple Intelligences. Any reader for whom motivation is a key issue should use the ideas to work out what their particular motivation might be and deliberately use it while reading these books.

MOTIVATION: p 291

Interest-oriented readers *continued*	2) Material can be written bearing in mind different motivations by presenting different perspectives. The suggested *ROUTES* on the *WEBSITE* for various reader groups are examples of catering for different perspectives.
Further comment	If two or more people are using the book together, the different styles of reading should be accommodated.

ROUTES
COMPANION @ WEBSITE

4.1   Exercise: reading style

Exercise: Reading style

Consider which styles of reading might suit you:
Why might they suit you?
Which have you tried already?
Which work most of the time/ sometimes/ never?
Which sound worth experimenting with?
What do you know already about your way of reading?

See examples in *DIFFERENT WAYS TO READ*: p 10

4.2   Something goes wrong with reading

If a dyslexic/ SpLD person is struggling with reading, it is important to check whether there is anything that can be done about it.

For example, going to sleep over reading can indicate that the brain is taking in too much material that has not been understood properly.

There are many approaches to make reading effective that do not involve the mechanics of reading.   The full discussion of reading is in *Gaining Knowledge and Skills with Dyslexia and other SpLDs* (Stacey, 2021). The discussion includes ways in which an author's style of writing is unhelpful to dyslexic/ SpLDs.

Stacey (2021)

Insight: External factors hamper reading

Reading difficulties can be made a lot worse by the way the text is written or presented. They aren't just from your dyslexia/ SpLD.

Insight: Word changes cause doubt

Some authors don't like to repeat the same word too many times, so they change the word even though the idea hasn't changed.

Do you ever find that you then start to doubt your reading ability? It's as if your mind is worrying because you may have missed some significant detail that the change of words indicates. Then gradually, your reading skill deserts you; you struggle; you end up sleeping over the text, even when you are very interested in it.

Sometimes in this series, I have deliberately not changed words, even though the repetition is rather tedious.

5   What do you want to explore?

One key tactic for making reading easier is to prime your mind, rather like warming up muscles. No serious sportsman would start their sport without warming up their muscles. The mind can be looked after in the same way.

Tip: Know your reason for reading

When you identify your main purpose for reading anything, you give your mind some guidelines for understanding what you are reading.

You then allow yourself to explore the text, looking to satisfy your purpose; reading is much easier.

Once a person has developed characteristics of dyslexia/ SpLD, the characteristics don't go away. They can be managed well, but the person is always vulnerable to the characteristics coming to the fore.

Ginny Stacey and Sally Fowler are both dyslexic, in different ways!

This book is worth reading because:

- it discusses influences that contribute to the persistence of dyslexia/ SpLD

- it compares the differing experiences of childhood and adulthood

- it looks at ways to teach so that the characteristics of dyslexia/ SpLD need not develop in 'at risk' children

- it proposes a new paradigm that will help to allow the needs of dyslexic/ SpLD children to be catered for by practice that is vital for them and good practice for all.

Any of these topics in the book could be part of your purpose for reading.

5.1 Initial purpose for reading

The following exercise is designed to help establish any reader's initial purpose: you are effectively creating your own dipping-in list.

Exercise: Initial purpose for reading

1   Use the *TEMPLATE: A1 - JOTTING DOWN AS YOU SCAN* to keep track of ideas.

1.1   Remember you are scanning for this exercise, not reading. You are finding the sections most interesting to you now.

TEMPLATES

COMPANION @ WEBSITE

2   Scan the following places to find ideas that catch your interest:
   2.1   point 1.1 above, to remember to scan
   2.2   the orange insight boxes in this chapter
   2.3   the table of *Reader Groups, §5.2*
   2.4   the themes in *§5.3, Reading to Find Out About a Theme*
   2.5   *§6, This Book: Development of Dyslexia and other SpLDs*
   2.6   *§7, The Series: Living Confidently with Specific Learning Difficulties (SpLDs)*
   2.7   the *Contents* of the book
   2.8   the *Index.*

§5.2: p 16
§5.3: p 18
§6: p 20
§7: p 23

Contents: p xv
Index: p 314

3   For each idea that catches your attention:
   3.1   note where in the book the idea is
   3.2   why the idea interests you
   3.3   how important the idea is to you immediately and in the longer-term.

4   Think about your life:
   4.1   What issues to do with dyslexia/ SpLD do you want to understand or solve?
   4.2   What situations in everyday life, employment or study are affected by your dyslexia/ SpLD, or might be affected?

NB: you are creating your personal dipping-in list.

5   Look at the list of ideas you have made.
   5.1   Are there any common threads that could be grouped together? Use *Templates: A5 - Collecting Ideas that Interest You* or *B1 - Collecting Ideas that Relate to You* to gather the common threads.
   5.2   Number the ideas in the order that you would like to explore them now.
   5.3   Write the ideas on the *Template: A2 - Bookmark – Purpose* in the order that you want to explore them. The *Bookmark – Purpose* will remind you what you have decided to explore.

Templates

6   Start reading. Use *Template: A4 - Jotting Down as You Read*, or any other template, to capture insights as you read.

5.2 Reader groups

One way of giving your mind the guidelines that assist reading is to recognise why you want to acquire any new information.

I have thought about different reader groups with different reasons for reading this book. These are shown in the *Box: Reader Groups,* with a list of some of the roles.

The *website*

has further reader groups for the whole series.

Reader groups	including
Tutors supporting adult and teenage dyslexic/ SpLD people and subject teachers	specialist support providers SENCOs school subject teachers university, evening class teachers sports coaches, etc. head teachers parents who actively teach their children
Professionals needing to know about the problem side of dyslexia/ SpLD and people with a general interest in dyslexia/ SpLD	• people in authority, having responsibility • employers • social workers, medical and legal professionals • counsellors • people offering a service • retailers • people living with, working with, taking action with dyslexic/ SpLD people • families • co-workers, team members • people dealing with indirect communication • writers of public communications • exam writers

SENCOs: Special Educational Needs Co-ordinators

Reader groups *continued*	including
Teachers and parents of dyslexic/ SpLD children	parents, grandparents, primary and secondary school teachers head teachers
Assessors and researchers	disability evaluators assessors and researchers
Policy makers, politicians and people in the media	all people concerned with disability issues
Readers in of all these groups could be dyslexic/ SpLD themselves	

Decide which reader group(s) you belong to.

Why do you choose the group(s)?

What information are you looking for? Use *READING TO FIND OUT ABOUT A THEME*, below, and *AIMS, OUTCOMES AND BENEFITS* to help you decide.

AIMS, OUTCOMES AND BENEFITS: p 21

Dyslexic/ SpLD readers

As well as belonging to one or more of the reader groups above, you may have a formal diagnostic assessment or you may suspect you belong to the dyslexic/ SpLD group. Working with this book could provide you with the opportunity to recognise and understand what happens to you as a result of your dyslexia/ SpLD. Build any insights into your own *INDIVIDUAL, PERSONAL PROFILE OF DYSLEXIA/ SPLD* and your own *REGIME FOR MANAGING DYSLEXIA/ SPLD* and take the opportunity to become more autonomous.

INDIVIDUAL, PERSONAL PROFILE OF DYSLEXIA/ SPLD: p 268

REGIME FOR MANAGING DYSLEXIA/ SPLD: p 268

5.3 Reading to find out about a theme

You may be a dyslexic/ SpLD reader and as such find it easier to read focusing on a particular theme of dyslexia/ SpLD that you want to explore first. In thinking how a dyslexic/ SpLD person might approach the material, I put together several different themes. The themes relevant to this book are listed below. The full list of themes in the series is on the *WEBSITE*, along with where the discussions can be found.

THEMES

has the themes for the whole series

 The themes that are relevant to this book include:
1) Problems of dyslexia/ SpLD

- Persistence of dyslexia/ SpLD

- Variations

- Recognising pitfalls: hazards and obstacles

- Accommodation

- Comparison with non-dyslexia/ SpLD

- General behaviour patterns of dyslexia/ SpLD

- Adulthood and childhood problems for:
  o Dyslexia
  o Dyspraxia
  o AD(H)D
  o Dyscalculia

2) Avoiding the problems of dyslexia/ SpLD
- Childhood
  - Teachers and parents
  - Evidence of problems
  - 1-1 support
  - Classroom support
- Research and teaching programmes
  - Cognitive profile
  - Skills
  - Confidence
  - Overlap of SpLDs
  - Research models of SpLD
  - New paradigm

The themes for the rest of the series come under the general headings of:

Living with confidence
- Individual, personal profile of dyslexia/ SpLD
- Regime for managing dyslexia/ SpLD

The wide impact in everyday life
- Organisation and problem solving
- Time and time management
- Space, place and direction
- Study and employment

Gaining knowledge and skills
- Other people involved
- Teaching, dialogue and indirect communication
- Policies and systems
- Foundations of knowledge and skills
- Input and output modes: reading, listening, doing, taking and making notes, writing, speaking and taking-action
- Social situations: exams, group work, driving, travel, job applications, eating out and finances

6 This book: *Development of Dyslexia and other SpLDs*

This book has new perspectives on the problems of dyslexia/ SpLD.

It discusses a variety of influences that contribute to the persistence and variability of dyslexia/ SpLD.

It encourages dyslexic/ SpLD people to be fully conversant with the pitfalls of their dyslexia/ SpLD as part of managing the effects.

It discusses teaching for children and adults struggling with basic skills.

It proposes a new paradigm to minimise the effects of dyslexia/ SpLD for the individual and for society.

Insight: Problems don't have to develop

Over a period of weeks, I noticed one person using many of the creative strategies of dyslexic people. I asked if she were dyslexic. "Not really. My mother is a dyslexic tutor. She saw my problems early and taught me strategies. Now I have a few wobbly spellings and lots of ways of working."

Full *Story: Best Case Scenario: Good Techniques, Minimal Dyslexia:* p 156

The 'At Risk' Child Can Avoid Many Of The Problems.

6.1 Aims, outcomes and benefits

Several clear aims emerge for this book:

- to give a clear understanding:
    - of the on-going nature of dyslexia/ SpLD when early problems are not addressed at the start
    - that the appropriate teaching can reduce the development of many of the problems
- to show that it is cost-effective to deal with the difficulties early
- to emphasise that approaches which are VITAL for dyslexic/ SpLDs are GOOD PRACTICE for all
- to present a new paradigm that matches a learner's skills and innate thinking to learning tasks.

The stories and insights in this book are written to bring life to the ideas. *KEY ELEMENTS OF THE STORIES IN THIS BOOK* has a table listing all the stories, with a few almost-stories. They are grouped according to the element being addressed; the key element is summarised.

KEY ELEMENTS OF THE STORIES IN THIS BOOK: p 133

The art of living with differences is fundamental to good relationships between people across the dyslexic/ SpLD and non-dyslexic/ SpLD divide. This divide happens in all situations of human life, not just education. It's difficult to know when the differences might be important because dyslexia/ SpLD are hidden[3]: you cannot look at one of this group of people and say, "That person has dyslexia/ SpLD, I need to be aware of that." A greater knowledge about dyslexia/ SpLD will allow you to recognise signs of dyslexia/ SpLD and to talk openly, with curiosity rather than judgement, about any differences that arise.

---

[3] The physical effects of dyspraxia are not always hidden.

I hope the outcomes will include:

- You will have a greater understanding of the issues and problems that dyslexic/ SpLD people face.
- You will be able to talk about these issues in a way that allows dyslexic/ SpLD people to know that they have been heard properly.
- You will be able to help them as they work to minimise the effects of their dyslexia/ SpLD.
- You will understand that early appropriate responses to a pupil's problems are the most effective approach, as well as being the cheapest.
- You will realise that approaches that suit dyslexic/ SpLD people are also good for many others.

- Dyslexic/ SpLD people will benefit from a greater openness that helps them to become autonomous learners and people.
- Dyslexic/ SpLD people will be able to contribute their full potential to the workforce, with good management of any problems that they have.

I hope the benefits will include:

- Society as a whole will benefit from the contributions made by dyslexic/ SpLD people who are capable and not handicapped by the effects of their dyslexia/ SpLD.
- Society, as a whole, will benefit in the long run when fewer human and financial resources are needed to deal with dyslexia/ SpLD.

The full benefits will come from using the other books in this series, too.

7   The Series: *Living Confidently with Specific Learning Difficulties (SpLDs)*

7.1   Readership/ audience

Living Confidently with Specific Learning Difficulties (SpLDs) is a series of books that look at the whole of the experience of living with these specific learning difficulties.

Descriptions in Ⓖ p 301 of 4 SpLDs:
dyslexia
dyspraxia
AD(H)D
dyscalculia

The ideas described in this series draw on work over 25 years helping individuals to find out how their minds work and how to use them effectively in study or everyday life.

Finding Your Voice with Dyslexia and other SpLDs and *Organisation and Everyday Life with Dyslexia and other SpLDs* are both written addressing dyslexic/ SpLD people.

Gaining Knowledge and Skills with Dyslexia and other SpLDs and *Development of Dyslexia and other SpLDs* both address people in roles alongside a dyslexic/ SpLD person.

Each book can be used on its own, but there are some concepts that spread over the four. The *KEY CONCEPTS* are summarised in *APPENDIX 3*.

APPENDIX 3: p 282

7.2   Summary of the series

Life is a journey. We need to find our way through it.

We need our own voice to help us navigate.

Living Confidently with Specific Learning Difficulties (SpLDs) is about living life to the full and enjoying the journey, each person using her maximum potential and minimising the effects of her dyslexia/ SpLD.

Book 1: *Finding Your Voice with Dyslexia and other SpLDs* (Stacey, 2019)
The book is written for dyslexic/ SpLD people and contains:

- building a personal, individual profile
  - thinking preferences
  - pitfalls
  - ways to pause well
  - accommodations

- four steps for managing dyslexia/ SpLD
  - recognising your pitfalls
  - pausing
  - using your thinking preferences
  - knowing your goal

- ideas from physiology and psychology that
  - relate to dyslexia/ SpLD
  - help make sense of some effects of dyslexia/ SpLD

- techniques for using the mind well
  - mind set
  - chunking
  - recall
  - memory consolidation
  - concentration
  - metacognition
  - objective observation
  - reflection
  - making connections
  - prioritising

- thinking preferences
  - senses: visual, aural/oral, kinaesthetic
  - framework or rationale
  - holistic vs. linear thinking
  - Myers-Briggs Personality Type, especially motivation
  - Multiple Intelligences

- thinking clearly: techniques for using maximum mental capacity
  - emotional hi-jacking
  - emotional states of mind
  - confidence
  - self-esteem
  - breathing
  - relaxation
  - Brain Gym
  - Neuro-Linguistic Programming (NLP)
  - the art of pausing and maintaining clear thinking

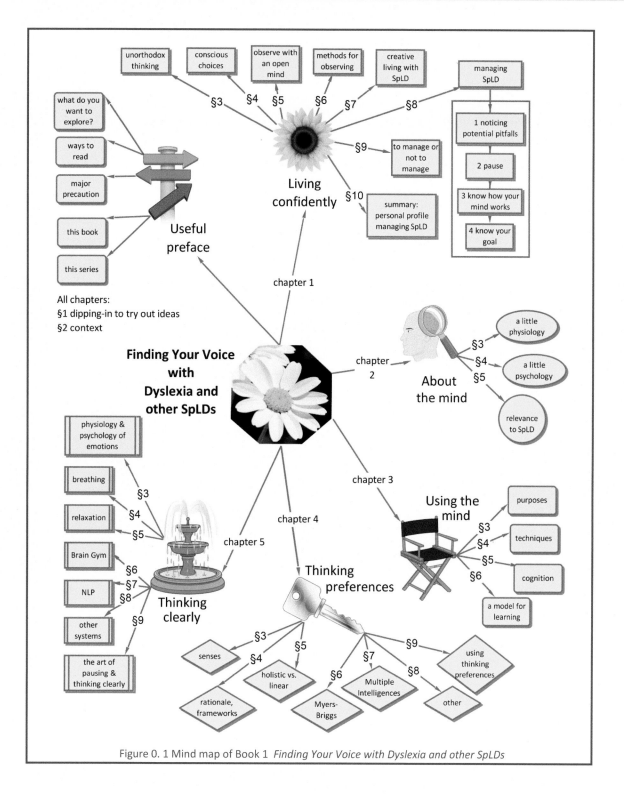

Figure 0. 1 Mind map of Book 1 *Finding Your Voice with Dyslexia and other SpLDs*

Book 2: *Organisation and Everyday Life with Dyslexia and other SpLDs* (Stacey, 2020a)

The book is written for dyslexic/ SpLD people and contains:

- a model for working out issues to do with organisation
    - materials and methods for working on any ideas
- general problem solving
- solutions applied to
    - time and time management
    - space, place and direction
    - everyday life
    - study peripherals
    - employment.

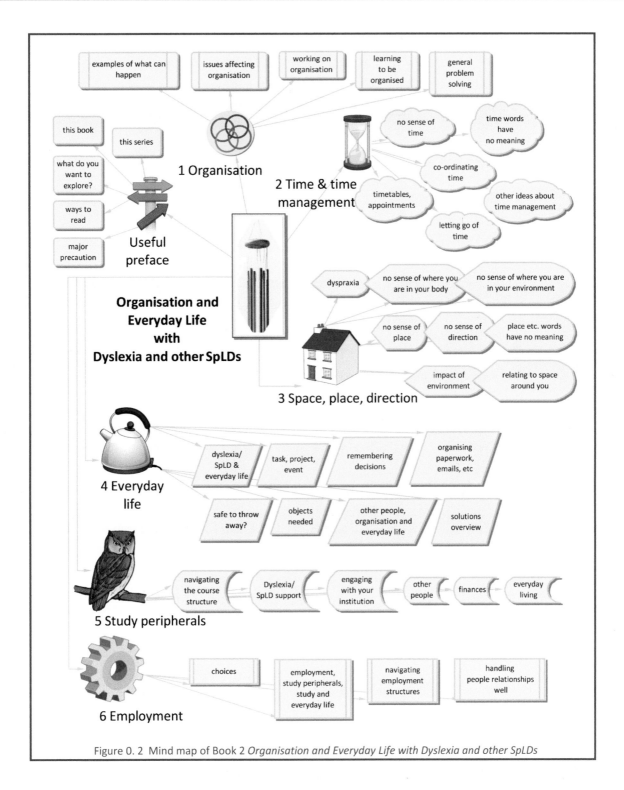

Figure 0. 2 Mind map of Book 2 *Organisation and Everyday Life with Dyslexia and other SpLDs*

Book 3: *Gaining Knowledge and Skills with Dyslexia and other SpLDs* (Stacey, 2021)

The book is written for people who assist dyslexic/ SpLD people to gain knowledge and skills, which includes everyone:

- when you tell someone the time of day or how to cook an egg, you are passing on knowledge and skills
- you can't immediately tell whether the person you are talking to is dyslexic/ SpLD.

The book contains:

- different roles people have:
  - 1-1 support teachers, subject teachers and lecturers
  - employers, managers and supervisors
  - professionals in positions of influence and authority: healthcare, legal, financial
  - family, friends, acquaintances, work colleagues,
  - designers and producers of indirect communications
  - policy makers
  - people in the media
- imparting knowledge and skills:
  - general approaches
  - teaching
  - dialogue
  - indirect communication
  - accommodation
  - policies and systems
- foundations for knowledge and skills:
  - model for learning
  - comprehension
  - knowing the goal
  - planning
- input modes: reading, listening, doing
- taking and making notes
- output modes: writing, speaking, taking-action
- situations: exams, group work (meetings, seminars, debates), driving
  - social examples: travel, job applications, eating out, finances.

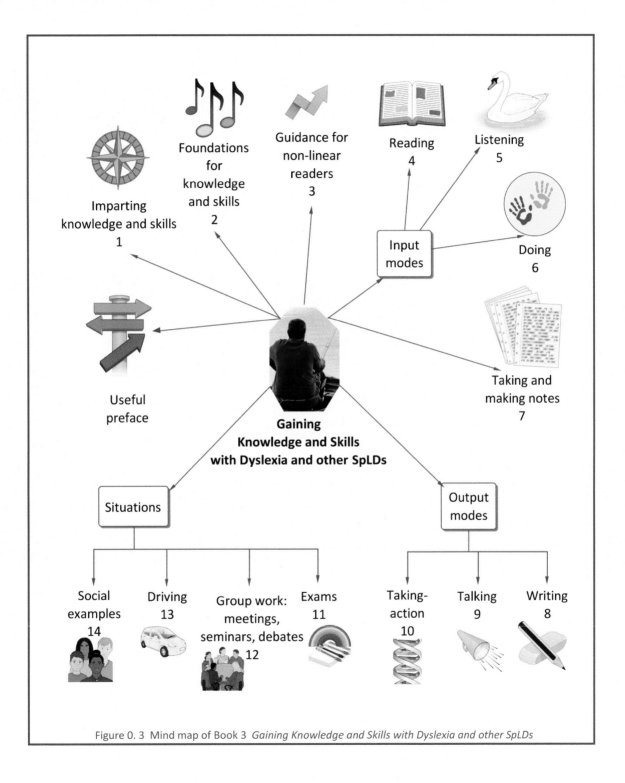

Figure 0. 3 Mind map of Book 3 *Gaining Knowledge and Skills with Dyslexia and other SpLDs*

Book 4: *Development of Dyslexia and other SpLDs* (Stacey, 2020b)

The book is written for those alongside dyslexic/ SpLD people and contains:

- ideas about the persistence of dyslexia/ SpLD and reasons to take dyslexia/ SpLD into account earlier rather than later, including:
  - learned confusion
  - neurons firing together, wire together
  - the persistence of dyslexia/ SpLD
  - problems masked by average language skills
  - levels of compensation
  - degrees of severity
- what goes wrong
  - discussion about the different SpLDs
  - discussion about similar problems experienced by non-dyslexic/ SpLD people
- adaptations of the ideas for younger children
- how to approach matching an individual's learning to what they are good at.

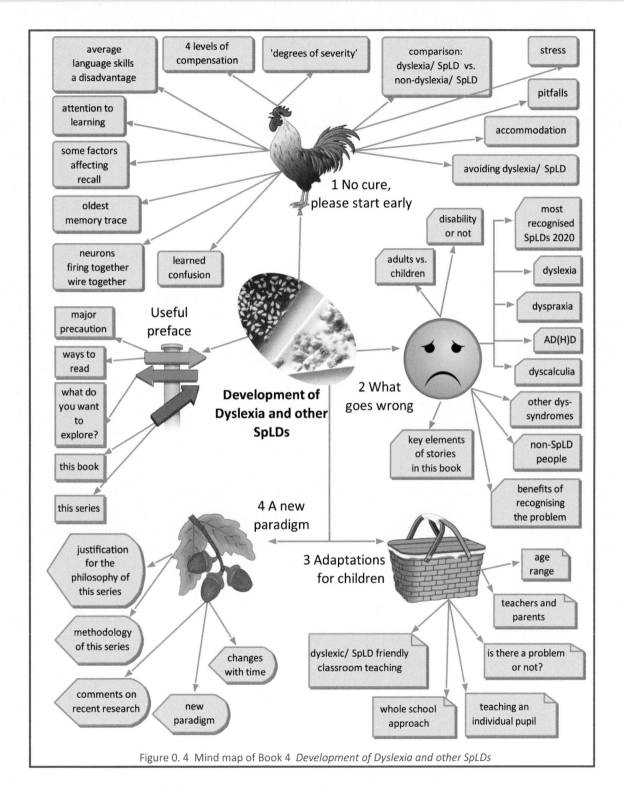

Figure 0. 4 Mind map of Book 4 *Development of Dyslexia and other SpLDs*

Applicable to all books in the series

Series Website

- has material to assist with using the books:
    - templates and check-lists
    - different ways to select the material most useful to you.

Useful Preface

- is mostly the same for each book
- the sections particular to each book are marked by the book icon and a blue line on the left hand margin.

It contains:

- the philosophy of the series
- a warning to avoid further dyslexic/ SpLD traits developing as new things are learnt
- some suggestions to make reading easier
- information about the book in question
- information about the series.

Appendix 1 Resources (The same in all 4 books except for referencing.)

will help you collect information together, decide on priorities and monitor progress.

Appendix 2 Individual, Personal Profile and Regime for Managing Dyslexia/ SpLD

(The same in all 4 books except for section 1 and referencing.)

will help you build the information about your dyslexia/ SpLD and how you manage it. Section 1, *LIVING CONFIDENTLY*, starts by stating the aim for dyslexic/ SpLD people to be as autonomous as possible. In books 2 - 4, a summary of the material in book 1 is included so that these books can be used independently of each other.

Appendix 3 Key Concepts (The same in all 4 books except for referencing.)

In order to allow the separate books of the series to be used on their own, summaries of the key concepts of the individual books are given in Appendix 3. These are the concepts I think are most important for living confidently with dyslexia/ SpLD.

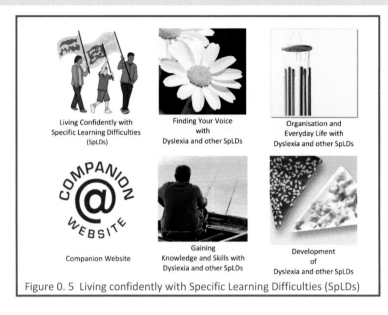

The book cover images:

The daisy represents growth.

Wind chime music represents life flowing well when organisation suits the individual concerned.

The fisherman recalls the saying: 'Give a man a fish and you feed him for a day; teach a man to fish and you feed him for a lifetime'.

The slices of cake represent changing 'That's the way the cookie crumbles' to 'It's a piece of cake'.

Figure 0. 5 Living confidently with Specific Learning Difficulties (SpLDs)

7.3   Aims and outcomes

The first group of aims of this series is that dyslexic/ SpLD people can:

- find out what their best ways of thinking are, how to use them and maintain their use
- understand how their specific learning difficulty affects them
- be able to pause when they recognise a pitfall has occurred
- know how to deal with the pitfall
    o   by using best ways of thinking
    o   knowing what needs to happen
- negotiate with those around them so that they are able to fulfil their potential in any situation and so that the dyslexic/ SpLD effects are minimised.

The general attitude at the end of the process is almost:

- OK, I'm dyslexic/ SpLD; I really enjoy the way I process information and the way I am
- everyone has some problems, mine just happen to have a label
- it's no big deal; I'll do well 'with a little help from my friends'.

In order to achieve this group of aims, a group of specialist support providers will need in-depth knowledge of dyslexia/ SpLD. Their knowledge and experience are usually a major contribution to the progress made by any dyslexic/ SpLD person.

The second group of aims is that:

- non-dyslexic/ SpLD people can understand better what the issues are for the people with dyslexia/ SpLD
- communication between the two groups can be improved to the benefit of all parties.

These two sets of aims produce different outcomes depending on whether you are dyslexic/ SpLD or alongside a dyslexic/ SpLD person. The *WEBSITE* has *OUTCOMES* for various reader groups more finely classified.

OUTCOMES

They have been divided into:

- the Skills and Knowledge,
- the Benefits, including changes of behaviour
- and some thoughts about the Potential Possibilities

There can be a lot of laughter and joyful living once good communication is established across the differences of dyslexia/ SpLD.

7.4   Distinguishing between the different SpLDs

Most of the series is not marked as more or less relevant to a particular SpLD. People are so varied even when their problems are given the same labels. The clearest separation I know is that organisation is the major problem for dyspraxic adults when it comes to thinking (the motor side of dyspraxia is not covered). But even in this group, I'm aware of one student with no dyslexic problems who needs to be aware of his thinking preferences in order to do justice to his knowledge.

Out of respect for the overlap of experiences (problems and solutions), most of this book makes no distinction between the different SpLDs.

One exception is *CHAPTER 2, WHAT GOES WRONG* which has sections focusing on the 4 main SpLDs: dyslexia, dyspraxia, AD(H)D and dyscalculia. The sections consider the differences between the child and adult experiences of each syndrome.

WHAT GOES WRONG: p 82

A second exception is *CHAPTER 4, NEW PARADIGM* which is mainly about dyslexia, since it is the most widely researched SpLD.

NEW PARADIGM: p 232

7.5   The way forward

The whole series is about the autonomy that allows dyslexic/ SpLD people to get out from under the difficulties. These difficulties have a label, may have various labels, but they aren't the only difficulties that people face. Negotiating accommodations should be done with understanding of the issues for all parties involved. The way forward could benefit many groups of people.

Ⓖ p 303: autonomy

What I hope people will get from the series:

Dyslexic/ SpLD people:

    a systematic way of observing strengths and weaknesses and using the strengths to help them manage the problems they face because of their dyslexia/ SpLD; the confidence to contribute to work, life, in their study, in a way that fulfils their innate potential and which is not masked or hampered by their dyslexia/ SpLD.

Those in supporting roles, whether in a 1-1 relationship or in a more general type of relationship:

    resources to understand the impact of dyslexia/ SpLD on the whole lives of dyslexic/ SpLD people and ways of making necessary adjustments to facilitate better communication.

Those who have to think about public communication and use of public spaces:

    an understanding of the difficulties encountered by dyslexic/ SpLD people and a recognition that making communication and access easier for them will also help many other people.

Politicians, other policymakers and people in the media:

    an understanding that dealing with dyslexia/ SpLD effectively as early as possible is the right thing for society to do; that done well it has cost benefits in many different ways and is therefore worth carrying through properly; that mutual respect and consideration between all members and levels of society are enhanced through the best approaches to dyslexia/ SpLD.

What I hope will happen for dyslexic/ SpLD children:
> that adults will listen to them and observe them so that they can grow up with maximum autonomy and management of their dyslexia/ SpLD; that many of the recognised problems might not develop for them.

What I hope will happen in general education is that the new paradigm I have put forward will be seen as teacher-friendly, effective, sensible, satisfying and cost saving.

Ⓖ p 303: paradigm

The *NEW PARADIGM* is:

NEW PARADIGM: p 232

- that systems are developed, and used, to explore how individuals, children and adults, learn
- that learners have the opportunities to tailor their learning tasks so that they can achieve the knowledge and skills being taught
- that teaching programmes are flexible enough to accommodate all learner approaches.

Final comment

When people are confident of their skills and not afraid to own and manage their weaknesses, they have many of the tools necessary to face the various situations in their life, see the *TOOL BOX FOR LIVING CONFIDENTLY*.

TOOL BOX FOR LIVING CONFIDENTLY: p 273

The voice is found; the potential is unlocked; living with dyslexia/ SpLD is done with confidence.

References

Gleick, James, 1997, *Chaos, The Amazing Science of the Unpredictable*, Minerva, London

Kolb, Bryan, 1995, *Brain Plasticity and Behaviour,* Lawrence Erlbaum Associates, Mahwah

Stacey, Ginny, 2019, *Finding Your Voice with Dyslexia and other SpLDs*, Routledge, London

Stacey, Ginny, 2020a, *Organisation and Everyday Life with Dyslexia and other SpLDs*, Routledge, London

Stacey, Ginny, 2020b, *Development of Dyslexia and other SpLDs,* Routledge, London

Stacey, Ginny, 2021, *Gaining Knowledge and Skills with Dyslexia and other SpLDs*, Routledge, London

Website information

Okabe, Masataka, Ito, Kei, 2008, *Color Universal Design (CUD) - How To Make Figures and Presentations That Are Friendly to Colorblind People*,
http://jfly.iam.u-tokyo.ac.jp/color/ Accessed 29 January 2017
Series website: www.routledge.com/cw/stacey

1 No Cure, Please Start Early

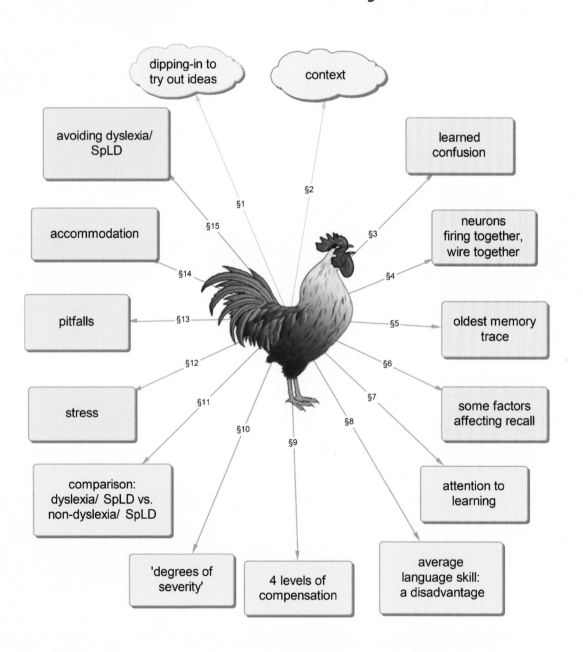

dipping-in to try out ideas

context

avoiding dyslexia/ SpLD

learned confusion

§1

§2

§15

accommodation

§3

neurons firing together, wire together

§14

§4

pitfalls

§13

oldest memory trace

§5

§12

§6

stress

§11

§7

some factors affecting recall

§10

§8

comparison: dyslexia/ SpLD vs. non-dyslexia/ SpLD

§9

attention to learning

'degrees of severity'

4 levels of compensation

average language skill: a disadvantage

Contents

List of key points and summaries

K = key points
S = summaries

Tip: The skills and knowledge dyslexic/ SpLD people can gain from this series

APPENDIX 3: KEY CONCEPTS has a list of the main skills and knowledge that dyslexic/ SpLD people can gain from this series of books. They fall into the categories of
> *THINKING CLEARLY*
> *USING THE MIND WELL*
> *THINKING PREFERENCES*
> *USEFUL APPROACHES*
> *ASPECTS OF DYSLEXIA/ SPLD*

APPENDIX 3: KEY CONCEPTS: p 282

Working with the chapter

The *TABLE: SYNOPSIS OF THIS CHAPTER* summarises the issues dealt with in this chapter. You should be able to explain these ideas to your student and discuss how any of them are relevant to the ways he experiences his dyslexia/ SpLD. As he explores the impact of his dyslexia/ SpLD, you should encourage him to build both his *INDIVIDUAL, PERSONAL PROFILE OF DYSLEXIA/ SPLD* and his *REGIME FOR MANAGING DYSLEXIA/ SPLD*.

TABLE: SYNOPSIS OF THIS CHAPTER: p 43

INDIVIDUAL, PERSONAL PROFILE OF DYSLEXIA/ SPLD: p 268

REGIME FOR MANAGING DYSLEXIA/ SPLD: p 268

Some of the boxes are addressed to dyslexic/ SpLD people; it's the only way they make sense. They are marked with the peach bar in the left hand margin.

Templates on the website

A1   *JOTTING DOWN AS YOU SCAN*
A2   *BOOKMARK – PURPOSE*
A4   *JOTTING DOWN AS YOU READ*
A5   *COLLECTING IDEAS THAT INTEREST YOU*
B1   *COLLECTING IDEAS THAT RELATE TO YOU* (specially for readers who are themselves dyslexic/ SpLD)
B8   *RECORDING TEMPLATE - 4 (5 EQUAL COLUMNS)*

TEMPLATES:

Appendix 1 Resources

APPENDIX 1: p 252

This appendix will help you and your student collect information about the way he does anything and how his dyslexia/ SpLD affects him. It collects together some of the general skills he will need in order to make progress.

If you are dyslexic/ SpLD, this appendix will help you gather the information you want from this book.

Appendix 2 Individual, Personal Profile of Dyslexia/ SpLD and Regime for Managing Dyslexia/ SpLD

APPENDIX 2: p 266

Tip: *NO CURE, PLEASE START EARLY* and building an *INDIVIDUAL, PERSONAL PROFILE OF DYSLEXIA/ SPLD* and a *REGIME FOR MANAGING DYSLEXIA/ SPLD*

As your student understands his dyslexia/ SpLD better and the way it varies, help him to be confident about himself. Help him to build the insights that emerge into his *PROFILE* and *REGIME*; these will allow him to become more autonomous.

Ⓖ p 303:
autonomous, profile, regime

Appendix 3 Key Concepts

APPENDIX 3: p 282

This appendix has a summary of the key ideas I cover when doing an audit of skills and knowledge with a dyslexic/ SpLD student. It shows which of the 4 books in the series covers each idea in full.

1   Dipping-in to try out ideas

Read
    § 2 CONTEXT
    §3 LEARNED CONFUSION which includes a discussion about having too many possible spellings for a given word
    §5 THE OLDEST MEMORY TRACE which has some thoughts as to why dyslexia/ SpLD keeps coming back even though your student has learnt other non-dyslexic/ SpLD ways to process tasks

§2: p 42
§3: p 44

§5: p 48

2 Context

As we learn or experience events, our minds in some way respond and our brains are altered (Baddeley, 1982; Kolb, 1995; Wolf, 2008). This chapter considers some important issues for dyslexia/ SpLD when these alterations come from confused initial learning.

Baddeley (1982)
Kolb (1995)
Wolf (2008)

The discussion of the issues is illustrated with experiences of dyslexic/ SpLD people. It is hoped that conversations will take place which allow dyslexic/ SpLD people to gradually relate to the descriptions and recognise more accurately what happens as a result of their own dyslexia/ SpLD. The benefit of recognition should be that the *Pitfalls* of dyslexia/ SpLD are no longer disruptive.

Ⓖ p 303: *pitfall*

Pitfalls: p 73

The most important message of the chapter is how crucial it is to work in the right way for individual brains from the start of learning, whether as a child or as an adult taking on a new subject or hobby.

The second important message is that dyslexia/ SpLD doesn't go away once better learning has also taken place. Understanding why it doesn't go away helps the process of dealing with the effects.

The third message is that flexibility to manage dyslexia/ SpLD makes life, learning and employment much easier for all concerned.

	Table: Synopsis of this chapter
§3 p 44	New correct learning doesn't erase older confused learning.
§4 p 47	If neurons don't fire together, they won't wire together: neural networks have to be energised at the same time for learning to take place. The way your student thinks is a crucial part of getting neurons to fire together.
§5 p 48	Once established, older learning is used in preference to newer learning and older learning is not modified by newer learning.
§6 p 51	Recall • can depend: 　　　　○　on place 　　　　○　on time and relevance 　　• may not be triggered on demand 　　• may occur at varying speeds which can lead to sequencing problems.
§7 p 56	Subliminal learning can't be relied on.
§8 p 57	When average achievement is below potential abilities, it can mask dyslexia/ SpLD.
§9 p 60	Managing dyslexia/ SpLD is not static; it varies even for one person.
§10 p 61	'Degrees of severity' are too simplistic and guidelines that relate to experience are proposed.
§11 p 65	Differences between dyslexia/ SpLD and non-dyslexia/ SpLD are discussed.
§12 p 67	Dyslexic/ SpLD people may be well practised at dealing with stress. Lack of understanding by those around can create unhelpful stress. Avoiding problems due to dyslexia/ SpLD can result in increasing them. Dealing with stress and the particular sources of stress is part of dyslexia/ SpLD management.
§13 p 73	Your student needs to recognise the pitfalls, the opportunities for error, of his dyslexia/ SpLD in order to manage them well.
§14 p 78	When managing pitfalls is either impossible or puts your student at a significant disadvantage, accommodations should be put in place to allow him to operate at a level consistent with his best abilities.
§15 p 78	If the learning needs of 'at risk' children are catered for in early childhood, many of the problems can be avoided.

Key point: The effectiveness of early intervention

This chapter has an accumulative message for those involved with children's learning, i.e. for policy makers, teachers and parents.

Early intervention pays dividends:

- the teaching practice that is Vital for dyslexic/ SpLDs is Good Practice for all, there is no robbing Peter to pay Paul

- much of on-going dyslexic/ SpLD problems can be avoided when an 'at risk' child is catered for early

- when dyslexic/ SpLD problems don't develop, the cost of later specialist tuition is avoided

- disruptive behaviour from unhappy, underachieving dyslexic/ SpLD children in the classroom shouldn't arise.

3 Learned confusion

It is alleged Mark Twain once asserted "it is a poor mind that only has one spelling for a word". One day thinking how to spell a word, I realised that there were a number of alternatives in my mind, but that none of them was labelled 'correct, use me'. These thoughts connect with some understandings about learning and the pruning of neural networks.

Ⓖ p 303: neural networks

In *Finding Your Voice with Dyslexia and other SpLDs* (Stacey, 2019), I discuss neural networks being produced as part of anyone's learning. In summary:

Stacey (2019)

- brain connections are progressively pruned to a single neural network that should be efficient for that person: e.g., spellings only have one version; see also *PARK PATHS AND PRUNING NEURONS*

- the mind learns to organise the information it deals with

- intended skills are acquired.

INSIGHT BOX: PARK PATHS AND PRUNING NEURONS: p 5

The contrast with dyslexia/ SpLD is that attempts to learn can leave the brain with many connections, networks that are inefficient and the mind with confusion (Davis, 1994).

Davis (1994)

Insight: Hand modelling as analogy for learning

An analogy I use in workshops compares learning with making a model of a hand out of modelling plastic. To make the hand model, you have to press your hand down onto a slab of plastic, *FIGURE 1.1*. The plastic concerned takes about 4 hours to solidify. You don't want to stand

Figure 1. 1 Initial imprint

with your hand there for 4 hours, so you take it away for as long as you can. You replace your hand at intervals for long enough for the details from your hand to be imprinted on the plastic again. By lining up your hand each time you press down, you get a reasonable cast of your hand, *FIGURE 1.2*.

The parallel with learning is that the first time you engage with a skill, or knowledge, that you want to learn, you pay a lot of attention and you can be fairly clear about what you are learning. If you do nothing else, you will forget over time; the plastic relaxes and details are lost, similarly the mind loses detail. Usually, people have to reinforce their learning by rehearsal or practice,

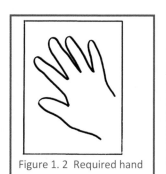

Figure 1. 2 Required hand cast

equivalent to the hand being repeatedly put back on the plastic. The outcomes are that 1) the hand model is clear or 2) learning is accomplished.

It is possible that the initial placing of the hand on the plastic was at an undesired angle but that subsequent placings were consistent with the first. The hand model is clear and you can rotate it or re-shape the surrounding material to achieve the desired orientation, *FIGURE 1.3*. An equivalent learning situation is those people who cannot immediately tell left from right but after a simple

Figure 1. 3 Hand cast good but at wrong angle

extra thought or movement have no trouble with left and right, for example, those who know which side is left by making an L shape with their left thumb and fingers or by remembering where their wedding ring is.

Dyslexia/ SpLD is equivalent to there being no consistency from one time to another as the hand is put down on the plastic, *FIGURE 1.4*. Trying to learn simply produces more confusion (chaotic neural networks) and as time passes the confusion becomes well established. *WHAT GOES WRONG* discusses the observed behaviour that results from the confusion.

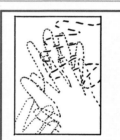

Figure 1. 4 'Dyslexic/ SpLD' hand cast

WHAT GOES WRONG:
p 82

When I have used this analogy in workshops, dyslexic people will often tell me that I should say some learning happens without the confusion. When someone in their childhood has had the "knack of putting 'it' the right way", there has been no confusion: in *FIGURE 1.5* just the tip of the index finger is as good as required

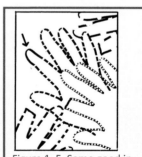

Figure 1. 5 Some good in the 'dyslexic/ SpLD' mix

This "knack of putting 'it' the right way" can range:

- from something as simple as drawing a few lines (visual thinking) while talking about something
- to explanations of a topic that suited the person's way of thinking (could be using any option for *THINKING PREFERENCES*).

THINKING PREFERENCES:
p 290

This analogy fits with the experience that dyslexic/ SpLD people can learn, but usually not in the same way as everyone else. As far back as 1989, Harry Chasty said 'If this child doesn't learn the way we teach, can we teach him the way he learns and then develop and widen his competences in learning?' (Chasty, 1989). This approach is still being advocated by leading professionals in the field (Chinn, 2017). Usually the quote ends at the word 'learns'. The full aim of the ideas in this series is to satisfy the second half of the quote as well.

Chasty (1989)

Chinn (2017)

The earlier people can learn the right way for them, the less confusion develops.

Summary: Dyslexia/ SpLD is not removed by better learning

When dyslexic/ SpLD people find their best way to learn and have good memory traces, say for language and spelling, they still have a problem: the new learning doesn't remove the old, so they have both network systems together in the brain.

The dyslexic/ SpLD network can often get triggered when a *PITFALL* happens.

PITFALLS: p 73

4 Neurons firing together, wire together

Ⓖ p 303*: neuron, neuron firing*

Neurons firing in the brain are a key element of neural networks being used. There are gaps between neurons, called synapses. Thoughts happening in the mind involve neurons firing signals that are communicated across the synapses by means of chemicals called neurotransmitters. Several neurons firing at the same time contribute to the way the signal is passed on. Once neurons have fired together, there is a higher probability that they will fire together again in the future. This phenomenon is often expressed as 'Neurons that fire together, wire together' even though part of the 'wiring' is chemical, (Stein and Stoodley, 2006, p 415). As they 'wire' together, they build neural networks.

Stein and Stoodley (2006, p 415)

To build up the neural networks that underpin efficient, effective learning, the learning processes need to involve any influences that will assist the most useful patterns to 'wire' together.

Find out what your student is thinking about when he attempts to learn anything. The neural networks associated with his thoughts, his emotions or his attitudes will be the ones that are firing while he learns.

> What is he thinking about?
>
> What is alive for him as he sets about learning?
>
> What emotions are around?
>
> What helps him to engage with the present material?

Questions like these will help you understand the influences that help or hinder his learning. You are aiming to help him achieve learning in line with *FIGURE 1.2* or *FIGURE 1.3* and to avoid confusion like *FIGURE 1.4*. Insights that you gain this way can be built into his *INDIVIDUAL, PERSONAL PROFILE OF DYSLEXIA/ SPLD* and the *REGIME FOR MANAGING DYSLEXIA/ SPLD*

INDIVIDUAL, PERSONAL PROFILE OF DYSLEXIA/ SPLD:
p 268

REGIME FOR MANAGING DYSLEXIA/ SPLD:
p 268

Summary: 'Neurons that fire together, wire together'

Neurons being 'wired' together means they operate as part of a consistent pattern; they become the efficient neural networks that should be the outcome of learning.

It is important to find out for each individual the way that their innate potential will enable the neurons to fire together.

For dyslexic/ SpLD people 'firing together' can be assisted by elements from both the *INDIVIDUAL, PERSONAL PROFILE OF DYSLEXIA/ SPLD* and the *REGIME FOR MANAGING DYSLEXIA/ SPLD.*

---

5 The oldest memory trace

Anyone would like to remember and use the good memory trace, but that may not happen. Jost's law, about durability and remembering, states that if two memory traces have the same strength, the older

one will be more durable and forgotten less rapidly. 'It is as if in addition to decaying in the short term, memory traces become resistant to decay once well established' (Baddeley, 1982, p 47).
To me, this makes sense of the frequent experience of many dyslexic/ SpLD people reverting to older, incorrect memory traces. The following are examples of the ways in which the persistence of memory creates problems for dyslexic/ SpLD people.

Baddeley (1982, p 47)

Insight: Always right in a test, not reliable in use

You can re-learn something so well that you always get it right in a test but, when you are trying to use it automatically as part of some other task, you struggle to get it right; for example, using the correct pronunciation of a word which you mis-pronounced as a child. It is as if your working memory is fully engaged with the present task and there is no capacity available to select the newly learnt version.

ⓖ p 303
working memory

Summary: Dyslexia/ SpLD comes back

The experience for many dyslexic people is that when they hit a *PITFALL* it is the older, dyslexic memories of spelling and language that get used, not the later correct ones.

PITFALLS: p 73

Story: Increasing stress and childhood spelling

One colleague says she can tell that her stress levels are rising when she writes 'any' starting with 'e', i.e. 'eny', the way she spelt it as a child.

Some of the initial teaching strategies become 'set in stone' in dyslexic children's minds.

Insight: Set in stone

Children are told early on that 'verbs are doing words', and they are taught the patterns of verbs using doing words. 'Verbs are doing words' becomes the oldest memory trace that can't be modified.

Some never get told that the other words with the same patterns are also verbs, even if they are words of being or having.

Story: Sleeping is not doing

One dyslexic student objected, "Sleeping is not doing; it cannot be a verb."

I have come across this reaction many times and it is very hard for the dyslexic students to recognise verbs in sentences[1] when they are not 'doing words'. This quality of 'set in stone' doesn't just affect spelling; many other incidents have been reported in which the initial perception has been taken as being complete and accurate, and it can be almost impossible to modify it in any way.

---

[1] Recognising the patterns of verbs can be a very useful tool for comprehension, especially while reading.

Another example is the way routes become set:

Story: Only one way from A to B

For one person, if she has gone from A to B via C, there is no other way to get from A to B. Even when she can see B while standing at A and you can point out a short direct route, she still has to go via C no matter how long that route is; see *FIGURE 1.6*.

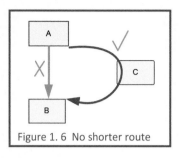

Figure 1. 6 No shorter route

6   Some factors affecting recall
6.1   Episodic memory

I discuss episodic memory in *Finding Your Voice with Dyslexia and other SpLDs* (2019). A journey is an episode remembered as a single package; the alphabet is a single entity. The experience of significant numbers of dyslexic/ SpLDs is that they only remember the complete episode; they cannot recall it in sections; they cannot use it in sections.

Stacey (2019)

Insight: The alphabet in strings

Many dyslexic/ SpLDs don't know where a letter is in the alphabet.

If they need to know where a letter is, some have to start at A and recite the alphabet until they come to it. Others know roughly where it is and take a running jump: they start a few letters before the required letter and recite until they come to it.

6.2 Importance of the place of learning

Baddeley and Godden (Baddeley, 1982, p 106) did some research on recall and recognition[2], and how they are affected by place.

Baddeley (1982, p 106)

Story: Recall and deep sea divers

Baddeley and Godden used deep sea divers, who were learning instructions, to investigate the effects of place. They gave divers words to learn while on land or under 10ft of water. They discovered that words were recalled better in the place that they were learnt. In contrast, when the divers were tested on the recognition of words, the place the words were learnt did not affect the results.

See also: STORY: REMEMBERING INSTRUCTIONS ONLY WHEN THEY ARE NEEDED, p 54 in which recall doesn't happen on its own but only when the work provides a prompt.

Story: Is 'do' the same at school and home?

One primary school boy was doing reading practice with me at his home. He came to the word 'do' and half said it, 'D… I've done it at school, but I haven't done it with you.' We then discussed that words stayed the same, no matter where you were using them.

Story: Is 'pat' the same on two different pages?

Another child learning to read had worked out 'pat' on one page of a book, but a couple of pages later had forgotten what the sound was. Going back to the original page, he knew the right sound, moving forward again, he didn't know it. The page seemed to be part of the recall mechanism.

---

[2] Recall is the process of bringing something out of memory.
Recognition is a process of knowing something when it is shown to you.

In the last 2 stories, the issue was the consistency of words from one place to another. In the following story, the presence of the student at the place of the photographs was key to recall happening.

Story: Recall from lecture notes

One student was having problems with the speed at which her lecturer was covering topics on her physics course. She could understand the lectures. She had a good way of dealing with her notes, but could not keep up week by week. Another feature of her learning emerged as we worked on methods for her to keep up.

In the process of our discussion, she showed me both the online lectures handouts and the photos she took of the writing on the board.

The online handouts were in his handwriting; he followed them very closely when writing on the board. The two sets were effectively identical.

Looking at the handouts online, the student could recall nothing of the physics involved. Looking at her photos, on the same computer, she was able to tell me exactly what the lecture was about. As I'm also a physicist, I could tell she understood what she was saying.

It was quite remarkable the way the photos that she had taken could trigger her memory and her understanding.

6.3 Moving around the classroom

The actual place of learning may have an impact that needs to be taken into account in schools. If the results of Baddeley and Godden's experiments apply to the classroom then work done on the same topic but in different places may not be co-ordinated in some children's minds.

For example, work on castles as a topic could involve the children:

- making castles in the modelling corner
- reading about them in the reading corner
- talking about them in the centre of the room all gathered round the teacher.

These activities could be done in preparation for some written work on castles. The expectation would be that the words would be easier to recall because of the previous work.

If writing is carried out in yet another place, any child for whom the place is an important part of the recall will be unable to recall the words and the writing will not benefit from the preparatory work.

6.4 Knowing instructions when needed, but not straight after they've been given

Several dyslexic people have told me that they cannot recall information 'as a pointless exercise'. For example, it feels a pointless exercise when you are told something and the speaker tries to check you have heard by asking you to repeat what they've said. However, this group of dyslexic/ SpLD people know that when they come to use the information, it will be readily available.

Story: Remembering instructions only when they are needed

A dyslexic gardener used to be given the week's instructions in one go. He could never repeat it back on the day, but come the time when he needed the information for his work, there was no problem with his recall.

Experience will show whether the recall is working for the actual situation.

It takes considerable confidence to avoid feeling inadequate when you can't recall something immediately after it has been spoken to you.

Students whose memories work in similar ways often need to direct their minds in specific ways so that they can answer exam questions, whether by writing or by speaking.

6.5   Varying speeds of recall

Some writing problems, and probably speaking ones, result from different parts of a sequence having different speeds of recall.

Insight: Recall at varying speeds

If you want to spell a word, the letters may all flow from your mind to the pen or computer, but some will flow faster than others and the spelling gets out of order (Newby, 1995).

Newby (1995)

The same happens with words; you are thinking about your ideas ahead of the place that your hands are writing and then words from your thinking get injected into the part of the sentence that you are writing: your writing becomes very disjointed.

Summary: Recall

Dyslexic/ SpLD people's recall of information and skills can be hampered by many factors. Patchy recall may contribute to *PITFALLS*.

PITFALLS: p 73

7 Attention to learning

It is widely assumed that subliminal learning occurs; for example, that:

- if you read a lot
    - you will learn how to spell
    - you will learn how the English language works to make sense
- if you write essays
    - you will acquire the skills needed for the task and gradually get better.

It is widely experienced by dyslexic/ SpLD people that this kind of subliminal learning doesn't happen for them.

Ⓖ p 303: subliminal learning

The episodic buffer is the component of working memory that controls the capacity of working-memory (Stacey, 2019; Baddeley, 2007). There are a limited number of storage places, called chunks, in which information can be held in the episodic buffer. The size of each chunk can be increased by pieces of information being strongly linked together.

Stacey (2019)
Baddeley (2007)
Ⓖ p 303: chunking

When spelling and reading become automatic, strong links exist between the letters and the words. The ideas conveyed by the words also can be linked strongly: the chunks of episodic memory can then be expanded to hold a lot of information. *FIGURES 2.3* and *2.4* show graphically what happens as the chunks are used up.

FIGURES 2.3 and *2.4*: p 105

When automatic spelling and reading do not develop in dyslexic/ SpLD people's minds, there will be no strong links between letter or words and especially not between ideas. They will always be struggling with basic language and numbers; they will not be making links between information. Their minds will not be able to link information together to use the chunks effectively and subliminal learning will not happen.

Key point: Absence of subliminal learning

Generally, subliminal learning should not be taken for granted for dyslexic/ SpLD learners. They need to pay attention in very specific ways to everything they need to learn and they need to use their individual thinking preferences.

Ⓖ p 303: subliminal learning

8 Average language skills: a disadvantage

Ⓖ p 301: descriptions of 4 SpLDs from DfES (2005)

Average language skills can lead to a disadvantage for a dyslexic/ SpLD person, when general intelligence[3] is not included in the definition or descriptions of the syndromes.

A working party for the Department for Education and Skills (DfES) produced guidelines to clarify acceptable evidence for dyslexia/ SpLD (DfES, 2005). Their description of the different SpLDs did not include general intelligence as a key component; it was described as 'extra evidence'. The working party was set up as a result of requests for clarity from Local Education Authorities, so their guidance has had an impact on the approach to dyslexia/ SpLD. There were good reasons for the change, however there are people who miss out because of it.

An alternative perspective is that general intelligence is a key component of dyslexia/ SpLD (Elbeheri and Everett, 2009) and that a discrepancy between general intelligence and the skills affected by dyslexia/ SpLD is an integral part of the definition of these syndromes. The view is sometimes called the deficit model for dyslexia/ SpLD.

Elbeheri and Everett (2009)

---

[3] The role of general intelligence in the definition is still debated, but it is outside the scope of this series of books.
The definitions of dyslexia/ SpLD do not affect the usefulness of the ideas in these books.

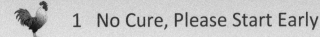

FIGURE 1.7 represents the distribution[4] of people when you compare reading level against intelligence level. The spread in both directions (vertical and horizontal) represents the range of abilities in reading and IQ. Since reading skills do not only depend on intelligence, the distribution is an oval at an angle[5]. The shading of the oval indicates the density of data points, i.e. the greatest number of individuals concentrated in the centre of the oval and fewer individuals towards the outside of the oval.

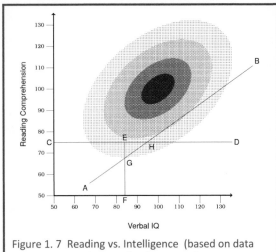

Figure 1. 7 Reading vs. Intelligence (based on data from Vellutino, 2000 and Bishop, 1989).

The numbers along the axes of FIGURE 1.7 are measurements of reading comprehension and verbal IQ. To make comparison easier, the average ability that is recorded testing people is converted to be 100. In the discussion below, cut offs are used to show people who have abilities sufficiently below the average to be a cause for concern. The value at which the such cut offs are made is different for different circumstances and often a source of difference of opinion. Where the cut off is taken does not invalidate the present discussion.

A double cut off process can be used to monitor for children with poor literacy skills. A line CD is the cut off for reading skills and EF is the cut off for intelligence (Bishop, 1989). Those above the line CD were deemed to be making adequate progress. Those in the area CEF have low intelligence and their low reading skills are not unexpected. Those in the area FED are those in need of help.

Bishop (1989)

Vellutino (2000)

---

[4] In order to compare data from different sources, statisticians often use the normal distribution. This distribution assumes the data are randomly distributed about a mean (average value), for example there is an average height for people and heights measured are randomly distributed above and below the average.

[5] The angle of the distribution is given by the correlation between reading comprehension and verbal IQ. The correlation coefficient has been taken as 0.6 (Vellutino, 2000). The plot uses a normal distribution for both reading comprehension and verbal IQ. The figure was created by A.E. Stacey and is used with his permission.

The deficit model uses a line AB to separate those with adequate skills and those without. Thus, the area DHB shows a group of children whose literacy skills are not matching their intelligence, but who are not seen as making too little progress when the line CD is used. These children do not get help at school; they often use their intelligence to find other ways round difficulties and it is not until adulthood that they are recognised as being dyslexic/ SpLD. A high percentage of students, about 40% (Singleton, 1999), are identified as dyslexic/ SpLD for the first time at university. Many women are not recognised as dyslexic/ SpLD until they go to university because the response of females to difficulties is much quieter than that of males; they don't create a disturbance, so their lack of progress is not picked up.

Singleton (1999)

When the discrepancy is not seen as worthy of attention, the pupils can be denied an early opportunity to recognise what their best way of learning is. Those affected make less progress than they could; they have to work harder than they need. They use their friends, parents and others to help them. Some become the class clown to distract attention from their lack of progress. It would be so much better all round, if the discrepancy were taken into account early and they were able to explore different approaches to learning.

Some are not so affected by the lack of recognition early on. There is something about their situation that allows them the freedom to develop the skills they need in their own way. They are not cause for concern.

Summary: Average language skills mask dyslexia/ SpLD

The average language skills of some dyslexic/ SpLD people are being regarded as adequate; they are not being compared with other signs of intelligence and a discrepancy goes unrecognised. This becomes a disadvantage when an individual's best way of learning is not established in early childhood.

9 4 levels of compensation

McLoughlin et al., (2001, p 50) discuss awareness of dyslexic weaknesses, and compensation by using strategies. They describe 4 levels of compensation:

McLoughlin et al., (2001, p 50)

1   'People at level 1 are not aware of their weaknesses and have developed no strategies to overcome them.

2   'Those at level 2 are aware of their weaknesses but have not developed strategies to overcome them.

3   'People at level 3 are aware of their weaknesses and have developed compensatory strategies, but have developed them unconsciously.

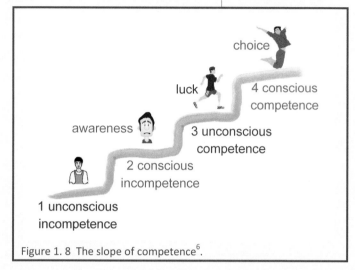

Figure 1. 8 The slope of competence[6].

4   'Finally, people at level 4 are aware of their weaknesses and they have consciously developed strategies to overcome them.'

These levels are shown in *FIGURE 1.8.* They useful in the discussion of dyslexia/ SpLD management and the impossibility of a 'cure'.

Key point: Intermittent nature of dyslexia/ SpLD

Being able to manage dyslexia/ SpLD is not equivalent to reaching level 4 and operating on that level consistently. Even when people mostly operate at level 4, a new situation, task or colleague can put them back to level 2 or even level 1.

Usually they are only put back to level 2 because they haven't yet developed the right strategies to deal with the new challenge, but

---

[6] Strategies at level 3 develop unconsciously, hence 'luck' in the diagram.

they are aware that the difficulties they face probably have something to do with their dyslexia/ SpLD.

Something 'new' has made them more vulnerable to their dyslexic/ SpLD *PITFALLS*.

PITFALLS: p 73

Part of managing dyslexia/ SpLD is a person recognising when he has come out of operating at level 4 and needs the ability to do something about getting back there. Some attention almost always has to be directed to thinking processes with an awareness as to which level of compensation he is on.

Summary: No Cure

When managing dyslexia/ SpLD is understood in terms of moving between levels of compensation, one can see that you can't assume a compensated dyslexic/ SpLD has been cured of the dyslexia/ SpLD; it's more akin to remission, being held under control.

10 'Degrees of severity'

Often there is discussion about 'degrees of severity' of dyslexia/ SpLD in the literature. For example:

- The committee report chaired by Singleton (1999) discusses the need for support in higher education in terms of the 'degree of severity'

Singleton (1999)

- Talli et al. (2016) studied the significance and frequency of deficits in developmental dyslexia and specific language impairment. They use the concept of 'severe deficit' in the discussion of their results.

Talli et al. (2016)

- Jefferies (2007) includes some case histories in her thesis on working memory. She includes the categories of mild, moderate and severe dyslexia, where appropriate, in the headings of the cases.

Jefferies (2007)

Some dyslexic/ SpLD people don't take their own problems seriously because they watch others who seem to have many more difficulties.

To me, it doesn't make sense of experience to talk about 'degrees of severity' as if:

- there were a continuous slope from severe to mild
- you could select a point on the slope to represent a person's degree of dyslexia/ SpLD
- you could expect a person to gradually move down the slope from severe to mild by learning to deal with the dyslexia/ SpLD, see *FIGURE 1.9.*

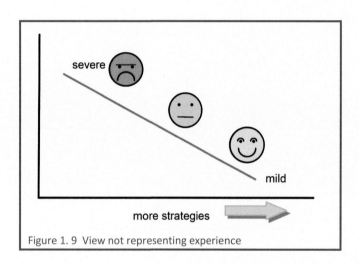

Figure 1. 9 View not representing experience

The effects that don't fit with severity of dyslexia/ SpLD are:

- that dyslexic/ SpLD memory traces are not destroyed when new strategies are developed
- that the oldest (dyslexic/ SpLD) memory trace often is more readily activated than the new strategy
- that people experience 'good and bad' days (Aldridge, 1995; Fawcett, 1995)

Aldridge (1995)
Fawcett (1995)

- that emotional hi-jacking can trigger a dyslexic/ SpLD mode of functioning (Stacey, 2019)

Stacey (2019)

- that stress can make you more vulnerable to dyslexic/ SpLD processing.

There are good reasons for wanting to be able to label degrees of dyslexia/ SpLD:

- dyslexic/ SpLD people want to know how their experience compares with others
- people with responsibility for making official provisions need some guidance as to which measures are appropriate
- people in charge of regulations need to know what is reasonable to meet most people's needs
- managers want to know what level of accommodation is appropriate
- people designing communications systems should consider the needs, including likelihood of misunderstandings, of dyslexic/ SpLD people.

For these reasons, and many others, some concept other than severity would be useful in the discussion of dyslexia/ SpLD.

For inter-person comparison, I suggest the issues to observe for each individual are:

- How many skills are vulnerable to dyslexia/ SpLD out of those known to be part of the syndromes?
- How many skills have no dyslexic/ SpLD complications?
- How often does someone experience dyslexia/ SpLD affecting them?
- How much effort does it take to maintain dyslexia/ SpLD management?
- When tipped into dyslexia/ SpLD, how easy is it usually to regain good functioning?
- How much does the person mind about the effects of dyslexia/ SpLD?

With these questions, you could get a feel for how much a dyslexic/ SpLD person's energy, confidence and self-esteem is governed by having to manage dyslexia/ SpLD.

Degree of severity is being replaced by

- number of skills affected
- frequency of being affected
- how far back a person tends to be pushed into non-management
- probable recovery time.

This is not as neat as a single 'degree of severity', but more realistic.

Summary: Measures of compensation

In terms of McLoughlin's 4 levels of compensations, for each person:

　What does level 4 consist of?

　How well can he maintain it?

　How often does he get triggered out of level 4, and by what?

　How much time and effort is needed for him to get back
　　to level 4?

When it comes to exam provisions or employment accommodation, you need to be thinking:

- what will allow the individual to succeed at a level consistent with their other, innate, intellectual capabilities?

　Ⓖ p 303: innate

- what buffer zone do they need to regain good functioning should dyslexic/ SpLD functioning get triggered?
- what safety net can be used to prevent a damaging outcome from any situation?

The variations experienced, even by one person from one time to another, mean that tailoring provisions or accommodations tightly to one person has to be done with caution.

Some things will be very particular and easy to define, e.g., the colour used for an exam paper or the changes in environment to reduce distraction from noise in an open office.

Others, such as a precise amount of extra time for exams[7], can't be predicted because it would depend on experience in each exam and would vary from one exam to another for a given person. Again, as above, not a neat, single concept to use but more realistic.

11 Comparison: dyslexia/ SpLD vs. non-dyslexia/ SpLD

It is difficult to explain what dyslexia/ SpLD is like. Very early in my work on dyslexia, I knew I would not believe what I was saying if I could not see the effects from the inside[8]. I devised exercises to generate dyslexic effects in non-dyslexic minds to help non-dyslexics experience and understand what I was explaining (Stacey, 2005).

Stacey (2005)

Even now, some 25 years later, many people will say:

- "I do ...(such and such), does that make me dyslexic?"
- they are "having a dyslexic moment"
    - when they can't think of the right word for something
    - they have some other problem similar to a dyslexia/ SpLD one
- there is a spectrum from non-dyslexic to very dyslexic and that we all fall somewhere on the spectrum.

Listening to many people's experiences in the workshops I've run and from the students I've supported, I have come to the following view.

---

[7] Good guidelines for extra time in exams exist for many different situations and within many different institutions. What I'm saying here is that you can't predict 3 minutes per hour (m/h) will be right for person A; 5 m/hr for B; 7 m/h for C; etc. Such precise predictions would work for neither the person concerned nor the institution.

[8] I had learnt to meditate and watch my thoughts as they happened, so I could see the effects of dyslexia from the inside.

For each SpLD, and independent of general intelligence, there are 3 groups, as shown in *Figure 1.10*:

Ⓖ p 303: intelligence

1 There is a group of people who have no difficulty with learning the skills that are undermined by the particular SpLD. You could teach this group quite badly and they would still learn the skills, because the skills are natural to them. The skills they learn are robust and function well, only breaking down under extreme conditions.

2 There is a group of people whose natural abilities are not so in tune with the desired skills, but their educational experience has suited them well enough and the skills have been learnt without any confusion. The skills are more vulnerable than those of the first group and they can let people down in ways that are similar to the experience of the dyslexic/ SpLD group. However, they have only a good set of neural networks relating to the skills, so after a glitch in processing, the skills are re-established in good working order.

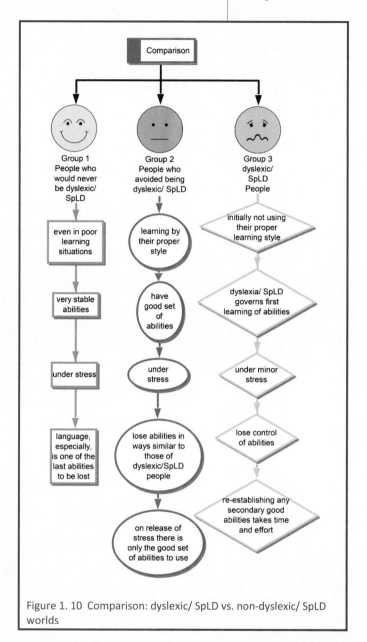

Figure 1. 10 Comparison: dyslexic/ SpLD vs. non-dyslexic/ SpLD worlds

3 The dyslexic/ SpLD group are those who have not learnt the skills in a way that suits the natural abilities; they have one or more chaotic neural networks relating to the skills in question; these neural networks can be activated and used in various ways

Ⓖ p 303: neural networks

See also: *Learned Confusion*: p 44

depending on circumstances. Later learning, done in the correct way for an individual, doesn't eliminate these chaotic networks, so a vulnerability to dyslexia/ SpLD remains even after good skills have been learnt.

If the constitutional origins of dyslexia/ SpLD are separable, a single person could be in different groups for different SpLDs; for example:

- person A could be in
    - group 3 for dyslexia
    - group 2 for dyscalculia
    - group 1 for dyspraxia and AD(H)D
- person B could be in
    - group 3 for dyspraxia
    - group 1 for dyslexia, dyscalculia and AD(H)D.

As more data is gathered for dyspraxia, AD(H)D and dyspraxia, it is found that the different SpLDs often co-exist, i.e., a person is in group 3 for more than one SpLD; see *OVERLAP OF SPLDS*.

OVERLAP OF SPLDS: p 224

12   Stress

For most people, stress makes any problem more difficult to deal with; dyslexic/ SpLD people are no exception.   Stress can range from feelings of mild pressure to a level of panic which stops clear thinking.

Managing dyslexia/ SpLD involves individuals being aware of their own thinking and being able to direct it in the best possible way (Stacey, 2019). They cannot rely on their minds being on auto-pilot and functioning well, e.g. for dyslexics, language can't be relied on. Dyslexic/ SpLD people have the added dimension that stress can activate the dyslexic/ SpLD neural networks and, once that has happened, reducing the stress may not restore order in the mind as quickly as it would for someone without the extra *PITFALLS*.

Stacey (2019)

PITFALLS: p 73

It is important to say that dyslexic/ SpLD people are often very good in stressful situations because such situations are nothing new: they have had to find out how to deal with so many different difficult situations that they have the skills to hand. Also, some people need a certain level of stress in order to make them get moving with tasks.

External sources of stress

There are two external sources of stress that are particularly worth mentioning in relation to dyslexia/ SpLD:

One is other people around not listening to them and not understanding that they have innate ways of thinking that are quite different to those of non-dyslexic/ SpLD people. It can be very tiring and frustrating trying to convince others, even other dyslexic/ SpLDs, to take your differences seriously.

The second is important enough to be in the following *INSIGHT BOX*.

Insight: Boring, safe options are unsafe

The other (external source of stress) is trying to avoid the effects of dyslexia/ SpLD by opting for a less interesting job or hobby; doing so can be counterproductive and increase levels of stress.

Because you are not interested, your mind will not be using interest to chunk information together and the capacity of working memory will not be enhanced (Stacey, 2019); as a result, the effects of your dyslexia/ SpLD can become worse, and will not be avoided.

CHUNKING: p 287

Stacey (2019)

By contrast, an interesting job or hobby can minimise the effects of dyslexia/ SpLD. Tackling tasks that are difficult or especially challenging for you can be empowering. You are more likely to bring something special to the job or hobby. Other people are more likely to be supportive when they can appreciate and value your different contribution.

Internal sources of stress

Early dyslexic/ SpLD experiences may have left dyslexic/ SpLD people with a lot of unhappy memories, especially around the problems they still encounter.

- Anything that revives one of those memories can trigger an emotional hi-jack and they will feel as if they are back in the scene where it first happened (Stacey, 2019).

Stacey (2019)

- It is important to be able to see that some of their emotion belongs to the original situation and possibly doesn't belong in the present at all.
- It may be that a present emotional hi-jack is indicating some problem that an individual still can't deal with and new insights might make it worth sorting out a way forward.

Exercise: Stress

Stress is rather a broad term and it could be useful to be more precise about it.

- Make a list of emotions that can produce it: frustration, dissatisfaction, worry...
- Think of several situations that you find stressful. Have you included all the emotions that produce the stress?

Precise naming of an emotion can be the beginning of a process to reduce its difficult effects, especially any damaging effects on thinking.

Exercise: Taking the stress out of PITFALLS - 1

Use the list you produced in the previous exercise.

- Do any of these emotions relate to your dyslexia/ SpLD?
- Is there some way you are not managing a PITFALL of your dyslexia/ SpLD?

PITFALLS: p 73

- Can you find similar stories in this book or on the series website?

COLLECTIONS:

- Can you use any of the observation suggestions on the series website to work out exactly what is problematic?
- Can you develop some strategy to deal with the PITFALL?
- Is there someone who could help you take the stress out of it?

There are many ways that people react to situations that make them uncomfortable.

They can:

- avoid them and pretend they don't exist
- analyse them
- try to find solutions
- carry on the story of the situation
- make judgements relating to the situation. (Stead, 2016)

Stead (2016)

In my experience of *PITFALLS*, their power to disrupt a student's life only diminishes when the student understands them and has ways to deal with them. Even then, *PITFALLS* can have an emotional impact that doesn't diminish until it is faced.

Exercise: Taking the stress out of *PITFALLS* - 2

Sit comfortably, but in an upright position.

Close your eyes.

Focus on your breathing in the abdomen; be aware of the movement of your stomach as you breathe in and out. (Don't do this step, if you start to breathe rapidly. Hold your breath for a count of 10 to calm your breathing and ignore this step.)

Choose a *PITFALL* you can deal with, but which still leaves you feeling uncomfortable. Don't choose the most difficult situation.

Think of one time recently when you encountered the *PITFALL*.

How were you feeling?

Where in your body are there any sensations connected to your feelings?

Keep your mind focused on that part of your body and just allow your feelings to be.

If you can use the breath, breathe into that part of the body; or else accept the way your body is feeling with compassion or sympathy.

Be open to anything your body might be able to tell you about the way you feel.

You may notice a shift in the sensations in your body.

When you feel ready, open your eyes and end the exercise.

This way of working with the sensations in your body often reduces the stress that comes with a *PITFALL*.

Physiological sources of stress

In order to process language or do any complex thinking, different parts of your mind need to be able to communicate. If action is needed as well, your mind has to be able to communicate with your body. These delicate interconnections can be impaired by several different mechanisms, including:

- strong reactions in the brain's stress centres in response to emotional states of mind
- hormones and other chemicals in the blood-streams being out of balance
- sickness.

This list is not expected to be complete.

Psychological sources of stress

There are psychological causes of stress as well as physical ones:

Insight: Sources of psychological stress

- you may compare your performance with that of others and expect yourself to be the same as them, without seeing where you have strengths that can be brought to the task or situation
- significant others (parents, teachers, employers etc) may expect you to think or learn in a way that simply won't work for you
- you may not have the confidence to use the abilities that you feel you have
- you may want to fit in with the crowd and not be different
- you may feel no-one takes you seriously
- you may feel no-one recognises what you can do well
- other[9].

This list is not complete.

These psychological causes of stress may well contribute to an overall lack of self-esteem or lack of self-confidence.

Some of these sources are external, driven by the people around them; some will be internal and be driven by dyslexic/ SpLD people's own perceptions. Their reactions to the psychological stresses can induce the physical stress reactions discussed above.

One important ingredient for dealing with the sources of stress is for people to understand their own dyslexia/ SpLD and know how to manage it well. Then they can get to a point when they see beyond dyslexia/ SpLD and they notice that many people have problems of some kind, which are often not grouped under a single label.

---

[9] Other sources of stress can be uncovered: for example, *Artist's Way at Work* (Bryan, 1998) gives a 12-week programme that allows a reader to explore subtle influences of stress that hamper their growth and progress.

13   Pitfalls

A pitfall is defined as a 'hidden or unsuspected danger, drawback, difficulty or opportunity for error' (OED Online, 2016).

('pitfall, n.'
OED Online, 2016)

Insight: Important characteristics of *PITFALLS*

- You can't always predict when one is going to open up.
- The earlier you recognise one, the better you will be able to lessen its effects on your life.
- It is difficult to organise *ACCOMMODATIONS* for unpredictable *PITFALLS*, you have to manage them as they occur.
- Some *PITFALLS* you will develop strategies to deal with; this sub-category I've called 'hazards'.
- Some *PITFALLS* are such major problems that you are not able to develop strategies for them; this sub-category I've called 'insuperable obstacles'.

ACCOMMODATIONS:
p 78 and *INDEX*

Ⓖ p 303*:* hazard,
obstacle

The earlier sections of this chapter have included:

the development of the chaotic neural networks of dyslexic/ SpLD functioning

the experience of dyslexic/ SpLD people that, even when they have good strategies, there are times when they function in their most dyslexic/ SpLD ways.

Key point: The importance of *PITFALLS*

It is the way we, the dyslexic/ SpLD community, get tripped into dyslexic/ SpLD functioning that makes *PITFALLS* so important.

While highlighting the importance of *PITFALLS*, it is also worth acknowledging that dyslexia/ SpLD can also produce a 'glitch', 'a sudden short-lived irregularity in behaviour'. A glitch is a time when dyslexia/ SpLD has an effect on your pupil's behaviour, but it is seen immediately and corrected. Any error is short-lived and there is no impact to prolong dyslexic/ SpLD functioning.

('glitch, n.'
OED Online, 2016)

Examples: Glitches

Introducing someone by the wrong name, e.g. Champion for Campbell because both start with C and are linked in your mind, but noticing it immediately and then using the correct surname.

Saying, "The dyslexic person beside me needs some food now." Then recognising you should have said "diabetic person" and correcting immediately.

It is the immediate correction that contains the pitfall as a glitch and prevents it becoming more of a problem.

The way you work with a pupil and his pitfalls will depend on his age. If you are working with a child you are trying to help him avoid developing dyslexia/ SpLD problems. With a pupil of any age, you will be trying to identify where his learning is getting derailed. If you are working with someone from teenage years and older, you will also need to uncover the pitfalls from his previous learning experiences.

For both[10] age ranges, you need to bear in mind that anything 'new' is problematic. The very initial steps of learning anything will underpin all that comes later. *TIP BOX: UNOBTRUSIVE, OBJECTIVE OBSERVATION OF A PUPIL* suggests finding out how your pupil functions using a topic that is not part of what he has to learn.

TIP BOX: UNOBTRUSIVE OBJECTIVE OBSERVATION OF A PUPIL: p 167

---

[10] *AGE RANGE*, p 154, divides pupils into 'children' at primary school and 'teenage+' at secondary schools and adults.

Exercise: Identifying a *PITFALL* with a child

Be objective and open minded.

Collect evidence using *TEMPLATE: B8 - RECORDING TEMPLATE - 4*
Headings:

A = date, and task or situation

B = what you expect the child to do

C = what he is doing

D = what you think the root of the problem is

E = next step

Observe using the following questions:

- What are the pointers that make you think the child is not doing tasks as easily as others?

- At what point does the task present a problem?

- What are the things that seem to frustrate him?

- What is he trying to do?

- What does he think he's trying to do? (The two may not be the same.)

- Is there one step in the task that is proving difficult?

- How can you change the teaching side of his learning to diminish his problem? Check the ideas about teaching in *TEACHING AN INDIVIDUAL PUPIL* and *WHOLE SCHOOL APPROACH*.

Keep an open mind; the answers may not be what you expect.

TEMPLATES
COMPANION @ WEBSITE

TEACHING AN INDIVIDUAL PUPIL: p 161

WHOLE SCHOOL APPROACH: p 176

When you are working with an adult student, you need to be able to talk about various difficulties he has in study, life and employment. Let him describe them to you and work with him to find out what's at the heart of them. I'll often suggest likely influences but I'm always ready to change my ideas when it is clear they are not matching his view of his experience. I work with my students with all the ideas in this series of books to find out what's at the root of their problems. It's how they have shown me so much and how I became a conduit for ideas and experiences to pass from one person to another.

As you gain insights about the way a student thinks and does things, you need to build up the insights into an INDIVIDUAL, PERSONAL PROFILE OF DYSLEXIA/ SPLD and a REGIME FOR MANAGING DYSLEXIA/ SPLD. You should be helping your student to become autonomous: understanding where he's got strengths and how to deal with problems when they occur.

INDIVIDUAL, PERSONAL PROFILE OF DYSLEXIA/ SPLD: p 268

REGIME FOR MANAGING DYSLEXIA/ SPLD: p 268

One of the difficulties about dyslexic/ SpLD PITFALLS is that non-dyslexic/ SpLD don't share them. They often share the manifest behaviour, but there is usually an underlying component that they don't share. Talking about the PITFALLS doesn't diminish them the way talking over problems often does. You can help a lot by the way you are prepared to accept what a dyslexic/ SpLD person says about their experience: acceptance of what is, with problem-solving in mind.

Story: Acceptance, with problem-solving

When I taught a group of dyslexic students at university, they complained that they couldn't use dyslexia as an excuse with me, because I'd just say, "OK. Let's find the way round that, then."

Story: PITFALLS at 60+

A dyslexic friend said:
"One of the delights of growing older is the arrival of grandchildren and the opportunity to take up knitting. Along with the knitting go knitting patterns – pieces of paper with tempting pictures and a page or two of indecipherable, impenetrable code. My non-dyslexic knitting colleagues were bemused by my inability

to knit a simple cardigan. My inability to translate the code into knitting prevented progress until I realised that this could be seen as a PITFALL and that there should be a way around it. My colleagues were able to help by converting the code into auditory instructions while I recorded them as a series of visual images.

"Interestingly, at the end I still couldn't interpret their code based on letters, and they couldn't interpret my diagrams."

In a classroom, pupils often don't discover the others who are also dyslexic/ SpLD, so they can't find solutions by sharing problems. Being with a group of others is good when there is recognition that people will have very different experiences.

Summary: Make friends with your PITFALLS

Find out:

- what they are
- how they impact on your life
- which ones you can do something about and have confidence in your strategies
- which ones are insuperable obstacles
- know what you are good at and enjoy it.

Gradually, you gain more control over the impact that dyslexia/ SpLD has on your life. You can then recognise that most people have problems of some kind or another. Your pitfalls just happen to be labelled dyslexic/ SpLD.

Dyslexia/ SpLD doesn't stop creating anything from havoc to mild amusement. But when you make friends with your PITFALLS, you can ease the emotional drain on you and everyone around you.

14 Accommodation

Accommodations are adaptations put in place to address or reduce the problems caused by dyslexia/ SpLD; sometimes called 'reasonable adjustments' or 'provisions'.

There are certain situations in which a PITFALL of your pupil's dyslexia/ SpLD is very likely to be a significant issue, and it is known in advance. For some of these situations, e.g. exams and tests, accommodations are well established, though they may need to be tailored to suit a particular student.

Other situations may be specific to your pupil's circumstances. You may need to work quite hard to convince those with the power to help him that the accommodation you are asking for is reasonable and in the best interest of all concerned in the long run. *GATHERING EVIDENCE IN THE EARLY STAGES OF DYSLEXIA/ SPLD* and *NEGOTIATING ACCOMMODATION* set out a protocol for backing your request.

GATHERING EVIDENCE IN THE EARLY STAGES OF DYSLEXIA/ SPLD: p 160

NEGOTIATING ACCOMMODATION: p 278

15 Avoiding dyslexia/ SpLD

Key point: Please start early

Once dyslexic/ SpLD neural networks have become established in a child's mind, they cannot be undone.

They are always there to be activated, possibly through stress or emotional hi-jacking etc.

When the mind is fully engaged on a task, there is not enough capacity to monitor keeping out of the dyslexia/ SpLD networks.

Different, more effective neural networks can be constructed as well, but they don't replace the dyslexic/ SpLD ones.

So There Is No Cure.

ADAPTATIONS FOR CHILDREN: p 140 deals with using the insights of this series of books with children.

Initially, one has a child 'at risk' of dyslexia/ SpLD. Helland et al. (2017) investigated techniques for identifying 'at risk' children. When you know the patterns of behaviour, the 'at risk' child can be recognised very early on (Saunders, 1995). With appropriate teaching, there is no need for most of the effects of dyslexia/ SpLD to develop. Elizabeth Henderson, as headmistress of two state primary schools, was able to guide the schools so that her dyslexic pupils were catered for by the ethos of the whole school (Henderson, 2003). One of her chief principles was that teachers needed to observe the children in their class; time for doing so was built into the teachers' contracts.

Helland et al. (2017)

Saunders (1995)

Henderson (2003)

Key point: Vital for dyslexic/ SpLDs, good practice for all

The other pupils in the school benefitted too: what is vital for dyslexic/ SpLD pupils is good practice for all. Avoidance of generating dyslexic/ SpLD networks is the way forward, which can be achieved through appropriate teaching.

Dyslexia/ SpLD do not just affect the early stages of learning. There are impacts on higher level processing, which will need appropriate teaching throughout life. Once dyslexic/ SpLD people, as adults, have understood how they think and learn they will be in a much better position to take control of their own learning and to negotiate with others what they need in order to contribute to the best of their ability. Avoiding creating new dyslexic/ SpLD neural networks is still a must, even as an adult.

The unorthodox thinking abilities of many dyslexic/ SpLD people need to be acknowledged and used, both during the avoidance of problems and in their own right. They contribute positively to the self-esteem and confidence of the individual and to the overall situation.

References

Aldridge, Joy, 1995, *The Dyslexics Speak for Themselves*, in Miles, Tim, and Varma, Ved (eds), *Dyslexia and Stress*, Whurr, London

Baddeley, Alan, 1982, *Your Memory: A User's Guide*, Penguin Books, London

Baddeley, Alan, 2007, *Working Memory, Thought, and Action*, Oxford University Press, Oxford

Bishop, D.V.M., 1989, *Quantitive Aspects of Specific Development Language Disorders*, in Munsat, T. (ed.), 1989, *Quantification of Neurologic Deficit*, Butterworths, Boston

Bryan, Mark, 1998, *The Artist's Way at Work*, William Morrow & Co., New York

Chasty, Harry , 1989, *The Challenge of Specific Learning Difficulties*, in Hales, Gerald, et al., 1989, *Meeting Points in Dyslexia, Proceedings of the 1st International Conference of the BDA*, BDA, Reading

Chinn, Steve, 2017, *Mathematics for Dyslexics and Dyscalculics* 4th ed., Wiley, Chichester

Davis, Ronald D., 1994, *The Gift of Dyslexia*, Souvenir Press, London

Elbeheri, Gad, Everett, John, 2009, *Dyslexia and IQ: from Research to Practice,* in Reid, Gavin, 2009, *The Routledge Companion to Dyslexia,* Routledge, Abingdon

Fawcett, Angela, 1995, *Case Studies and Some Recent Research*, in Miles, Tim, Varma, Ved (eds), *Dyslexia and Stress*, Whurr, London

Helland, T., et al., 2017, *Detecting Preschool Language Impairment and Risk of Developmental Dyslexia*, in *Journal of Research in Childhood Education*, 31(2), pp 295-311

Henderson, Elizabeth, 2003, *How to Have a Dyslexia Friendly School*, Beacon Office, Oldfield School, Maidenhead

Kolb, Bryan, 1995, *Brain Plasticity and Behaviour*, Lawrence Erlbaum Associates, Mahwah, NJ

McLoughlin, David, et al., 2001, *Adult Dyslexia: Assessment, Counselling and Training,* Whurr, London, 6th re-print

Newby, Michael, 1995, *The Dyslexics Speak for Themselves*, in Miles, Tim, Varma, Ved (eds), *Dyslexia and Stress*, Whurr, London

Saunders, Roger, 1995, *Stress Factors within the Family,* in Miles, Tim, Varma, Ved (eds), *Dyslexia and Stress*, Whurr Pub Ltd, London

Singleton, Chris, Chair, 1999, *Dyslexia in Higher Education: Policy, Provision and Practice,* The University of Hull, Hull

Stacey, Ginny, 2005, *A Taste of Dyslexia*, Oxfordshire Dyslexia Association, Oxford

Stacey, Ginny, 2019, *Finding Your Voice with Dyslexia and other SpLDs SpLD*

Stead, Tim, 2016, *Mindfulness and Christian Spirituality: Making Space for God,* SPCK, London

Stein, John, Stoodley, Catherine, 2006, *Neuroscience, An Introduction,* Wiley, Chichester, UK

Talli, I., et al., 2016, *Specific Language Impairment and Developmental Dyslexia: What are the Boundaries? Data from Greek Children*, in *Research in Developmental Disabilities*, 49-50, pp 339-353

Vellutino, F.R., et al., 2000, *Differentiating between difficult-to-remediate and readily remediated poor readers: More evidence against the IQ-achievement discrepancy definition of reading disability*, Journal of Learning Disabilities, Vol 33 (3), pp 223-238

Wolf, Maryanne, 2008, *Proust and the Squid*, Icon Books, Cambridge

Website information

DfES Report, 2005, https://www.patoss-dyslexia.org/Resources/DSA-Working-Guidelines Accessed 10 June 2020

Jefferies, Sharman, 2007, *Education-Related Learning Difficulties and Working Memory Function,* https://ethos.bl.uk
Accessed 19 April 2017

OED Online, June 2016, Oxford University Press Accessed 29 August 2016

Series website: www.routledge.com/cw/stacey

2 What Goes Wrong

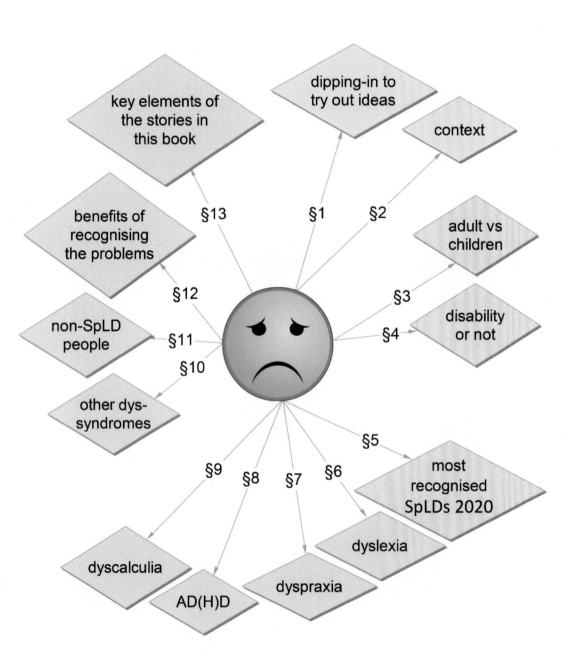

Contents

List of key points and summaries

K = key points
S = summaries

**Tip: The skills and knowledge SpLD people
can gain from this series**

APPENDIX 3: KEY CONCEPTS has a list of the main skills and knowledge that SpLD people can gain from this series of books. They fall into the categories of

> *THINKING CLEARLY*
> *USING THE MIND WELL*
> *THINKING PREFERENCES*
> *USEFUL APPROACHES*
> *ASPECTS OF DYSLEXIA/ SPLD*

APPENDIX 3: KEY CONCEPTS: p 282

Working with the chapter

Explore the advanced difficulties of the SpLDs and *MANIFEST BEHAVIOUR OF SPLDS* with your student. Find out her internal perspectives. Talk through the *STORIES, SUMMARIES* and *KEY POINTS* with her, especially the 2 using the wheelchair analogy. Find out what helps her to have a constructive perspective of her SpLD experiences.

Tables containing advanced difficulties:
DYSLEXIA: p 103
DYSPRAXIA: p 113
AD(H)D: p 118
DYSCALCULIA: p 123

MANIFEST BEHAVIOUR OF SPLDS: p 98

Work with *PITFALLS* to identify the way any of the problems impact on her life, study and employment. Help her build the insights into her *INDIVIDUAL, PERSONAL PROFILE OF DYSLEXIA/ SPLD* and her *REGIME FOR MANAGING DYSLEXIA/ SPLD*.

PITFALLS: p 73

INDIVIDUAL, PERSONAL PROFILE OF DYSLEXIA/ SPLD: p 268

If the scarring from her childhood experiences is very deep, encourage her to work with a counsellor who understands the impacts of the SpLDs.

REGIME FOR MANAGING DYSLEXIA/ SPLD: p 268

Templates on the website

A1   *JOTTING DOWN AS YOU SCAN*
A2   *BOOKMARK – PURPOSE*
A4   *JOTTING DOWN AS YOU READ*
A5   *COLLECTING IDEAS THAT INTEREST YOU*
B1   *COLLECTING IDEAS THAT RELATE TO YOU* (specially for readers who themselves have an SpLD)

TEMPLATES

Appendix 1 Resources

This appendix will help you and your student collect information about the way she does anything and how her SpLD affects her. It collects together some of the general skills she will need in order to make progress.

If you have an SpLD, this appendix will help you gather the information you want from this book.

APPENDIX 1: p 252

Appendix 2 Individual, Personal Profile of Dyslexia/ SpLD and Regime for Managing Dyslexia/ SpLD

APPENDIX 2: p 266

   Tip: *WHAT GOES WRONG* and building an *INDIVIDUAL, PERSONAL PROFILE OF DYSLEXIA/ SPLD* and a *REGIME FOR MANAGING DYSLEXIA/ SPLD*

As your student understands her SpLD better and which problems she encounters, help her to be confident about herself.

Help her to build the insights that emerge into her *PROFILE* and *REGIME*; these will allow her to become more autonomous.

Ⓖ p 303: autonomous

Appendix 3 Key Concepts

APPENDIX 3: p 282

This appendix has a summary of the key ideas I cover when doing an audit of skills and knowledge with a SpLD student. It shows which of the 4 books in the series covers each idea in full.

1   Dipping-in to try out ideas

It may help to brainstorm about one or two students before following these dipping-in suggestions.

Read: THE PERSPECTIVE FROM WHICH AN SPLD IS DESCRIBED, §2.1
       ADULTS VS. CHILDREN, §3
       the INSIGHT and STORY boxes.

Scan: MANIFEST BEHAVIOUR OF SPLDS, §5.2
       the summary tables of problems encountered by people with
          the 4 SpLDs, §§6, 7, 8, 9
       the rest of the chapter, looking for anything that catches your
       attention.

As you read and scan, jot down anything you want to come back to, with where it is in the chapter.

Ⓖ p 303: brainstorm

§2.1: p 89
§3: p 91

§5.2: p 98

§6: p 103
§7: p 113
§8: p 118
§9: p 123

Read those parts that are relevant to your students or your current interest.

2   Context

> N.B. This chapter distinguishes between the different syndromes. Therefore, the phrases dyslexia/ SpLD and dyslexic/ SpLD are not used unless relevant to another part of the book. SpLD is used as the umbrella term and the names of the four individual, most recognised syndromes are used.

This chapter focuses on the learning and processing problems of the different SpLDs; it doesn't cover the physical and medical problems of dyspraxia and AD(H)D. The other books of the series also contain information, including stories, about the problems of the SpLDs but the emphasis there is on finding solutions to the problems (Stacey, 2019, 2020, 2021).

Stacey (2019, 2020, 2021)

As an umbrella term, SpLD means that:

1   there is some area of processing that your student's mind does not carry out as well as would be expected from her general achievements

2   there are other areas of processing that she can carry out significantly better.

Since only some areas are affected, the profile of attainment seen from diagnostic testing shows a 'spiky profile' with highs as well as lows (Jones and Greenwold, 2012).

Jones and Greenwold (2012)

SpLDs are not the same as a general low ability to learn; however, they are more difficult to determine in the presence of general low ability.

The areas of processing affected by each SpLD have a progression. As children grow, they are expected to gain certain skills with language, attention, movement and maths. The children will start by learning a basic set of sub-skills, which will be developed as they progress through school. Some of the skills will be taught directly, some the children will be expected to acquire subliminally.

Ⓖ p 303: subliminal learning

Beyond the basic set of sub-skills there are sets of advanced skills. The sections dealing with the dyslexia, dyspraxia and AD(H)D have tables listing the basic and advanced skills that are affected by the SpLD. The table for dyscalculia has 2 perspectives on maths problems.

DYSLEXIA: p 103
DYSPRAXIA: p 113
AD(H)D: p 118
DYSCALCULIA: p 123

Most non-SpLD adults gain the advanced sub-set of skills to a level adequate for their jobs and lives. Some develop the skills to a much higher level. For example, most people can move about very easily, but sports people, dancers, musicians, and similar people, have learnt to move in highly trained ways.

Much of the work teaching people with SpLD is concerned with the basic set of sub-skills. The work with students at university and college is to do with the advanced set of sub-skills, which can be as affected by the underlying SpLD as the basic sub-set.

It is recognised that many SpLDs co-occur (co-exist, or 'are co-morbid') and that the problems experienced can stem from different underlying causes; academic research in this area is discussed in *OVERLAP OF SPLDS*.

OVERLAP OF SPLDS: p 224

The aims and objectives of this series of books do not depend on the final definitions or a universally agreed recognition of the causes. They relate to individual people:

- what is happening in their heads
- how they can discover the thinking processes that help them
  - realise their potential
  - minimise the effects of their SpLD.

Key point: Enable people to recognise dyslexia/ SpLD

The purpose of this chapter is to enable people, with SpLD or not, to recognise the symptoms and behaviour relating to the different SpLDs. Part of managing any SpLD is recognising the PITFALLS, knowing as much as possible about the underlying causes of problems so that the right solutions and learning methods are used by each individual SpLD person.

PITFALLS: p 73

This *CONTEXT* ends with some ideas about internal and external perspectives of SpLD problems. The chapter then discusses:

- adult and child experiences of SpLDs
- disability issues, including the existence of dyslexia
- SpLDs in general
- individual SpLDs
- other dys-syndromes
- non-SpLD people's experience
- the benefit of recognising the problems.

KEY ELEMENTS IN STORIES IN THIS BOOK, at the end of the chapter, has a list of all the stories. They are sorted according to the key elements with a brief comment about the message of each story.

KEY ELEMENTS IN STORIES IN THIS BOOK: p 133

2.1   The perspective from which an SpLD is described

There are various ways of presenting the symptoms and problems of SpLD. Two that can be quite different are:

1   you can make a list of skills that teachers and parents expect children to acquire, and assess failure and behavioural problems; here the perspective is that of the outside observer

2   you can describe situations from the SpLD person's point of view, which gives an internal perspective.

The following 3 boxes contain examples of different perspectives.

Insight: Changed perspective 1: attention given to objects

Many dyslexic people are acutely aware of their surroundings and some have a feeling for order and symmetry. During a conversation or meeting, such a person can move her body or head so that objects line up neatly or aesthetically with each other and the person she is talking to, see FIGURE 2.1. All her attention is taken with this task.

It maybe that non-dyslexic people line up objects too, but they often have minds that store the words spoken around them in short-term memory. When they need the words, they simply play the tape in their heads and contribute to the discussion. Without this short-term memory facility, the dyslexic person has lost the thread of the conversation and cannot access the lost information.

The outsider's perspective is that this dyslexic person has a poor attention span.
The inside perspective is that of being engaged with the aesthetics of the surrounding environment.

Figure 2. 1 Lining up objects

Story: Changed perspective 2: "What difficulty?"

One of the questions on a check-list for dyslexia is: Do you have difficulty finding your way around a strange town? One student answered no, so I asked how he did it.

"I just enjoy getting lost. I've seen more of Paris in one weekend than most people do in several holidays."

External perspective: he gets lost.
Internal perspective: enjoyment and many possibilities.

Story: Changed perspective 3: "I got one spelling right!"

A teacher was looking at some work with Lucy and commenting on the spelling. Lucy had spelt one particular word many different ways, including one that was right.

Lucy's tactic was to use as many different versions in the hopes that one would be right.

The teacher was puzzled by the variety and said to her, "Look you've got it right here, so why didn't you get it right every time?" Lucy, internally, was gleeful and thinking, "Yes, I got it right once!"

The external and internal views about the spelling were so different that there was no discussion about it, nor any development of spelling strategies; so Lucy made no progress from the conversation.

This story is not an unusual one. It shows a behavioural outcome from LEARNED CONFUSION.

LEARNED CONFUSION:
p 44

Summary: Internal and external perspectives

The internal and external perspectives of an SpLD can be quite different. Work with *PITFALLS* to find out your student's perspectives.

PITFALLS: p 73

3 Adults vs. children

Many SpLD adults have gained considerable insights 1) into the contribution they can make to the world around them and 2) into the working of their minds or the management of their SpLD.

Key point: Adults' insights

What adults have to contribute to the knowledge about their type of SpLD should be used to the benefit of children, even at a very early age. One hope I have for this series of books is that many more SpLD adults will feel better able to describe their SpLD experiences.

Each SpLD is known by the difficulties in certain skills. The various skill sets develop as an individual grows. For simplicity in this book, the basic skills are those usually learnt at primary school; the advanced ones are those usually learnt at secondary school and beyond. The SpLD difficulties are similarly called basic and advanced.

There are patterns of behaviour that can also be recognised by those who have seen them before. Saunders (1995) says that a grandmother is often the first one to see the characteristics of SpLD in her grandchild. She remembers similar behaviour in her child and wants to lessen the emotional hardships of her grandchild. Students are often recommended to investigate SpLD by tutors who recognise the patterns because they have seen similar behaviour in previous students with SpLD.

Saunders (1995)

Basic difficulties

The basic difficulties are the most widely recognised problems: the ones that affect learning in childhood and the ones that have attracted the most research.

Many adults have mastered the basic difficulties of their SpLD. They may take time, or extra attention, to deal with the different difficulties, but by and large they can do so and it is only fairly infrequently that they get caught out, see *4 Levels of Compensation*. Others experience frequent trouble with the basic difficulties.

Advanced difficulties

The advanced difficulties are not as well recognised, even for dyslexia. Many SpLD people do not even realise that ways they have of processing information are part of the SpLD patterns of adulthood. It is hard to conduct research with adults of a wide spectrum of abilities as they are no longer all together in a single institution as they were in schools. The work done in universities to support students with SpLD is one of the best sources of good practice.

Some adults manage the effects of their SpLD without realising what they are doing; they have found ways round and they simply stick to them through thick and thin; some do it with grace and others have a defensive attitude towards their own ways of processing information, learning or tackling a task, as is demonstrated in *Two Dyslexic Sailors*.

Confidence and security

Adult SpLDs also can have a different standing with those who try to help them. They can take a perspective on the difficulties that is quite difficult for most children. They can discuss the issues on a more equal footing; they may feel much better equipped to contribute ideas about what does or doesn't happen to them and what will or won't sort out a problem; and they can be quite strong about ideas that will not help them. As a result, their insights could be significant for a better understanding of the experiences of children: the adults' experiences should allow the children to be heard with greater understanding.

For basic and advanced difficulties see:
Dyslexia: p 103
Dyspraxia: p 113
AD(H)D: p 118
Dyscalculia: p 123

4 Levels of Compensation: p 60

Two Dyslexic Sailors: p 4

Story: Not making excuses

I remember explaining to my guitar teacher one week why I hadn't made the progress we both expected. She said, "It sounds like excuses to me!" I knew I wasn't making excuses. I knew I had tried very hard to overcome the difficulty. I set about proving to her what I meant (which took several lessons). I was lucky in that she was prepared to listen and we both learnt a lot.

Adults who don't feel secure will often try to hide the SpLD from spouses, employers, in fact everyone, and they can keep up the front for many years.

Summary: Acquisition of skill set

By the time a SpLD person is an adult, she will have acquired a lot of experience relating to her SpLD. You can consider her experiences in terms of:

- how good she is at the basic difficulties of the SpLD
- how she manages the advanced difficulties
- what her level of confidence or insecurity is, and her level of self-esteem.

Ⓖ p 303: confidence, self-esteem

4 Disability or not

Many people with SpLD object to being labelled 'disabled', as do many with physical disabilities. However there is a problem in that SpLD people process information in ways that do not help communication with the rest of the population.

Key point: Wheelchair analogy for SpLD disadvantage

Wheelchair users are dis-abled when there is no ramp to give them access to a building. Dyslexic people are dis-abled when information is written in long solid paragraphs with long sentences. These are two simplistic situations in which the environment puts the person at a disadvantage.

SpLDs are not like short-sightedness, which can be corrected by means of a simple aid (glasses); it is more like diabetes which has to be constantly monitored and controlled (by diet and/or medication) all the time. Management of SpLD can involve continual mental monitoring, see MENTAL ENERGY TO MANAGE DYSLEXIA/ SpLD. Even the parallel with diabetes is not very good, since the problems that trip a mind into its SpLD functioning are not completely predictable; they have variable effects and may well persist for variable amounts of time.

MENTAL ENERGY TO MANAGE DYSLEXIA/ SpLD: p 269

Slowly, as the whole population changes its attitude towards differences and comes to values them, there will be no stigma to disability and no-one will object to the linguistic convenience of giving groups names like disabled, dyslexic and non-dyslexic. Utopia, I know, but one has to aim in the positive direction. Denying the distinction doesn't resolve the real problems.

4.1   Does dyslexia exist or not?

Because dyslexia/ SpLD are not obvious, there will inevitably be people who question whether or not these syndromes exist. There is broad agreement between the majority of professionals in this field, but nevertheless there is room for debate about the details. I don't think these issues should prevent support being available to children as early as possible and to adults when they recognise they have difficulties.

One reason people give for reluctance to provide support is that it is unfair to divert funds to assessing dyslexia, specialist teaching and research.

People also argue that dyslexia doesn't exist; that no distinction should be made between poor readers with general poor intelligence ('garden variety' poor readers) and poor readers with intelligence above their reading ability. They argue that:

- there is a continuum of reading and spelling abilities
- the early problems are shared by all children
- the teaching and support that works for dyslexic children is also appropriate for 'garden variety' poor readers
- that people will shelter behind the label of dyslexia.

Key point: Don't wait for failure, avoid it

I have also heard people argue that you cannot recognise or assess dyslexia until a child is about 7 when they've had a couple of years struggling to learn literacy and failing.

My response is: the teaching that is VITAL for SpLDs is GOOD PRACTICE for all – so why not just include it in general practice?

You don't have to wait for failure. Singleton (1987, 1988) showed that the cognitive aspects of dyslexia (STM weakness, etc.) could be identified well before the child learns (and fails) to read.

Singleton (1987, 1988)
Ⓖ p 302 STM

The VITAL practice has been included in general practice. Elizabeth Henderson (2003) was head of 2 state primary schools which catered successfully and naturally for the dyslexic children.

Henderson (2003)

With a regime such as Henderson's: the 'at risk of dyslexia' child doesn't develop too many of the dyslexic problems:

- the literacy skills develop in parallel and to the same level as other skills
- the VITAL teaching practices are continued throughout the years of education
- the funding of specialist support becomes unnecessary because students learn the skills in the best possible way for them.

I've put forward what I see as necessary in *New Paradigm*.   An example of the right education from an early age is given in *Story Box: Best Case Scenario: Good Techniques, Minimal Dyslexia*.

New Paradigm: p 232

Story Box: Best Case Scenario: Good Techniques, Minimal Dyslexia: p 156

Without the appropriate learning:

- the confusions of dyslexia can develop
- they are always there to be activated even when a person has good management skills
- support and accommodation are necessary to allow the individual to achieve at her highest potential.

Questioning whether dyslexia/ SpLD exist, or haggling about the details, should not be used as an excuse to avoid putting good practice into place.

5   Most recognised SpLDs in 2020

In August 2005, guidelines were put on the DfES[1] website for the assessment of SpLDs in Higher Education (DfES, 2005). They covered four types of SpLD:

DfES (2005)

Descriptions of the 4 SpLDs from the guidelines are in the *Glossary*, Ⓖ p 301, and in the sections on the separate SpLDs.

dyslexia   dyspraxia   dyscalculia

attention deficit disorder with or without hyperactivity (AD(H)D).

Dyspraxia is also known as 'developmental co-ordination disorder' (DCD).
Dyslexia is the most widely researched.

The guidelines gave descriptions of the four SpLD rather than definitions.
The core problems for each SpLD are:

Dyslexia	the learning process in aspects of literacy
Dyspraxia	impairment or immaturity of movement
Dyscalculia	learning difficulty with basic aspects of arithmetic
Attention deficit disorder (with or without hyperactivity)	problems with attention span and impulsivity (with or without hyperactivity)

---

[1] DfES: Department for Education and Skills

The tables in the sections below on dyslexia, dyspraxia, and AD(H)D give a summary of the basic and advanced skills affected by each syndrome. The advanced ones are the same list for these three SpLDs, since basic problems can affect the same advanced processes, though not necessarily in the same way. Beside the summaries, the descriptions from the DfES guidelines are set out in bullet points instead of linear sentences (which can be found on Ⓖ p 301).

Dyslexia: p 103
Dyspraxia: p 113
AD(H)D: p 118
Dyscalculia: p 123

The descriptions for dyspraxia and AD(H)D both contain the phrase 'characteristics common to many SpLDs'. Dyslexia is the SpLD which first attracted attention and a considerable amount of research. The other SpLDs are often discussed by comparison with dyslexia; either the problems that are in common are highlighted, as in the descriptions from the DfES, or the significant differences are highlighted. Therefore the paragraph about *Dyslexia* is more detailed than the paragraphs about the other SpLDs.

Dyslexia: p 103

Dyscalculia is different in that maths doesn't become a carrier for other subjects in the same way that language does. You go on studying maths at higher levels; you are usually expected to acquire the higher levels of language as you study other subjects; hence there is a difference in the way maths problems are recognised – and supported.

This section

- discusses the importance of *Knowing Which SpLD* is behind manifest behaviour and suggests how that might be determined
- it lists the *Manifest Behaviour of SpLDs* by category
- it discusses *Variations in Manifest Behaviour*
- it presents a *Model for SpLD* that can be used to discuss the physiological, psychological and behavioural levels of the SpLDs.

Knowing Which SpLD:
p 98
Manifest Behaviour of SpLDs: p 98
Variations in Manifest Behaviour: p 100
Model for SpLD:
p 102

5.1   Knowing which SpLD

It can be important to know which SpLD is causing a problem; the solutions will depend on the cause as well as the *THINKING PREFERENCES* of your student.

THINKING PREFERENCES: p 290

Example: Which SpLD is behind poor notes?

Writing notes can be necessary:

- in many jobs
- for students
- to take telephone messages.

Among the reasons for poor notes are:

- dyslexia: not being able to spell words
- dyspraxia: fatigue setting in when writing; badly written words
- AD(H)D: lack of attention means there are gaps in the information.

Determining which SpLD is causing the problems and how it is doing so involves *OBJECTIVE OBSERVATION* and *MONITORING PROGRESS* systems to build up an accurate record of what is happening. The observation and monitoring carried out with your student is far more important than the precise label that is given to the SpLD because even within one label there are so many *VARIATIONS IN MANIFEST BEHAVIOUR* and because she may experience the symptoms and problems of more than one SpLD, see *OVERLAP OF SPLDS*.

OBJECTIVE OBSERVATION: p 288

MONITORING PROGRESS: p 263

VARIATIONS IN MANIFEST BEHAVIOUR: p 100

OVERLAP OF SPLDS: p 224

5.2   Manifest behaviour of SpLDs

My experience of supporting students showed me that individuals with the same SpLD present different clusters of symptoms and problems and that many of the problems are common across the different SpLDs, as the DfES descriptions affirm. The disrupting effect of any manifest behaviour is dealt with in *PITFALLS*. *KEY ELEMENTS OF THE STORIES IN THIS BOOK* is also relevant to the way dyslexia/ SpLD affects people's lives.

PITFALLS: p 73

KEY ELEMENTS OF THE STORIES IN THIS BOOK: p 133

It is more useful to categorise the problems by area of problem than by SpLD type; in the following list, the problems are described from an external perspective, not an internal one; see 3 *STORY BOXES: CHANGED PERSPECTIVE.*

STORY BOXES: CHANGED PERSPECTIVE: p 90

Processing

- noticeable inconsistency between what can be achieved on 'good' and 'bad' days
- difficulty becoming fluent in a new skill to the point where it becomes automatic, for example reading, writing and driving a car
- poor short-term memory for carrying out instructions or copying from the board or remembering what has just been read and/or said
- poor attention span and concentration
- difficulty retaining the visual image of words, signs, symbols, formulae, musical notation

Confidence and stress

- lack of confidence
- particular susceptibility to stress, which may be associated with deadlines or examinations or meetings

Organisation

- poor at organising work and other aspects of life
- taking longer than other people to complete tasks
- a poor sense of passage of time, mixing up dates, times and appointments
- directional confusions, getting easily lost, having problems using maps or finding the way to a new place

Language

- lack of comprehension, despite appearing to read fluently
- poor reading of text due to visual distortions such as blurring or moving letters
- difficulty sequencing letters in spelling, or numbers and signs in maths
- difficulties using dictionaries, encyclopaedias and directories
- difficulty remembering phone numbers and dialling them accurately
- difficulties taking messages

Motor control

- mispronunciations and poor word retrieval when speaking, both caused by motor problems or difficulties in discriminating sounds
- poor motor control resulting in a range of difficulties including handwriting, inaccurate reading and spelling

Maths

- sequencing, such as instructions and mathematical procedures, sequencing of numbers or letters

(The above lists have been re-organised from SpLD Working Group 2005/DfES Guidelines (DfES, 2005))

DfES (2005)

5.3 Variations in manifest behaviour

Don't expect any systematic patterns for the problems experienced by people with each SpLD:

- one person may not have all the problems
- the level of difficulty will not be consistent for all the problems one person encounters
- the level of difficulty can vary from one time to another, and over quite a short length of time
- a person can have no difficulty at all with one of the classic problems.

NON-SPLD PEOPLE discusses the way non-SpLD people experience the problems.

NON-SPLD PEOPLE:
p 129

Key point: Variability undermines acceptability

The variability in manifest behaviour has been one of the difficulties in getting SpLDs taken seriously by those who have very little to do with an SpLD person.

Story: Contrasting behaviour

One dyslexic and dyspraxic student had a very cheerful outlook on life despite facing many problems with study and everyday life. The way her memory focused in the present was both good and bad for her.

The good thing was that, for most of the time, she could completely forget her considerable problems.
The bad thing was that asking her questions didn't access her knowledge.

When her subject tutor asked her questions about an essay she had just written, she couldn't recall anything. It sounded as if she didn't know anything. I started by asking her questions, but fairly quickly drew a mind map of the essay title. Then she produced all the information in the essay. It was in her memory, just not accessed by questioning.

The same response to questions happened in a tribunal. The chair of the tribunal completely failed to get her story from her in the official setting. He was asking the right questions, but her answers added up to "there aren't too many problems". Of course, by the time she remembered what the problems really were and started talking about them, the contrast was so great that the real story was completely undermined. This pattern of behaviour prevented many an attempt to help her resolve the problems.

5.4   Model for SpLD

FIGURE 2.2 shows a *MODEL FOR SPLD* including an analogy with computers. The hardware represents the brain, the constitutional basis; the software, the cognitive characteristics which are a combination of the mind and psychological level (Stacey, 2019).

Stacey (2019)

The operator of the computer represents the SpLD person using the brain and cognitive characteristics; this is the behavioural level of functioning and includes the manifest problems of the SpLDs. The receivers of output represent the other people who might be getting emails or reading documents written by an SpLD person.

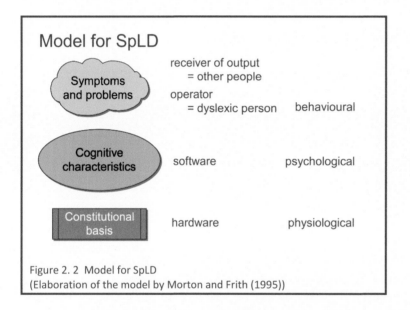

Figure 2. 2 Model for SpLD
(Elaboration of the model by Morton and Frith (1995))

Physiological research is concerned with the differences in the constitutional basis that underpins the functioning of SpLD. A good understanding of what is happening at this level should allow many more people to get beyond questioning the syndromes to dealing with them empathetically. The discussion of the physiological level is beyond the scope of this book, though the concept of neural networks is used, see *PARK PATHS AND PRUNING NEURONS*.

Ⓖ p 303:
neural networks

PARK PATHS AND PRUNING NEURONS: p 5

The psychological and behavioural levels are the concern of this series of books. The other 3 books are about making the right changes so that interactions with those around SpLD people work effectively. This book is about understanding the impact of the problems, why they persist and how their development might be avoided. This chapter is about the symptoms and problems that occur at the behavioural level with some insights from the psychological level.

6 Dyslexia

Table 2.1 Summary of problems encountered by dyslexics

In childhood, dyslexia affects: Basic skills	In adulthood, dyslexia, dyspraxia & AD(H)D affect: Advanced skills
•single word reading	•organisation of ideas
•spelling	•comprehension
•handwriting	•organisation of self
•fluent reading	•management of time
•creative writing	•management of place
•organisation dealing with time and space	•all forms of spoken and written language

Three different ways of putting the experience of dyslexia into words come from:

- the summary above of basic and advanced difficulties
- the description from the DfES guidelines
- the cognitive characteristics listed below.

They all have their uses.

- The first is a list of skills.
- The second is descriptions of the problems experienced.
- The third gives four cognitive characteristics that can be used to understand the effects of dyslexia.

Description from DfES guidelines (DfES, 2005)

- Dyslexia is a combination of abilities and difficulties; the difficulties affect the learning process in aspects of literacy and sometimes numeracy.

- Coping with required reading is generally seen as the biggest challenge at Higher Education level due in part to difficulty in skimming and scanning written material.

- A student may also have an inability to express his/her ideas clearly in written form and in a style appropriate to the level of study.

- Marked and persistent weaknesses may be identified in working-memory, speed of processing, sequencing skills, auditory and/or visual perception, spoken language and motor skills.

- Visuo-spatial skills, creative thinking and intuitive understanding are less likely to be impaired and indeed may be outstanding.

- Enabling or assistive technology is often found to be very beneficial.

I explain dyslexia in workshops to non-dyslexic people by presenting them with activities that generate dyslexia, temporarily, in their minds and then interpreting their processing and reactions in terms of the four cognitive characteristics of dyslexia (Stacey, 2005).

Stacey (2005)

The power of the activities is that non-dyslexic people see for themselves the experiences that dyslexic people try to explain. Very few people have remained sceptical after a workshop. The cognitive characteristics used to explain the problems are those discussed by Singleton (1999):

Singleton (1999)

(G) p 303: working memory

- 'A marked inefficiency in the working or short-term memory system, which is regarded by many experts in the field as the fundamental underlying difficulty experienced by people with dyslexia.

- Inadequate phonological processing abilities, which affects the acquisition of phonic skills in reading and spelling so that unfamiliar words are frequently misread, which may in turn affect comprehension.

- Difficulties with motor skills or coordination. Nicholson and Fawcett have noted that people with dyslexia can show a particular difficulty in automatising skills.

- A range of problems connected with visual processing, which can affect reading generally, but especially when dealing with large amounts of text.'

Summary: Cognitive characteristics of dyslexia

- inefficient working-memory
- inadequate phonological processing
- lack of automatisation of skills
- visual processing problems

NB: Not everyone has the same pattern of cognitive characteristics. Variations occur similar to *VARIATIONS IN MANIFEST BEHAVIOUR.*

VARIATIONS IN MANIFEST BEHAVIOUR: p 100

Working-memory

Baddeley (2007) describes the episodic buffer of working-memory as having a capacity that is limited to 4 chunks of information; these are analogies to a series of 4 pigeon-holes, see *FIGURE 2.3*. You can put information into a pigeon hole so long as it is connected together as it is stored. Once there is a break in the connections, the next pigeon-hole is used. When all of them contain information, the first one is used again, but the new information replaces that already there; it is not added to it, see *FIGURE 2.4*.

Baddeley (2007)

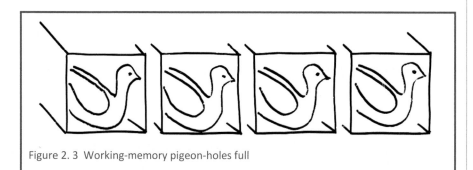

Figure 2. 3 Working-memory pigeon-holes full

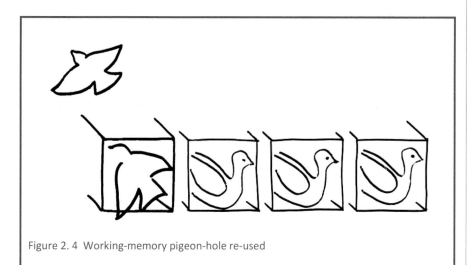

Figure 2. 4 Working-memory pigeon-hole re-used

The implications for dyslexia are wide-reaching.

1   When a dyslexic person is struggling with reading or spelling, their minds will not be making meaningful connections between the letters; in struggling with one sentence, single letters could be put into each pigeon hole, so that only 4 letters would be held in working-memory before the first one is replaced by the 5th, or with single words so that only 4 words at a time are held in working-memory. It is not easy to make sense of language under these constraints. There are so many instances where this lack of connections hampers dyslexic people when they are trying to use language.

2   You can't remember decisions for very long: if working-memory is too inefficient, you will think of something, possibly important, and very shortly afterwards it has gone from your mind.

3   Meaning is not securely linked to words: if your student doesn't link information together, she may not have enough working-memory to follow a conversation.

Insight: Words lose their meaning

I was once in a group of parents talking about new school maths teaching techniques. The language wasn't very technical; someone said a sentence with 'multiplication' in it.

My maths got me into Oxford University, but suddenly I couldn't remember that 'multiplication' had anything to do with maths.

By the time I had worked out the connection, the conversation had moved on. My working-memory had retained nothing; I couldn't pick up the threads again.

My self-confidence evaporated.

4   Concentrating so hard on one part that anything else is missed:

Story: Filing using the 3rd letter

If I have to file some papers under a name which has a 'difficult' letter part way through, such as k in 'Atkinson', I am so unsure about the 'k' that I file the papers under 'K' and not 'A'.

Tip: Chunking

Chunking is the process of making connections, on links, between pieces of information so that more is stored in each chunk and the capacity of working memory can be expanded.

Organisation

Few dyslexics find organisation just happens with minimal effort.

- Either people are super organised because that is the only way to function at all well in life, even with fairly trivial tasks.

- Or people never achieve a satisfactory method of dealing with organisation.

- Even for those who are well organised, anything that is new is likely to put them back into the un-organised group initially.

Phonological processing abilities

- Sounds don't register in the right order, so syllables in words get transposed.

- You read something and say it back to front: read 64 and say (or dial!) 46.

- You have to look at a speaker's lips to process what they are saying, which makes telephoning difficult.

- Words can lose their meaning, even very familiar ones, as in STORY BOX: WORDS LOSE THEIR MEANING above, and you lose the context of a book or conversation.

- The mental processing needed to read leaves no working-memory for understanding what you've read; first reading is not first learning.

Difficulties with motor skills or co-ordination

- So much attention is paid to the movement of spelling or writing that the meaning of the words is lost. The movement includes details like: the shape of letters, keeping on the line, leaving a gap between words.

- The mind isn't making organizational sense of any movements, so organization of thoughts does not mature as expected

- There's difficulty in copying letters in a fluent movement.

Example: Meaning of words disconnected from the movement of writing

In workshops I run, there's a task designed to show people how easy it is for meaning to become disconnected from the words they write (Stacey, 2005).

I have a slide with 'line' and 'reel' written in ordinary joined-up writing and in 2 colours, with one colour for the letters and one for the joining lines see FIGURE 2.5.

I ask people to write 'jump', 'run' and 'stand' in the same 2 ways.

When they have written the 3 words in both styles, I ask who is thinking about 'jumping', 'running' or 'standing'.

No-one ever is. Everyone is far too busy concentrating on getting the letters written in the right pen to think about the meaning. Some are working out reliable strategies for the job, like writing all the letters first and then putting in the linking lines.

STORY BOX: WORDS LOSE THEIR MEANING: p 106

line
reel
line
reel
jump
run
stand

Figure 2. 5 Two pens for joined-up writing

This exercise is a very good illustration of the mind not making organisational sense of the movement, i.e. the mind doesn't connect the movement with the meaning of the words. Then, organisation of thoughts that depends on the meaning of the words will not mature as a result of writing words.

Visual processing

- Eyes don't move properly across the page. During normal reading the eyes do not move continuously across the text but in small jumps called saccades. If a dyslexic person tries to read in a different way, such as sweeping the eyes continuously across each line, then saccadic movement will be suppressed. When this happens, the fine detail required to understand words and sentences is not processed.

- In some cases of dyslexia, a dominant or reference eye is not sufficiently established. To look at anything clearly, both eyes need to focus on the same place together; the dominant eye effectively guides the other to look at the right place. Without a dominant eye, the 2 eyes present images to the mind that don't overlap properly. In the case of reading, accurate perception of text is impaired.

- Eyes can see more clearly with different colour backgrounds; and when the backgrounds are not right, the mind has difficulty deciphering what it sees.

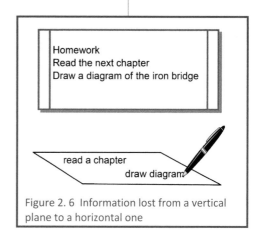

Figure 2. 6 Information lost from a vertical plane to a horizontal one

- The mind has difficulty correlating images in a vertical plane with those in a horizontal one, see *FIGURE 2.* 6.

- Anything not in view is not available to the mind for processing.

Insight: Out of sight is out of mind

There are many times that I've discussed how easily SpLD people don't remember anything that is out of view.
The situations include:

- of a pile of books or papers, only the top one can be thought about

- difficulty in remembering information on one website in order to work with it on another website; both need to be completely in view

- ideas for a big project have to be spread out so that they are all in view together.

Problems with recall from memory

Many dyslexic people's thinking is triggered by their immediate surroundings: if there is nothing in the surroundings that relates to what they need to think about they may not recall anything useful.

Insight: Forgetting intermittent pain

Being sent to a consultant in a hospital with an intermittent pain; if the pain is not felt while the consultant asks questions, his questions may not trigger any memory of the pain.

For me, it was only the puzzled look on the consultant's face as he got to the end of his questions that shocked me into thinking: "Why am I here?" Most of my answers had to be revised.

Concentration

All these various difficulties require mental capacity in working-memory to carry out processes that should have become automatic, but haven't, so working-memory becomes overloaded. There will be too little working-memory capacity to concentrate on whatever task the dyslexic person is trying to do. The external perception will be that the dyslexic person lacks concentration; the internal perception will be of hard work.

Deep and surface dyslexia and similar effects

Deep and surface dyslexia are sometimes used to refer to different sources of confusion within dyslexia. They both refer to problems with word recall. In deep dyslexia the problem is at the semantic level, so words that have similar or related meaning get confused. In surface dyslexia the problem is at the phonological level, so words with similar or related sound or spelling get confused.

Insight: Deep dyslexia interfering with a mnemonic

There is a mnemonic to remember the notes of music on the treble clef, which is 'every good boy deserves fruit' giving E, G, B, D, F. If deep dyslexia interferes with the recall, the mnemonic could come out as 'every good boy deserves cake', in which case the top note is recalled as C instead of F and the mnemonic has failed.

This is an example of deep dyslexia where the context of food has been retained.

Example: Surface dyslexia confusions

Surface dyslexia causes problems with connecting the right sound to the spelling of a word:

* pint is read to rhyme with mint
* confusion with sound-spelling relationships, such as: loose and lose, choose and chose. I really struggle with which spelling to use for the sound in my head.

Other pitfalls of dyslexia result in similar difficulties. Letter confusions can result in a word that fits the context of the original text or can be a redistribution of the letters.

Insight: Confusions from dyslexia

When reading out loud if the word 'apples' is replaced by 'pears', deep dyslexia is involved because the context has been retained; if it is replaced by 'please' then the letters have been jumbled, and surface dyslexia is involved.

Sometimes an initial misread leads to continual adjustment to agree with the misread.

Story: Everything consistent with a single first misread

A 30-year-old man was practising reading a very basic book about oak trees. The book had the word 'bud' and he read it as 'buds'. For the rest of the book, he automatically changed the grammar to agree with the plural word. He didn't realise what he was doing; he was more aware of difficulty in reading single words and he was not able to appreciate the skill he was showing by altering the grammar.

You get some inklings as to what is happening in the mind by observing over a long period of time and by using the observation methods suggested in *Finding Your Voice with Dyslexia and other SpLDs* (Stacey, 2019). I remember one psychologist telling me that it was no good asking individuals about their thinking because that is too subjective and psychology needs to be objective. However, I've also had several students come back questioning the findings of their assessment because they are aware of their thinking and know they had used methods that were not expected in the test, see STORY BOX: ASSESSMENT TEST SIDESTEPPED.

Stacey (2019)

STORY BOX: ASSESSMENT TEST SIDESTEPPED:
p 199

7   Dyspraxia

Table 2.2 Summary of problems encountered by dyspraxics

In childhood, dyspraxia affects: Basic skills	In adulthood, dyslexia, dyspraxia & AD(H)D affect: Advanced skills
•fine motor control	•organisation of ideas
•gross motor control	•comprehension
•laterality and bilateral integration	•organisation of self
•visual perception	•management of time
•auditory perception	•management of place
•body awareness in movement	•all forms of spoken and written language
•proprioception (where the body is)	
•organisation dealing with space	

Description from DfES guidelines (DfES, 2005)

- A student with dyspraxia/DCD may have an impairment or immaturity in the organisation of movement, often appearing clumsy.

- Gross motor skills (related to balance and co-ordination) and
      fine motor skills (relating to manipulation of objects)
   are hard to learn and difficult to retain and generalise.

- Writing is particularly laborious and keyboard skills difficult to acquire.

- Individuals may have difficulty organising ideas and concepts.

- Pronunciation may also be affected and people with dyspraxia/DCD may be over/under sensitive to noise, light and touch.

- They may have poor awareness of body position and misread social cues in addition to those shared characteristics common to many SpLDs.

The underlying brain characteristic for dyspraxia is that motor movement skills, touch and proprioception (the sense of the body from joints and other skeletal sources) do not develop in the same way as they do for the vast majority of people. Either gross or fine motor movement is affected, or both; there is a lack of a central core stability and hence no stable body image; and no consistent body memory to assist the growth of effective neural networks.

Again, there are variations in the extent to which a person is affected by dyspraxia and there are variations in the behaviour patterns that result, see *VARIATIONS IN MANIFEST BEHAVIOUR*.

VARIATIONS IN MANIFEST BEHAVIOUR: p 100

Story: Satisfaction for one dyspraxic on a rock face

One dyspraxic child was away on summer camp. Climbing was the activity for the first part of one afternoon. The dyspraxic child spent the whole session standing at the bottom of the artificial climbing wall. He was wearing a helmet and safety harness, but was completely paralysed by anxiety. His class mates were moving past him, up and away. Unable to move, he was focused on lifting his foot up onto the first foothold.

As an observer it was a memorable lesson in understanding how difficult it is for dyspraxics to move beyond the confines of the body.

By the end of the session and with immense will power and motivation, he was able to stand on two footholds 9 inches off the ground.

He was so pleased with his achievement.
It was a vivid demonstration of mind over matter and will power.

Dealing with the motor problems comes under occupational therapists and often involves physical work and stimulating the movement systems of the body.

One of the cognitive effects is that a person does not have a sense of where they are in their body, so they have to continually move because the movement defines their body for them.

Key point: Dyspraxia and perpetual movement

There is no point is asking them to be still; that seems to consume so much energy that there is no mental capacity for any other thoughts.

People around have to be able to concentrate in such a way that a dyspraxic's perpetual motion doesn't disturb them. The amount of movement varies from time-to-time and person-to-person.

Dyspraxia has the potential to affect all types of learning because motor systems are involved all the time, even as basically as eye movements, mouth and hand movements.

Story: Capital J in four pieces

One pupil had difficulty writing letters with continuous strokes; her strokes would get broken at every crossing or at deviations from a straight line. J would be written as 4 or 5 strokes instead of 2, see *FIGURE 2.7*. The teacher wondered whether the letters were seen as a whole; possibly they were just seen as parts.

Figure 2. 7 Dyspraxic capital J

With the perpetual motion and lack of a body image, there is no platform on which to build organised representations of the world around, nor of the many tasks of life; organisation remains a major problem. In the *FIGURE: 'DYSLEXIC/ SPLD' HAND CAST*, it would be the motor system that is interfering with the alignment of different learning situations, producing the confusion.

FIGURE 1.4: 'DYSLEXIC/ SPLD' HAND CAST:
 p 46

One of the main differences in the assessment of dyspraxia by comparison with dyslexia is that dyslexic problems are not apparent in the language skills of dyspraxic people. Writing can be bad due to poor motor skills, but spelling and use of language can be very good for someone whose problems are almost only due to dyspraxia.

As far as giving support to dyspraxic students is concerned, I usually find I do not have to be aware of their thinking preferences. The ideas from *THINKING PREFERENCES* may be useful, but they are unlikely to be essential in the same way that they are for most dyslexic people.

THINKING PREFERENCES:
 p 290

Organisation and dyspraxia

Since their body image is not organised, it seems that nothing else gets organised. For dyspraxic people, therefore, organisation of everyday events is likely to be a major effort all the time. Having systems in place well in advance of tasks can be very important for dyspraxic people, but even that may not be possible.

Story: Residential school outing

A specialist SpLD school had organised a residential outing. Five girls were in one dormitory; one of them, Alison, was dyspraxic with no idea about organisation. The outing was for four days and Alison's mother had put her clothes into four carrier bags in her case; with each bag labelled for the day it was to be used. The first thing Alison did was to empty all the carrier bags into a heap, thus losing the order her mother had set up for her.

She couldn't think about the activities she was told would be happening and select the correct clothing. She couldn't think "I am going hiking today; I will need strong shoes and trousers". She had no idea which garments went together: she would wear stout walking shoes at the same time as a frilly skirt.

At the end of the outing when all five girls had finished their packing, there was a pile of clothes in the middle of the room. The girls had no concept that these clothes would belong to any of them, since the room had been empty when they arrived. Their teacher went through the clothes asking what belongs to whom and nobody could recognise anything. Most of the pile belonged to Alison.

Alison always had difficulty with her shoes; she could select a pair but always had them on the wrong feet.

In contrast to these dyspraxic difficulties, Alison could write beyond her years.

If your student is dyspraxic, she may benefit by deliberately being conscious of organisation before she starts any task or continues with one already started, e.g. to think about the next several steps in a task that she's doing, or to think about the structure of a subject she is studying.   She could use *MIND SET* to switch on this deliberate consciousness.

MIND SET: p 287

You can show some dyspraxic people how to work on organisation and they will be able to use what they've learnt in another situation.

For others, organisation never penetrates their thinking to the point that they remember that they have to pay attention to it.

Concentration

The external perception of concentration and the internal experience of dyspraxia can lead to misunderstandings and difficulties.

Many people find too much movement disrupts their concentration so that when they observe the constant movement of dyspraxic people they decide the dyspraxic people cannot be concentrating.

However the mental effort to stay still would leave dyspraxic people with very little mental energy for concentration.

Therefore it is very important to allow dyspraxic people to move as much as they need in order to concentrate on the task in hand.

8   AD(H)D: Attention Deficit Disorder, with or without hyperactivity

Table 3.3 Summary of problems encountered by AD(H)D people

In childhood, AD(H)D affects:	In adulthood, dyslexia, dyspraxia & AD(H)D affect:
Basic skills	**Advanced skills**
•attention	•organisation of ideas
•following instructions	•comprehension
•having the right equipment	•organisation of self
•the ability to stay still	•management of time
•taking turns	•management of place
•social integration	•all forms of spoken and written language
•impulsivity	

In Attention Deficit Disorder, with or without hyperactivity, AD(H)D, a core disability is that attention is not controlled in the same way as it is for most people. AD(H)D is often treated through medication with programmes to build skills and modify behaviour; some people advocate support programmes without medication.

Description from DfES guidelines (DfES, 2005)

- Attention Deficit Disorder (ADD) exists with or without hyperactivity.

- In most cases people with this disorder are often 'off task', have particular difficulty commencing and switching tasks, together with a very short attention span and high levels of distractibility.

- They may fail to make effective use of the feedback they receive and have weak listening skills.

- Those with hyperactivity may act impulsively and erratically, have difficulty foreseeing outcomes, fail to plan ahead and be noticeably restless and fidgety.

- Those without the hyperactive trait tend to daydream excessively, lose track of what they are doing and fail to engage in their studies unless they are highly motivated.

- The behaviour of people with ADD can be inappropriate and unpredictable; this, together with the characteristics common to many SpLDs, can present a further barrier to learning.

Insight: Nothing heard

One specialist tutor thought her pupils heard 40 - 50 % of what was said to them and for one pupil her guess was that he heard 20% during a day.

Her observation of the latter pupil was that there seemed to be 3 modes of operation:

- listening to what she was saying
- being completely distracted and paying attention to something else
- being completely switched off.

Key point: ADD and AD(H)D people missing out

When their minds have switched to something else, or switched off, people with AD(H)D miss what is being told to them, which is a considerable disadvantage in communication and learning. In *FIGURE 1.4, 'DYSLEXIC/ SPLD' HAND CAST*, the lack of consistent attention will contribute to the growth of confusion.

You need to be especially aware of ADD people since their lack of hyperactivity and quieter behaviour will not draw attention to their lack of concentration.

FIGURE 1.4: 'DYSLEXIC/ SPLD' HAND CAST: p 46

The medical treatment is beyond the scope of this book, but the programmes to deal with skills and behaviour will be very similar to those for the other SpLDs. The descriptions of manifest behaviour are similar, even though the cause is different, giving a bias towards the unexpected behaviour and not towards the language difficulties of dyslexia, nor the problems with motor movement and body stability of dyspraxia.

2 What Goes Wrong

As with all the other SpLDs, there is variation in the way people experience AD(H)D, see *VARIATIONS IN MANIFEST BEHAVIOUR*.

VARIATIONS IN MANIFEST BEHAVIOUR: p 100

When reading about the central executive of working-memory, and the supervisory attentional system, SAS, (Stacey, 2019, Baddeley, 2007) it struck me that the SAS does not seem to be working well for people with AD(H)D.

Stacey (2019)
Baddeley (2007)

Lack of progress makes AD(H)D people very vulnerable to low self-esteem and loss of confidence. The hyperactive ones may do well when they have external pressure to get on with a task, such as meeting deadlines; they may feel a negative reaction when one compelling deadline is met and nothing has taken its place. They need to look after themselves in the face of swings of mood.

Those without the hyperactivity probably also need the deadlines to get them going in the first place; sometimes there can be a fear of engaging with a task in case they can't do it or can't finish it.

There can be a need to move incessantly. Children need to get up and move around the classroom or house. Adults may tap their feet endlessly.

Insights: AD(H)D as lived

One of my AD(H)D students commented:

> "The DfES description of AD(H)D problems as 'lack of attention' isn't as accurate as, say, 'variability in attention' because we do pay attention – the problem is that what we

pay attention to changes very quickly! Our minds jump to other thoughts without our control (even with medication!)

If this happens in class, it is as if the teacher has stopped talking altogether but unfortunately we realise a few minutes later (when our attention comes back to the present task) that the teacher kept going and we didn't hear what was said.

The DfES calls this daydreaming but this isn't accurate – often when this happens to me I am sorting out a problem I was thinking about previously or I remember something that I have forgotten to do."

Organisation and AD(H)D

Organisation and using the thinking preferences can both be important in managing the short-term attention span of AD(H)D. The organisational structures need to be external so that they are stable and not disrupted by the breaks in attention.   Finding whether anything in particular causes the attention to be broken could be important.

Following instructions presents problems, in particular remembering, or doing things, in the right order. This affects maths, running errands and school work, etc.

It's really important for there to be one place for things, like a pencil case. People living or working with AD(H)D people need to understand how important strategies like this are for dealing with organisation.

Concentration

Since it is hard for attention to be given to one thing for any length of time, concentration on a task, or topic, will be hard to maintain for most AD(H)D people. Using technology to hold information will help, as will other techniques for effective use of the mind. Careful observations will be needed to work out the best ways forward for each individual.

Insight: An AD(H)D perspective on attention

One student said, "The tricky thing about AD(H)D is that we are either paying complete attention on something or none at all, because all the attention has switched to something else. It isn't the same as half paying attention."

Story: To London for a cup of coffee

One student was settling down to write his essay, and decided a cup of coffee would help. He found he'd run out of coffee, so he went down the corridor to borrow some from a friend. As the friend was out, he decided to go to the local shop and get some. The coach for London was picking up passengers outside the shop. So he got on and went to London.

9   Dyscalculia

Table 2.4 Summary of problems encountered by dyscalculic people

In childhood and adulthood: Basic and advanced difficulties
There are 2 different professional perspectives: 1) Dyscalculia is difficulties with maths concepts and maths procedures.
2) Dyscalculia is difficulties with basic arithmetic but other aspects of maths concepts could be OK.
There are professional views that attribute maths problems to a variety of underlying causes. These professionals generally prefer not to use the term dyscalculia.

Description from DfES guidelines (DfES, 2005)

- Dyscalculia is a learning difficulty involving the most basic aspect of arithmetical skills.

- The difficulty lies in the
    reception
    comprehension
    production of quantitative and
        spatial information.

- Students with dyscalculia may
    have difficulty in understanding
        simple number concepts
    lack an intuitive grasp of numbers
    have problems learning number
        facts and procedures.

- These can relate to basic concepts such as
    telling the time,
    calculating prices,
    handling change.

Maths, rather like language, is a subject in its own right and a carrier of information for other subjects, so if someone can't learn maths they may be at a disadvantage in the communications that are an essential and necessary part of everyday life, study and employment.

There is a difference in the way language and maths carry information for other subjects: language is used for a subject's concepts which need have nothing to do with language; the information maths carries is mathematical in nature.

Example sentences:	Comment:
When your internet connection goes down, you lose contact with many people until it is reconnected	This sentence is using language, but it is telling you nothing about language.
When your internet connection is broken, your productivity could increase by 40%.	This sentence is using maths; '40%' is mathematical in nature.

Variations in problems, behaviour and solutions between people and from one time to another for one person are just as important for those with dyscalculia as for the other SpLDs, see VARIATIONS IN MANIFEST BEHAVIOUR.

VARIATIONS IN MANIFEST BEHAVIOUR: p 100

Steve Chinn is one of the leading specialists in the field of dyscalculia and maths difficulties. From his book, *The Trouble with Maths: A Practical Guide to Helping Learners with Numeracy Difficulties* (Chinn, 2017), I find the following ideas:

Chinn (2017)

- some people have maths problems but are not dyscalculic
- the label 'dyscalculic' doesn't mean a person cannot gain maths skills
- with the right teaching and learning environment, pupils with maths problems can gain skills and catch up with their peers
- the history of underachievement is more important than the dyscalculia label
- the core teaching and learning principles to suit those with maths problems are most likely to come from those that suit dyslexic pupils.

Story: Colour coding forces

One engineer with maths problems couldn't work out a problem relating to forces on a beam until we colour coded the forces; the problem evaporated with the colour coding, see *FIGURE 2.8*.

He didn't have fundamental maths problems; his problem was being able to read the diagram well.

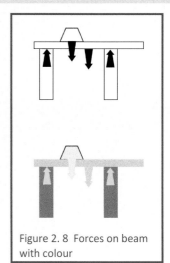

Figure 2.8 Forces on beam with colour

Story: No concept of placement values

There are many parts of basic arithmetic that I didn't understand until my children learnt them, by which time I had 2 degrees in physics, both of which involved high order maths.

For example, I didn't understand number placement until I was 37: that in 405 the 4 signifies four lots of one hundred and it means the same in all numbers with 4 in the hundreds place.

I saw the Dienes apparatus, *FIGURE 2.9*, at my children's school and then I understood numbers in a new way.

At school, I did sums by carefully lining up numbers, which works very well.

I'm sure I would be classified as dyscalculic if I'd learnt maths in the present, very wordy way because the words would have obscured the underlying maths.

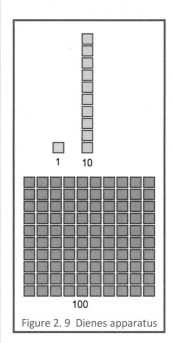

Figure 2.9 Dienes apparatus

Story: 100m is larger in a bigger stadium

One student wanting to work in nutrition had maths problems; he was also a runner and had a coach. He could not understand that a 100m race is always the same length; he is of the opinion that 100m is longer in a big stadium. He was going with his maths support tutor to a race in France. He planned to buy a tape measure so that they could see the difference between an English distance and a French one.

This student has fundamental problem with maths concepts beyond basic arithmetic.

These stories are three different experiences of maths problems and care needs to be taken to find the right solutions.

OBJECTIVE OBSERVATIONS: p 288

Some of the other problems encountered are:

- numbers: counting, remembering the order 0-9
- times tables
- direction: reading numbers you go left to right, but calculating you go right to left
- PIN numbers
- technical vocabulary
- direction: signage can be meaningless
- estimating
- time: telling the time, estimating how long something takes
- space, place and direction: not having a grasp of these concepts.

This book doesn't cover the teaching of maths concepts any more than it deals with language learning, but the principles of *OBJECTIVE OBSERVATIONS*, looking for *THINKING PREFERENCES*, *USING THE MIND WELL* and being able to keep *THINKING CLEARLY* will still be useful in finding solutions for the problems of dyscalculia.

THINKING PREFERENCES: p 290
USING THE MIND WELL: p 287
THINKING CLEARLY: p 285

Organisation and dyscalculia

Stacey (2021)

Good organisation of maths can help with maths working and understanding the concepts (Stacey, 2021), for example:

- setting sums out in organised patterns helps with calculations
- methodical copying from one line to the next of a proof helps your student to keep track of the processes
- using squared paper, not blank or lined; one number per square.

There are many ways an understanding of maths concepts impacts on the organisation of everyday life:

- estimating quantities and carrying out mental arithmetic can be helpful, for example when you go shopping, so not having these abilities puts you at a disadvantage
- managing time is important in organising everyday life: being on time, getting tasks done, not losing time looking for something
- difficulty with place and direction can disrupt everyday life: not being able to find things because you have no concept of place; not being able to find your way around
- dealing with money and finances uses maths.

There are many other ways the concepts from maths help to organise general living, and having problems with maths can be disruptive.

Concentration

As with all SpLDs, dyscalculia will make it hard for a person to concentrate. If your student is not making progress and has little motivation to achieve the end result, it will be difficult for her to engage with any task involving maths. Rote learning is unlikely to help if no understanding is involved at the same time.

Key point: Dyscalculia

Maths problems come from many different causes. You have to find out the underlying difficulty before you can help your student.

She may be a gifted mathematician at the higher levels despite being labelled dyscalculic.

127

10   Other dys-syndromes

Miles (1993) assessed many dyslexic children and adults over a considerable period. He gathered the problems he observed together in a very comprehensive way, not trying to make everyone fit the same pattern of difficulties, but accepting variations. As someone who has been officially assessed as dyslexic, the descriptions given by Miles seemed much more realistic than work that tries to narrow one label to a single core deficit.

Miles (1993)

For some time, dyslexia only included problems arising from the phonological processing deficit with the result that those people with similar problems but good phonological processing couldn't be called dyslexic and another name for them had to be found. Initially, new names started with dys- but that prefix implied something is wrong, and the field is trying to get away from the medical model of something wrong. There are now several terms: hidden disabilities, neurodiversity, autistic spectrum, specific language impairment, etc., all covering different aspects of non-expected, uneven development.

The *OVERLAP OF SPLDS* is one current topic of research. For example, Bishop (2008) compared the behaviour of children with specific language impairment (SLI) with that of dyslexics and those with autism. There was considerable overlap of behaviours of these syndromes and she considered whether dyslexia and SLI are on the same spectrum with different levels of severity and whether autism is SLI+, i.e. with additional impairments. Attention to the details of the behaviours shows significant differences that point to distinct combinations of causes, and distinct approaches to interventions.

OVERLAP OF SPLDS:
p 224

Bishop (2008)

It would be interesting to know the primary cause of the SpLDs because it helps non-SpLD people to engage more easily and it reassures those with an SpLD, but while research is being carried out, we cannot put the people on ice awaiting their true label; they still have to live, work and join in with life. Their descriptions of their experiences should be central in support work with them. They need respect as people who have gifts to contribute to society.

11   Non-SpLD people

The previous sections, DYSLEXIA, DYSPRAXIA, AD(H)D, and DYSCALCULIA, have been about problems at the behavioural level with some discussion of the cognitive characteristics involved. This section is a look at some experiences of non-SpLD people to show why the problems are of a different calibre for SpLD people.

DYSLEXIA: p 103
DYSPRAXIA: p 113
AD(H)D: p 118
DYSCALCULIA: p 123

Insight: Non-SpLD person learning calligraphy

One participant in a dyslexia workshop described how she had experienced learning calligraphy; in the early stages, when she was concentrating on the letter formation, she lost sight of spelling and frequently made mistakes. Gradually as the letter formations became familiar, her ability to spell resurfaced.

In the early stages, her working-memory capacity was all engaged with the new task and none was available for spelling. As the letter formations were automatised in her long-term memory, she had working-memory available again to deal with spelling.

Some of the difficulty about persuading non-SpLD people to recognise the SpLDs is that they experience many of the same difficulties and can't see what all the fuss is about. The initial experience learning calligraphy, as above, is very similar to the everyday experience of dyslexic people working with words.

For the calligraphy learner the ability to spell eventually came back; the dyslexic person working with words has the LEARNED CONFUSION of dyslexia in the background and she may not be able to get back to any acceptable language skill. So there are parallels in the observed experience, but the neural network possibilities are quite different.

LEARNED CONFUSION:
p 44

Teachers expect children to 'grow out' of making the mistakes, because this is what happens for most of them: their minds naturally fit the pieces of information together and gradually construct successful neural networks for the various tasks they have to master: the usual experience is that hard work and persistence will produce learning. See *NEURONS FIRING TOGETHER, WIRE TOGETHER*.

NEURONS FIRING TOGETHER, WIRE TOGETHER: p 47

Story: Subconscious spelling rules, subliminal learning

Stacey (2005)

One of the dyslexia simulations I use (Stacey, 2005) has legitimate letter combinations for sounds replacing the letters in a word[2]:

> Thairs wair yew meyt hunters, and trapers faw the Cerkooses, proding along chayned bairs and muzled wolvs. Yaw poeni shies at them, and yaw men lauf.[3]

Once, a participant protested about my spelling quite strongly, commenting, '... but you never put xx[4] at the end of a word. I didn't know I knew that!' Her mind had stored that rule about spelling, and probably many others; it isn't one that is often recited. She had been using knowledge of spelling in an unconscious way, without having to stop and think about it; she had learned the rule subliminally.

This synthesis of a consistent set of brain connections doesn't seem to happen for SpLD people; they are often processing information as if for the first time, and unable to use the automatic processing that the non-SpLD people can use.

COMPARISON: DYSLEXIA/SPLD VS. NON-DYSLEXIA/SPLD discusses three groups of people in terms of how vulnerable or stable certain skills are. The significant difference in the experience of non-SpLD people is that they have robust language and other skills that either don't desert them or that will re-establish reliably.

COMPARISON: DYSLEXIA/SPLD VS. NON-DYSLEXIA/SPLD: p 65

---

[2] Letter combination changes for sounds: phishing for 'fishing' is common on websites; ghoti as a spelling of fish is popularly attributed to Bernard Shaw: 'gh' as in cough; 'o' as in women; 'ti' as is station.

[3] The original is : 'There's where you meet hunters and trappers for the Circuses, prodding along chained bears and muzzled wolves. Your pony shies at them and your men laugh.' (Kipling, 1906)

[4] xx: I have forgotten the rule that I had broken and my knowledge of spelling rules is sufficiently sparse that I can't supply a likely candidate.

The manifest problems of non-SpLDs at the behavioural level in the *MODEL FOR SPLD* may seem the same, but the underlying cognitive characteristics may be significantly different, as well as there being a fundamental, underlying difference in brain structure (the constitutional basis in *MODEL FOR SPLD*) which is outside the scope of this book.

MODEL FOR SPLD:
p 102

Key point: To apply effort or not

Applying effort may be the right way forward for non-SpLD people; applying effort without finding out what's the best way to do something or think about something is a thankless, useless task for SpLD people.

When I have run workshops which include activities that generate SpLD effects in non-SpLD minds (Stacey, 2005), the overwhelming majority of people have understood the difficulties and frustrations because they can see their own reactions to the activities. They have been able to recognise significant differences between the problems presented by the activities and the way they experience problems in their own lives.

Stacey (2005)

12   The benefit of recognising the problems

I've heard it said: "You just have to get on with life and stop making such a fuss."

Key point: Wheelchair analogy for accommodations

It would be a bit tough to expect a person with no legs to get on with life without a wheelchair; study support is about teaching SpLDs to design the 'wheelchair' they need, incorporating the strengths of their individual minds.

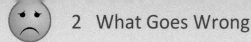

Wheelchair users need a ramp, or other mechanism, to get from one level to another; and these are put into buildings and spaces now.

The equivalent ramp for dyslexia is comprehensible dialogue with others and easier processing of information[5], so the dyslexia ramps are not one-off items that can be put in place and 'Hey-presto!' the problem's solved.

Hence, accommodation is an ongoing process.

Recognising the problems as precisely as possible helps your student to solve them with minimum disruption, effort and expense. The combination of knowing what abilities can be used and what *PITFALLS* need to be avoided allows the *REGIME FOR MANAGING DYSLEXIA/ SPLD* to be effective in a wide range of situations. The earlier appropriate action is taken the better the outcome will be for everyone.

PITFALLS: p 73

REGIME FOR MANAGING DYSLEXIA/ SPLD:
p 268

Story: Not told as a child

Sam was in his fourth and final year of a degree course when he first came for support.

He had been assessed while still at school. So his parents had known he was dyslexic since he was 15. They didn't tell him the result of the assessment because they were afraid he would use it as an excuse and not continue working. Sam thinks they were right at that time of his life.

---

[5] *DIFFERENT WAYS TO READ* describes choices made in writing this series of books to help dyslexic/ SpLD people find the information they need as easily as possible. *Gaining Knowledge and Skills with Dyslexia and other SpLDs* (Stacey, 2021) is about teaching them to make the best choices for themselves, as far as possible.
DIFFERENT WAYS TO READ: p 10

He struggled in the first years of his university degree, which is often the case even when someone knows they are dyslexic. He didn't really communicate his struggles to his parents and so it wasn't until partway through his third year that anybody thought the way he was struggling had anything to do with dyslexia or that there might be effective solutions to his problems.

Sam acknowledged that he had effectively wasted 2½ years struggling when he could have been learning how to manage his dyslexia effectively.

The benefits of recognising SpLD as early as possible can be enjoyed by everybody, individually and as a society, and not just by SpLD people.

Summary: VITAL for SpLDs, good practice for all

The teaching practice and consideration that is VITAL for SpLD people is good practice that could benefit everyone. The earlier someone with SpLD learns to manage her SpLD, the more proficient and confident she becomes; the lower the cost of any special accommodations; and the better she integrates with society as a whole.

13   Key elements of stories in this book

The following table has a list of the stories in this book with the key element and a comment. There are a few 'almost stories' too. They are all grouped by the key elements:

Analogy	Recall	Language
Compensation level	Place	Dyslexia
Expectations	Episodic memory	Dyspraxia
Learning	Stress	AD(H)D
Teaching	Thinking preferences	Maths problems
Feedback	Adult experience	

The three *Expectation* stories contrast the optimal situation with a couple of ways diagnosis can be mishandled.

The stories under *Learning* show several ways learning goes wrong; there's one story of learning helped and a couple of stories of non-dyslexic/ SpLD learning.

Recall and *Place* both contribute to several different stories.

The cumulative message of the stories is that knowing more precisely what is happening allows better choices to be made to help learning and so much more that happens in life.

Page	Box title or text	Key element Comment
p 131	WHEELCHAIR ANALOGY FOR ACCOMMODATIONS	*Analogy* Accommodation is to enable opting-in.
p 235	SEARCHING IN THE WRONG PLACE	*Analogy* It's no good looking in a way that doesn't cover the whole lives of dyslexic/ SpLD people.
p 5	PARK PATHS AND PRUNING NEURONS	*Analogy* Showing how learning doesn't settle to one standard process for a task, for example spelling a word.
p 90	CHANGED PERSPECTIVE 2: "WHAT DIFFICULTY?"	*Compensation level 3* Delightful example of the 'luck' in FIGURE 1. 8: THE SLOPE OF COMPETENCE: p 60.
p 209	TEARS IN APRIL 2017	*Compensation level 2* Example of strategies not working for all situations.
p 156	BEST CASE SCENARIO: GOOD TECHNIQUES, MINIMAL DYSLEXIA	*Expectations* A child expected to learn.
p 145	A DYSLEXIC PASSENGER	*Expectations* A child who used dyslexia as an excuse became a student who got challenged.
p 132	NOT TOLD AS A CHILD	*Expectations* A child not told, expected to learn but becoming a failing student.

Page	Box title or text	Key element / Comment
p 8	A PROBLEM CREATED AT AN INITIAL STAGE	*Learning* Earliest learning not altered by later experience.
p 50	SET IN STONE	*Learning* Earliest learning not being altered by later experience; the earliest teaching was too simplified.
p 50	SLEEPING IS NOT DOING	*Learning* Earliest learning not being altered by later experience.
p 175	A SHORT CUT THROUGH APOSTROPHES	*Learning* An insight into how learning can be missed.
p 175	CORRECT WORDS BUT NO SPELLING LEARNT	*Learning* Making a task more satisfying avoids learning spellings.
p 188	CONFUSION WITH SPELLING RULES	*Learning* A spelling rule misapplied and not amended.
p 243	INHIBITING THINKING	*Learning* Knowing what's unhelpful and removing it.
p 130	SUBCONSCIOUS SPELLING RULES, SUBLIMINAL LEARNING	*Learning* Subliminal learning of spelling.
p 129	NON-SPLD PERSON LEARNING CALLIGRAPHY	*Learning* Early stage of non-SpLD person's learning.
p 165	I'LL DRESS MYSELF	*Teaching* Frustration managed.
p 172	PUPIL RELUCTANCE	*Teaching* The right teaching overcoming pupil reluctance.
p 178	GEOGRAPHY BY 3 METHODS	*Teaching* Teaching covering several different learning needs.
p 76	ACCEPTANCE, WITH PROBLEM SOLVING	*Teaching* Accepting the student's perspective and looking for ways round problems.
p 90	CHANGED PERSPECTIVE 3: "I GOT ONE SPELLING RIGHT!"	*Feedback* Dialogue that didn't enable learning.

Page	Box title or text	Key element Comment
p 53	RECALL FROM LECTURE NOTES	*Recall* Personal presence affecting recall.
p 110	OUT OF SIGHT IS OUT OF MIND	*Recall* For many, what they can't see, they cannot bring to mind: in a pile of books, only information in the top one can be recalled.
p 54	REMEMBERING INSTRUCTIONS ONLY WHEN THEY ARE NEEDED	*Recall* Information recalled at need not otherwise.
p 55	RECALL AT VARYING SPEEDS	*Recall* Recall at varying speeds doesn't help.
p 101	CONTRASTING BEHAVIOUR	*Recall* Recall non-existent when the prompts are questions.
p 110	FORGETTING INTERMITTENT PAIN	*Recall* Recall non-existent when questioned about a different situation.
p 51	ONLY ONE WAY FROM A TO B	*Place* No flexibility with place; no confidence to experiment.
p 52	RECALL AND DEEP SEA DIVERS	*Place – recall* Influence of place on recall.
p 52	IS 'DO' THE SAME AT SCHOOL AND HOME?	*Place – learning* Learning influenced by physical place.
p 52	IS 'PAT' THE SAME ON TWO DIFFERENT PAGES?	*Place – learning* Learning not transferring from one page to another within a short length of time.
p 89	CHANGED PERSPECTIVE 1: ATTENTION GIVEN TO OBJECTS	*Place* Absorption with environment.
p 51	THE ALPHABET IN STRINGS	*Episodic memory* Inability to break memories into sections.
p 49	INCREASING STRESS AND CHILDHOOD SPELLING	*Stress – pitfall* Childhood spelling triggered by stress.

Page	Box title or text	Key element Comment
p 168	DRUM KIT IN A STORY	*Thinking preferences* A story that can be used to tease out thinking preferences.
p 4	TWO DYSLEXIC SAILORS	*Thinking preferences* The differences caused a clash. I had no phonological processing to retain information and use it.
p 199	ASSESSMENT TEST SIDESTEPPED	*Thinking preferences* An internal switch going unnoticed.
p 202	FEYNMAN ON TESTING THINKING	*Thinking preferences* Experiments carried out.
p 210	MANAGING MY DYSLEXIA THROUGH THIS RESEARCH	*Thinking preferences* Working in a way that suits.
p 76	PITFALLS AT 60+	*Thinking preferences* People with different thinking preferences able to help without understanding each other's way.
p 7	JOHN IS TYPICAL ...	*Adult experience* Ways successful dyslexics got through.
p 93	NOT MAKING EXCUSES	*Adult experience* Adult relationship with teacher.
p 112	EVERYTHING CONSISTENT WITH A SINGLE FIRST MISREAD	*Language* Advanced language skills present with poor reading skills.
p 106	WORDS LOSE THEIR MEANING	*Dyslexia* Words and meanings get separated.
p 107	FILING USING 3RD LETTER	*Dyslexia* Difficulty using the alphabet.
p 111	DEEP DYSLEXIA INTERFERING WITH A MNEMONIC	*Dyslexia* Right concept, wrong word.
p 112	CONFUSION FROM DYSLEXIA	*Dyslexia* Jumbled letters, wrong word.
p 114	SATISFACTION FOR ONE DYSPRAXIC ON A ROCK FACE	*Dyspraxia* Difficulty moving.

Page	Box title or text	Key element Comment
p 115	CAPITAL J IN FOUR PIECES	*Dyspraxia* Lack of smooth movement; no concept of the letter as a whole.
p 116	RESIDENTIAL SCHOOL OUTING	*Dyspraxia* No concept of organisation.
p 120	AD(H)D AS LIVED	*AD(H)D* An internal perspective of AD(H)D on attention and daydreaming.
p 122	AN AD(H)D PERSPECTIVE ON ATTENTION	*AD(H)D* Switching attention is not the same as half paying attention.
p 122	TO LONDON FOR A CUP OF COFFEE	*AD(H)D* How attention switching can lead an AD(H)D person a long way off track.
p 125	COLOUR CODING FORCES	*Maths problem* Presentation obscuring the maths.
p 126	100M IS LONGER IN A BIGGER STADIUM	*Maths problem – dyscalculia* No grasp of maths concept.
p 125	NO CONCEPT OF PLACEMENT VALUES	*Maths problems* Arithmetic problems and grasp of maths concepts.

References

Baddeley, Alan, 2007, *Working Memory, Thought, and Action,* Oxford University Press, Oxford

Bishop, D.V.M., 2008, *Specific Language Impairment, Dyslexia, and Autism: Using Genetics to Unravel Their Relationship*, pp 67-78 in Norbury, C.F., Tomblin, J.B. and Bishop, D.V.M. (eds), 2008, *Understanding Developmental Language Disorders: from Theory to Practice,* Psychological Press, Hove

Chinn, Steve, 2017, *The Trouble with Maths: A Practical Guide to Helping Learners with Numeracy Difficulties,* Routledge, Abingdon, 3rd ed.

Henderson, Elizabeth, 2003, *How to Have a Dyslexia Friendly School,* Beacon Office, Oldfield School, Maidenhead

Jones, Anwen, Greenwold, Lynn, 2012, *Dyslexia Contact*, p 24-30, Vol. 31, No 3, Sept 2012

Kipling, Rudyard, 1906, *Puck of Pook's Hill,* MacMillan and Co., London

Miles, Tim, 1993, *Dyslexia: the Pattern of Difficulties,* Whurr, London, 2nd ed.

Morton, John, Frith, Uta, 1995, *Causal Modelling: A Structural Approach to Developmental Psychopathology*, Ch 13 in *Developmental Psychopathology*, Vol. 1 pp 357-390

Saunders, Roger, 1995, *Stress Factors within the Family,* in Miles, Tim, Varma, Ved (eds), 1995, *Dyslexia and Stress*, Whurr, London

Singleton, C.H., 1987, *Dyslexia and Cognitive Models of Reading*, Support for Learning, Vol. 2, pp 47-56

Singleton, C.H., 1988, *The Early Diagnosis of Developmental Dyslexia*, Support for Learning, Vol. 3, pp 108-121

Singleton, C.H., Chair, 1999, *Dyslexia in Higher Education: Policy, Provision and Practice,* University of Hull, Hull

Stacey, Ginny, 2005, *A Taste of Dyslexia DVD,* Oxfordshire Dyslexia Association, Oxford

Stacey, Ginny, 2019, *Finding Your Voice with Dyslexia and other SpLDs,* Routledge, London

Stacey, Ginny, 2020, *Organisation and Everyday Life with Dyslexia and other SpLDs,* Routledge, London

Stacey, Ginny, 2021, *Gaining Knowledge and Skills with Dyslexia and other SpLDs,* Routledge, London

Website information

DfES Report, 2005, https://www.patoss-dyslexia.org/Resources/DSA-Working-Guidelines Accessed 10 June 2020

Series website: www.routledge.com/cw/stacey

3 Adaptations for Children

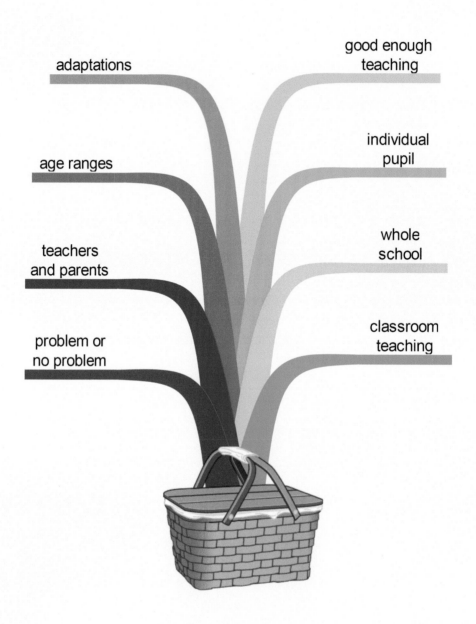

adaptations

age ranges

teachers
and parents

problem or
no problem

good enough
teaching

individual
pupil

whole
school

classroom
teaching

Contents

Vital for dyslexic/ SpLDs, good practice for all

Teaching practice that is VITAL for dyslexic/ SpLD children is also good practice for all children. The ideas about teaching in this chapter can be used with all children.

A school that caters well for dyslexic/ SpLD children need not divert resources, of money or people, from the majority of children to a minority.

THINKING PREFERENCES are highlighted in orange in this chapter.

 List of key points and summaries

K = key points
S = summaries

Working with the chapter

There are 3 aspects of working with children that are covered by this chapter:

- deciding whether dyslexia/ SpLD is an issue for a child
- working with an individual child
- catering for dyslexic/ SpLD children within whole school approaches.

Templates on the website

TEMPLATES:

For the initial approach to the chapter, use:

A1	JOTTING DOWN AS YOU SCAN
A2	BOOKMARK – PURPOSE
A4	JOTTING DOWN AS YOU READ
A5	COLLECTING IDEAS THAT INTEREST YOU
B1	COLLECTING IDEAS THAT RELATE TO YOU (specially for readers who are themselves dyslexic/ SpLD)

To collect information about a pupil, use:

B3	COMPARE EXPECTATIONS AND REALITY
B4	ACTION, RESULTS, NEXT STEP
B8	RECORDING TEMPLATE - 4
B12	QUESTIONS TO ASK A CHILD TO EXPLORE INNER THINKING

To work on thinking preferences, use:

E1   LIST OF OPTIONS FOR THINKING PREFERENCES
E2   TABLE OF THINKING PREFERENCES (SPATIAL)
E4   THINKING PREFERENCES (SPATIAL)
E5   THINKING PREFERENCES (LINEAR)
E7   THE BOX 'OTHER'
B11   MONITORING PROGRESS

To work on language and reading, use:

G1   THE FUNCTIONS OF 'ROUND' AND OTHER WORDS
G5   BASIC SENTENCES FROM A COMPLEX ONE.
G6   EYE SPAN EXERCISES 1 & 2
G7   EYE SPAN EXERCISE 3

Appendix 1 Resources

APPENDIX 1: p 252

The first 2 sections of this appendix will help you collect information about the way your pupil does anything and how his dyslexia/ SpLD affects him. The rest of the appendix has skills that you need to teach your pupil in order for him to become autonomous.

If you are dyslexic/ SpLD, this appendix will help you gather the information you want from this book.

Appendix 2 Individual, Personal Profile of Dyslexia/ SpLD and Regime for Managing Dyslexia/ SpLD

APPENDIX 2: p 266

Tip: *ADAPTATIONS FOR CHILDREN* **and building
an** *INDIVIDUAL, PERSONAL PROFILE OF DYSLEXIA/ SPLD* **and
a** *REGIME FOR MANAGING DYSLEXIA/ SPLD*

As the effects of your pupil's dyslexia/ SpLD become clearer, build the insights into a *PROFILE* and *REGIME* for him and give him ownership of them.

Help him to understand how he thinks best, what happens as a result of his dyslexia/ SpLD and the way it varies.

Help him to be confident about himself and see that there are ways round many of the effects of dyslexia/ SpLD.
Let him be as autonomous as he can be.

Ⓖ p 303:
autonomous

Appendix 3 Key Concepts

APPENDIX 3: p 282

This appendix has a summary of the key ideas I cover when doing an audit of skills and knowledge with a dyslexic/ SpLD student. It shows which of the 4 books in the series covers each idea in full.

1 Dipping-in to try out ideas

Decide what your immediate interest is:

1   to establish whether there is a dyslexic/ SpLD problem or not

2   to work with an individual pupil

3   to cater naturally for dyslexic/ SpLD pupils within a whole school approach.

For interest 1:
Scan *WHAT GOES WRONG* and sections §§3 - 7 in *NO CURE, PLEASE START EARLY*.

Read:
TEACHERS AND PARENTS, §4
IS THERE A PROBLEM OR NOT?, §5
Beginning of *TEACHING AN INDIVIDUAL PUPIL, §6*
IMPORTANT STAGES OF LEARNING, §6.1
FINDING OUT HOW YOUR PUPIL THINKS WELL AND WHAT MOTIVATES HIM,
    § 6.2.

WHAT GOES WRONG:
p 82
NO CURE, PLEASE START
EARLY, §3 - §7:
p 44-57

§4: p 156
§5: p 158
§6: p 161
§6.1: p 164
§6.2: p 165

For interests 2 and 3:
Read, from *NO CURE, PLEASE START EARLY:*
    NEURONS FIRING TOGETHER, WIRE TOGETHER, §4
    LEARNED CONFUSION, §3
    THE OLDEST MEMORY TRACE, §5
    SOME FACTORS AFFECTING RECALL, §6
    ATTENTION TO LEARNING, §7.
Scan: *WHAT GOES WRONG* and the rest of this chapter; note any behaviours that are relevant to your current pupils.

§4: p 47
§3: p 44
§5: p 48
§6: p 51
§7: p 56

WHAT GOES WRONG:
p 82

For interest 2:
Work with *TEACHING AN INDIVIDUAL PUPIL* and add the ideas to the programmes you use.

TEACHING AN INDIVIDUAL
PUPIL: p 161

For interest 3:
Read: From *NO CURE, PLEASE START EARLY:*
    AVERAGE SKILLS A DISADVANTAGE, §8
    4 LEVELS OF COMPENSATION, §9
    DEGREES OF SEVERITY, §10

§8: p 57
§9: p 60
§10: p 61

Work with, from this chapter:

> *Dyslexic/ SpLD Friendly Classroom Teaching, §8*
> *Teaching an Individual Pupil, §6*
> *Whole School Approach, §7.*

In this chapter:
§8: p 178
§6: p 161
§7: p 176

2 Context

It is an obvious statement, but worth making: the adult dyslexic/ SpLD person was once a child dyslexic/ SpLD. The patterns of behaviour established in childhood can influence those of the adult, as in the following story.

Story: A dyslexic passenger

One student knew he was dyslexic at a young age. He'd had support at school. He was good at sport and had a confident, cheerful outlook on life. He continued support at university. I was aware that he wasn't gaining anything useful from the support sessions with me.

I gave him an overview of the effects of dyslexia and how to deal with it. I told him nothing would develop in his mind until he could see it was relevant to him. I told him coming to support was a waste of his time until he wanted to make progress. We kept the lines of communication open.

He eventually came back saying my comments had made him reflect. He realised he hadn't put any effort into learning as a child; he'd used dyslexia as an excuse; he'd gone to the support sessions as a passenger.

He had treated support at university in the same way: as a passenger. He has now recognised the impact of his dyslexia and comes for support with a readiness to develop skills. He even wants to learn how the English language works. He felt my comments were the first time he'd been challenged to face up to his dyslexia and deal with it.

The series *Living Confidently with Specific Learning Difficulties* (Stacey, 2019, 2020, 2021) has insights, information and strategies for adults and teenagers dealing with dyslexia/ SpLD. This chapter is about adapting those ideas to apply to younger children and primary schools. It is about helping an 'at risk' child avoid many of the difficulties. It is also about helping others who are learning basic skills.

Stacey (2019, 2020, 2021)

In the context of the 'at risk' child, NO CURE, PLEASE START EARLY makes the case for taking dyslexia/ SpLD seriously from the first signs that progress is slower than would be expected for the individual child. This will be especially true for families who have a history of dyslexia/ SpLD[1]. It should also be remembered that the patterns of behaviour of these syndromes vary from one person to another. Dyslexia/ SpLD should not be ruled out because another member of the family is affected in quite a different way.

NO CURE, PLEASE START EARLY: p 38

ADAPTATIONS, the next subsection, sets out the material from the rest of the series that is relevant to children. GOOD ENOUGH TEACHING summarises qualities that assist dyslexic/ SpLD children to learn in mainstream schools.

ADAPTATIONS: p 147

GOOD ENOUGH TEACHING: p 151

Summary of the chapter

The chapter has 3 parts:

- who the adaptations are for: children in primary school and others learning basic skills, §3
- whether to think about a disability or not and how to collect evidence, §§ 4 and 5
- teaching suitable for dyslexic/ SpLD children:
    o on an individual basis, §6
    o in whole school approach, §7
    o in classroom teaching, §8.

§3: p 154

§4: p 156
§5: p 158

§6: p 161
§7: p 176
§8: p 178

---

[1] 'A history of dyslexia/ SpLD' may not always be known, since these syndromes have not been widely recognised in the past. But you may find people saying something like, "Uncle Joe was just like that."

2.1 Adaptations

This series of books (Stacey, 2019) has been divided into:

Book 1: processes and knowledge for dealing with dyslexia/ SpLD well

Book 2: applying the knowledge and skills of Book 1 to organisation and everyday life

Book 3: imparting knowledge and skills to dyslexic/ SpLD people in formal situations, informal ones and indirect ones

Book 4: a focus on the manifest behaviour and problems of dyslexia/ SpLD and their avoidance (this book).

The series is intended for adults, but several of the concepts apply to children as well.

The first table below contrasts this chapter with the other 3 books. The subsequent tables summarise the concepts and what's important about them.

Stacey (2019, 2020, 2021)

Books 1 - 3:	Adaptations for Children (this chapter):
deal with adults, often with a history of problems	deals with children[2] at early stages of learning
include organisation and everyday life impacts of dyslexia/ SpLD	expects organisation to be done for children
usually expect language and numeracy to be carriers of other topics.	is concerned with language and numeracy learning.

Important concepts	Comment
Where to start (Book 3)	It is important to start by gaining the child's co-operation and showing him that progress is possible and satisfying. Starting with material that interests him can help him to engage.
'New' is problematic (*MAJOR PRECAUTION*, p 8 or Book 1)	The beginning stages of anything can be really important. Early confusion can make a lasting impact that is almost impossible to get rid of.
Positive use of mistakes	Mistakes need to be seen as opportunities and not failures.

---

[2] See *AGE RANGE*, p 154, for discussion with respect to others learning basic language and numeracy.

Important concepts	Comment
Find out what the child thinks he's been asked to do (Book 2)	Instructions can be misinterpreted for many reasons: he may have missed some words; he may have made a consistent set of instructions that don't happen to be the ones you gave.
Find out his best THINKING PREFERENCES (APPENDIX 3, p 282, or Book 1) (THE BOX: 'OTHER')	You need to know the full possible range and be prepared to use *TEMPLATE: E7 - THE BOX: 'OTHER' when his way of doing a task doesn't fit what you know. Make sure you include the kinaesthetic sense with visual and verbal strengths; also include frameworks and rationale.
Find out what motivates him or what his interests are (Book 2)	Motivation and interest can be key to getting neurons to fire together and so wire together.
In finding solutions, probe behind the presenting problem (Book 2)	Often there is a point of confusion behind an obvious problem. You need to find out what it is in order to solve the issues.
Understanding pitfalls (This book)	A child needs to gradually understand where his difficulties lie and what he can do about them to get round them: deliberate strategies; ways to pause; accepting some difficulties are obstacles for which he needs help. He needs to maintain his self-confidence and self-esteem.

* TEMPLATES ⓒ

Useful information about the mind (Book 1, except for Place and Time: Book 2)	
Episodic memory	often can't be broken into sections.
Subliminal learning	can't be relied on; work may need to be done deliberately.
Rote learning	often is an unproductive way of learning.
Being alert	can be a challenge for dyslexic/ SpLD people. Under certain circumstances the arousal system of the body does not stay alert and learning is impeded.
Recall	can go wrong for a number of reasons; there are ways for improving it, but they will be individual.
Place and time	may cause significant problems because of the way they affect memory. Care needs to be taken with any issues that arise.

Techniques to assist learning (APPENDIX 3, p 282, or Book 1)	
Mental set Chunking Recall Memory consolidation Systematic reviews Metacognition	These are techniques that make a significant difference to the efficiency of learning. They are skills non-dyslexic/ SpLD children may learn subliminally through their work. They are skills dyslexic/ SpLD children need to learn in a deliberate, transparent way.

Other ideas about teaching (discussed in this chapter)	
Stages at which learning style is important	Learning may not happen if the style is wrong at certain stages.
Different ways to teach, to present material	By having a series of different ways you can cover a range of learning styles.
Static content	Too many things changing at once can produce confusion; sometimes keeping elements the same allows learning.
Objective observation	You need to be able to listen well and to observe what the child does. You need to explore your observations and interpretations further to be sure that they are accurate.
Know your own assumptions	You need to know what your own assumptions are and to be able to put them aside when a child is telling you something that doesn't fit your assumptions.

Understanding the problems	
In dealing with dyslexia/ SpLD in children or those 'at risk', it is good to bear in mind the discussions in *WHAT GOES WRONG* about some of the issues around dyslexia/ SpLD: whose perspective is used to discuss the observed behaviour manifest behaviour organisation basic and adult difficulties confidence whether to recognise a disability or not. In *KEY ELEMENTS OF THE STORIES IN THIS BOOK,* the stories are grouped according to the key elements, with comments that summarise the point of the story. *NO CURE, PLEASE START EARLY* discusses reasons why there is no cure for dyslexia/ SpLD. These reasons can be part of the initial difficulties in learning.	*WHAT GOES WRONG:* p 82 *KEY ELEMENTS OF THE STORIES IN THIS BOOK:* p 133 *NO CURE, PLEASE START EARLY:* p 38

Outcomes for the child	
The child learns at a level consistent with his best abilities	Potential is maximised with minimal distortion from dyslexia/ SpLD.
The child gradually becomes autonomous	It is in the best interest of the child to become autonomous. You won't always be there to help him unravel the problems as they occur.
INDIVIDUAL, PERSONAL PROFILE OF DYSLEXIA/ SPLD (p 268, or Book 1)	It is not always possible to avoid all the problems of dyslexia/ SpLD. His *PROFILE* should include strengths and ways of pausing, as well as the problems he has and accommodations he needs.
REGIME FOR MANAGING DYSLEXIA/ SPLD (p 268, or Book 1)	His *REGIME* is for managing unexpected moments when his dyslexia/ SpLD interferes with life.

2.2 Good enough teaching

A major theme of this series is that of listening attentively to each other, and to ourselves. There needs to be a curiosity to find out how another person thinks and how the internal maps that we make of the world are either similar or different. This attitude is also part of good teaching wherever teaching takes place: listening to a pupil through what he says or through what he does. I've used the phrase 'good enough teacher' to include flexibility and a continual approach to change.

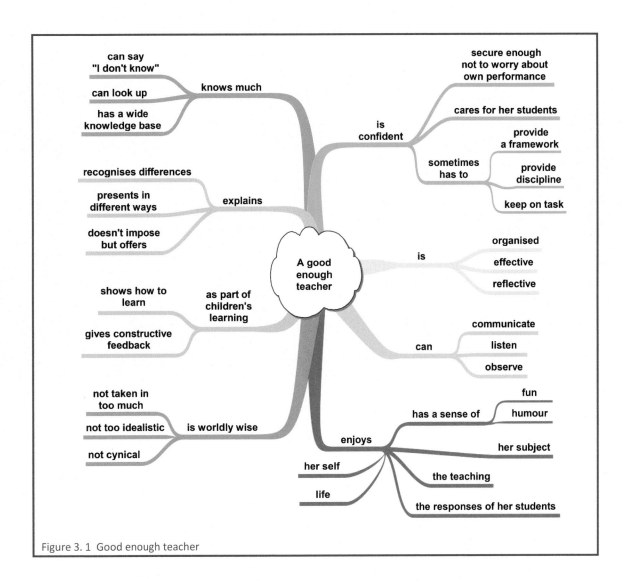

Figure 3. 1 Good enough teacher

Insight: A good enough teacher

- is organised, effective and reflective

- can communicate, listen and observe

- is confident:
    doesn't worry about her* own performance
    cares for her students
    can provide a framework and discipline as necessary
    can keep on task

- enjoys: her subject, students and teaching
    herself and life
    a sense of humour and fun

- knows much; can say "I don't know"; and can look up

- explains, using different presentation styles and recognising individual learning approaches; doesn't impose but offers

- as part of children's learning: shows how to learn skills; gives constructive feedback for skills and knowledge

- is worldly wise: not too idealistic; not taken in too much and not too cynical.

*With apologies to male teachers, I couldn't find a straightforward way to make this text gender neutral.

Listening and observing are more effective if you know your own intrinsic assumptions. In any conversation, we assume that other people will be thinking the same way that we are. When I run workshops and do an activity that allows people to be aware of the way they think, they are usually surprised at the different approaches shown by other participants. Knowing your assumptions should help you avoid misinterpreting anything that is happening for your pupil.

Exercise: Identifying assumptions

Look at the stories in the book and the MANIFEST BEHAVIOURS OF SPLDS.
List anything that relates to your pupils.
List any other situations that relate to your pupils.

Use TEMPLATE: B8 - RECORDING TEMPLATE - 4 with headings:
A = date and place
B = situation, description of situation
C = what you assume will happen
    what you assume your pupil is thinking
    what assumptions are made from teaching theories and
    practice
D = what actually happened
E = any clarification that you would like from your pupil
    what changes you could make to affect a different outcome.

MANIFEST BEHAVIOURS
OF SPLDS: p 98

TEMPLATES:

The insights you gain from this process will help you be more effective
in teaching those who learn in unorthodox ways.

Key point: Flexibility of a good enough teacher

A good enough teacher is likely to be flexible enough to allow
most 'at risk' children to find their own way through education.
Several ideas from such teachers have informed my practice and
are included in this series.

Key abilities are to observe and listen to children, and to put aside
any influence from your own assumptions of how to learn and
think.

3 Age range

The age range of pupils for these adaptations is more a question of the age at which certain skills are expected to develop and less to do with the actual age of learners.

The ideas presented in the whole series are directly relevant to individual adult experience, with the exception of learning basic skills of language and numeracy. The ideas should also be directly relevant to individual children in secondary education.

Once children are in secondary education, they are no longer expected to be learning the basic skills. Their learning is focused on advanced skills, and knowledge that will be useful to them in their adult life. Language and numeracy are often expected to carry other subjects in secondary school and adult education; they are no longer expected to be part of the curriculum.

Expectations and reality are not always the same. There are children in secondary school who are still struggling with the basic skills of language and numeracy. Some of them leave school and become adults who are still struggling to acquire these skills.

For simplicity, I have referred to two age groups:
 'children' covers primary school aged children
'teenagers+' covers secondary school children and adults who are still struggling with basic language and numeracy skills.

It is important to have respect for the actual age of the learners.

Teenagers+ may not learn well if they feel they are being patronised. Children may be hindered if too much is expected of their social immaturity.

The content of material used for teaching the basic skills needs to be related to the actual age of the pupil.

With children, it is appropriate to have lesson plans. Lesson plans can be useful with teenagers+, but you need to be prepared to be flexible; to abandon any plan and be guided by any pressing need or problem or immediate interest.

On the whole, children are not expected to organise their lives and work with them is likely to be only about learning the basic skills. Work with the teenage+ group should include the wider impact of dyslexia/ SpLD on everyday life and all the ramifications of organisation; it may also include subject specific work; the necessary material is covered in *Organisation and Everyday Life with Dyslexia and other SpLDs* and *Gaining Knowledge and Skills with Dyslexia and other SpLDs* (Stacey 2020, 2021)

Stacey (2020, 2021)

Children and teenagers+ can both suffer from low self-esteem and low self-confidence. You need to be careful of deep scars that many teenagers+ have from their childhood experiences of trying to learn despite their dyslexia/ SpLD. For both groups you need to be aware of underlying fears about being inadequate.

> For simplicity of style, this chapter is written in terms of children; but it also applies to the teenagers+ group.

4   Teachers and parents

Story: Best case scenario: good techniques, minimal dyslexia

One student was doing a vacation job for a few weeks alongside me.

I observed her ways of working for several weeks. She had many strategies that dyslexic students use but didn't seem to have any dyslexic problems.

I asked if she were dyslexic. She told me that she had a few quirky spellings, but she knew what they were. She explained that her mother was a specialist teacher for dyslexics and that her mother had recognised the early symptoms of problems and had taught her how to overcome them right from the start.

This student enjoyed all the riches of her strategies and thinking preferences without experiencing most of the problems, and without being bothered by those she did have.

Parents and teachers are both in good positions to observe that a child is not making as much progress as would be expected.

I have met many adults who were struggling with their study and feeling quite bad about themselves. Many of them have said that parents or teachers used to comment on their lack of progress. They may even tell me of one particularly significant adult who, for a while, was able to help and encourage them when they were a child. But nothing else was done about their difficulties and so often these signs have been have been missed or ignored.

The result is an adult who is struggling with education, in employment and with many everyday tasks and whose difficulties are magnified by low self-esteem and low self-confidence.

There are a range of attitudes that don't help in establishing co-operation between teachers and parents.

Parents can often feel that the teachers are the experts and have all the necessary training; consequently, they may place over-reliance on the teacher instead of trusting their own judgement. Teachers feel that parents are worrying too early and putting undue pressure on children and so they may fail to take parents' worries seriously enough.

The financial system can also be unhelpful in that acknowledging a child has a difficulty has resource implications.

Parents and teachers can also feel undermined if it is inferred that they are failing in some way. What's needed is a co-operative approach with observations shared between parents and teachers.

Sometimes, parents are afraid that a child will make excuses and will not try because of being labelled dyslexic/ SpLD, as the child in *Box: A Dyslexic Passenger* above. The *Philosophy of This Series* is to look for ways a child, or adult, can achieve their best at the same time as minimising the effects of the dyslexia/ SpLD. The child in the *Story: Best Case Scenario: Good Techniques, Minimal Dyslexia* demonstrates the benefit of the constructive help from her mother. She was certainly not expected to do less than her best.

Box: A Dyslexic Passenger: p 145

Philosophy of This Series: p 5

Story: Best Case Scenario: Good Techniques, Minimal Dyslexia: p 156

Another response of teachers and parents is to feel that taking notice is going to involve more time and resources than are available.

Key point: A little good help early prevents a large need later

It is worth remembering that a small amount of effort and resources used early will save a great deal of effort and resources later on.

It is very much less wearing to have co-operative children than ones who are fighting you every day of their childhood.

Anything that helps the jobs of teaching and parenting is valuable! Much of the practice that is VITAL for dyslexic/ SpLD children is good practice for all, so the resources used should benefit all.

Summary: Co-operation between teachers and parents

When there is a difference of opinion between the teachers and parents about a child's progress, those who think there is a problem need to collect evidence about the problem with evidence of achievement in other areas. *GATHERING EVIDENCE IN THE EARLY STAGES OF DYSLEXIA/ SPLD* suggests how to gather the evidence that may help to make a convincing case for the problems to be taken seriously. The evidence needs to be presented with the aim of gaining the co-operation of the other party.

GATHERING EVIDENCE IN THE EARLY STAGES OF DYSLEXIA/ SPLD: p 160

Teachers are in a position to make changes and to help a child even if the parents deny there's any problem. It is more difficult for parents when teachers are the ones who say there's no problem.

If as a parent you do not have a co-operative school teacher, it is still worth learning how to help your child, and the earlier the better.

5   Is there a problem or not?

The early stages of developing dyslexia/ SpLD are very difficult to distinguish from the natural trial and error of learning. Any signs of uneven progress need to be explored with the child and investigated. It is possible that a child knows there's something different about the way he learns or does tasks. He may be afraid of the differences and may try to hide them, which also doesn't help the early identification of problems.

There have been many stories of parents being told "He'll grow out of it.", which is generally what happens for most children (Augur, 1983). However the difficulties that are caused by the early signs not being recognised make it worth taking a second look to see whether there is a problem or not. The approach to learning that caters for dyslexic/ SpLD children is not a disadvantage to other children. Careful observation of how a child learns and what seems to motivate him are important parts of finding a suitable program, both of which can be helpful to any child.

Augur (1983)

It seems to me a cruelty to allow the attitude of 'he'll grow out of it' to be a reason for taking no early action.

Key point: Mistakes contribute to learning

A positive attitude towards mistakes can also be an important part of dealing with any difficulties. If a mistake is viewed as an opportunity to find out more about the way a child is learning or approaching tasks, it can be seen as beneficial.

Mistakes can be viewed as evidence to assist learning rather than failures which sap the self-confidence of the learner.

There has been a stigma about disability; to a large extent because society is not good at celebrating differences. Children often compare their own performance with that of their peers. They know when something is working differently for them. When they see they are not making the same progress as their peers, they can become very worried. It is worse for them if the dyslexia/ SpLD is ignored to the point that it has become a major problem. It would be much better for the problem to be identified, labelled and addressed without their self-confidence and self-esteem being damaged. An upbeat approach to finding solutions is a healthy attitude to adopt. The result would be a confident child (*FIGURE 3.2*) who can take responsibility for his own learning and his approach to tasks.

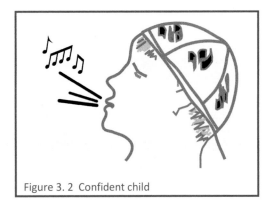

Figure 3. 2 Confident child

5.1 Gathering evidence in the early stages of dyslexia/ SpLD

The term Specific Learning Difficulties is useful. It means there are difficulties in an individual person's learning in specific areas and, by implication, in other areas there are achievements. You need to collect evidence about both. The achievements can give the learner confidence as well as showing up the problems.

5.1.1 Problems

It is worth collecting together the observations and experiences that are making you wonder whether dyslexia/ SpLD is an issue. Use *TEMPLATE: B8 - RECORDING TEMPLATE - 4*, with the headings in the *MARGIN:*

- List the actions and tasks that are causing you concern. (B)

- What is it about these tasks that causes you concern? (C)

- How frequently do you see these things happening? (C)

- What does your child say about them? (D)

- How does he describe his emotional attitude towards them? (D)

- Compare the list of problems encountered by your child (B) with those discussed in *WHAT GOES WRONG*, specially:

   o *§5.2, MANIFEST BEHAVIOUR OF SPLDS*

   o *§6, DYSLEXIA*

   o *§7, DYSPRAXIA*

   o *§8, AD(H)D*

   o *§9, DYSCALCULIA*

   or consult any list on the Internet from an authoritative website. (B)

- How many of these problems describe the experiences of your child? What do you think underpins his problems? (E)

TEMPLATES

Suggested headings:

A = Date

B = Actions or tasks

C = Comments by adult

D = Comments by child

E = Specify: type of difficulty

§5.2: p 98
§6: p 103
§7: p 113
§8: p 118
§9: p 123

5.1.2 Achievements

You can use a similar process to provide evidence that your child is making progress in other similar or more difficult tasks; you only need to change the heading for column E and the bullet point relating to E. These show that the difficulties you are worried about are not part of general slow learning.

Use *Recording Template - 4* as above, with E = specify type of achievement:

- Write the tasks in (B).

- How do these tasks demonstrate the child's intelligence? (C)

- What does your child say about these tasks? (D)

- What common themes are there in your child's achievements? (E)

Finding Out How a Child Thinks Well and What Motivates Him has suggestions for ways to establish your child's intelligence.

Finding Out How a Child Thinks Well and What Motivates Him: p 165

Try using these insights to improve the tasks that cause you to worry. Collect the evidence that they make a difference using *Template B4 - Action, Results, Next Step*.

Templates

Summary: For both problems and achievements

Describe what happens as precisely as possible. Take photographs of his achievements. It can help discussion if you have dates and times of day. If you can mount the information in a notebook, it will help you to tell a consistent story. By collecting evidence systematically, you have material to discuss with the other people involved with the child's learning, including the child himself.

---

6 Teaching an individual pupil

A fundamental element of working with an individual pupil is that you are immediately looking for *Thinking Preferences* that make learning effective for him. You are aiming to avoid the chaotic results of

Thinking Preferences: p 290

LEARNED CONFUSION. Each learning session builds systematically on the previous work in a way that makes sense for the learner, see *NEURONS FIRING TOGETHER, WIRE TOGETHER*. Those things that build the consistency for the learner are used consciously; those which produce confusions for the learner, or which are unnecessary, are avoided. *DYSLEXIC/ SPLD FRIENDLY CLASSROOM TEACHING* also discusses ideas that are important for 1-1 work with an individual pupil.

LEARNED CONFUSION: p 44
NEURONS FIRING TOGETHER, WIRE TOGETHER: p 47

DYSLEXIC/ SPLD FRIENDLY CLASSROOM TEACHING: p 178

There are many excellent programmes available for teaching dyslexic/ SpLDs. A good teacher who is observing what the pupil does will gradually select those programmes that produced the best success. An unobservant teacher may tend to see dyslexic/ SpLDs pupils as a homogenous group and focus on general, overall strategies.

Parents can use the ideas in *GATHERING EVIDENCE IN THE EARLY STAGES OF DYSLEXIA/ SPLD* to monitor the progress of their child. The evidence will either reassure them that the school has chosen the right programmes and is delivering them appropriately, or will be material to use in discussions with the school to look for more suitable approaches.

GATHERING EVIDENCE IN THE EARLY STAGES OF DYSLEXIA/ SPLD: p 160

It is the attention to the learner's processing that has to be added to the many programmes available. This attention is necessary whether in 1-1 work or in the classroom.

Tip: Some underlying principles of paying attention to the learner's processing

Working memory, long-term memory and recall can be improved when information is held together in a way that works for the individual, see *CHUNKING*.

CHUNKING: p 287

1st step:	to find out how your pupil thinks well and what motivates him
2nd step:	build an initial profile and test it
3rd step:	apply the insights to material that has to be learnt
4th step:	keep modifying the profile in the light of experience.

Ⓖ p 303: profile

Tip: Recognise individuality in children

It is not enough to say that dyslexic children need a multisensory approach to learning and then to give each one exactly the same tasks and materials. For example, many dyslexic people are holistic thinkers, but not all; so there are some who get nowhere with mind maps. Therefore, a major component of working with an individual pupil is *OBJECTIVE OBSERVATION*.

HOLISTIC VS. LINEAR: p 291

OBJECTIVE OBSERVATION: p 288

Key point: Adding particular strengths to programmes

The components that need to be added to the programmes used for a dyslexic pupil's learning are:

- selection from a very broad range of ways of learning, including 'other' when a pupil's learning seems to fit no known pattern
- catering for a pupil's natural way of learning
- using his interests and the strengths of his learning style.

From these components, a learning profile for the pupil will emerge. The profile should be added to the school's pupil passport, or any equivalent document. It will be part of his *INDIVIDUAL, PERSONAL PROFILE OF DYSLEXIA/ SPLD* and his *REGIME FOR MANAGING DYSLEXIA/ SPLD*.

INDIVIDUAL, PERSONAL PROFILE OF DYSLEXIA/ SPLD: p 268

REGIME FOR MANAGING DYSLEXIA/ SPLD: p 268

The pupil then needs to understand his *PROFILE* and know how he can best adapt his learning environment so that he becomes an autonomous learner.

6.1 Important stages of learning

I have found that there are certain stages of learning when it is very important to pay attention to how my student is learning. These are shown in *Figure 3.3* and listed in the text beside the figure. These are the stages at which you want neurons to fire together and so wire together.

Neurons Firing Together, wire Together: p 47

Important stages of learning

Input: any time new information is given.

Immediate use: very shortly after input.

Feedback loop: when what is being learnt is checked against what is intended to be learnt.

Recall: information is brought back from memory some time after input.

Direct use: information and skills are used exactly as they were input.

Developed use: knowledge and skills are modified in some way.

Long-term memory: knowledge and skills are established in long-term memory, and can be recalled.

Understanding: an appreciation of significant concepts has happened.

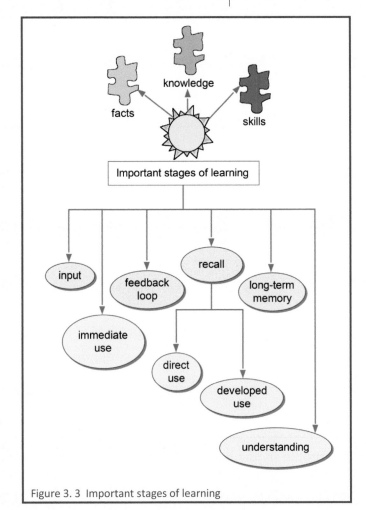

Figure 3. 3 Important stages of learning

Somewhere in the process, information given by you becomes knowledge and skill that he owns and he has gained a depth of understanding.

Recall may be a particularly difficult stage; there are several stories involving recall in the *Key Element of the Stories in This Book.* If your pupil is having difficulty with recall, you need to start with something

Key Element of the Stories in This Book: p 133

that he can recall easily, explore with him how he does it and then adapt the insights to what he needs to learn. Recall as part of a systematic review scheme helps to establish knowledge and skills in long-term memory (Stacey, 2019).

Stacey (2019)

Summary: Check he is thinking the right way for him

At all the *IMPORTANT STAGES OF LEARNING*, you should check that your pupil is thinking the right way for him. The right way may be different from stage to stage and time to time.

6.2 Finding out how your pupil thinks well and what motivates him

Even from an early age, it is possible to observe how children do things and what they are struggling with. How to collect your observations in a systematic way has been described under *ACHIEVEMENTS* and *PROBLEMS*.

ACHIEVEMENTS: p 161
PROBLEMS: p 160

Story: I'll dress myself

One 18-month-old wanted to dress himself and fought against his mother doing it. He was getting very frustrated with his lack of success.

It seemed that he couldn't work out how a crumpled heap of T-shirt became a T-shirt on him. He was a very orderly child; every possible line on the floor had a neat line of parked cars.

A step-wise approach solved the dressing problem. The clothes were put in front of him, with the openings towards him and in an order that he could put them on.

End of frustration, end of fights, shorter time getting dressed. A win-win solution.

One approach is to observe your pupil in a detached way with curiosity and to compare observations with others who can also observe the pupil.

TEMPLATES

Record your observations using *TEMPLATE: B8 - RECORDING TEMPLATE - 4,* with the headings in the *MARGIN*

- List the actions and tasks in (B)
- What strategies do you see your pupil using? (C)
- What does your pupil say about the way he does a task? (D)
- What *THINKING PREFERENCES* do you both think are being used? (E)

Suggested headings:
A = Date
B = Actions or tasks
C = Comments by adult
D = Comments by pupil
E = Strategies used, *THINKING PREFERENCES* demonstrated

Use the *TEMPLATE: E1 - LIST OF OPTIONS FOR THINKING PREFERENCES* to help you decide which ones are being used. Use *TEMPLATE: E7 - THE BOX 'OTHER'* for anything you want to remember but which doesn't fit readily into a particular category.

THINKING PREFERENCES: p 290

TEMPLATES

You need to consider whether the child learns by using all the senses (visual, verbal or kinaesthetic), a combination of two, or just one. The kinaesthetic sense is not used as deliberately as the visual and verbal senses. Stacey (2019) describes the way eye movement can show which sense is being used.

SENSES: p 290

Stacey (2019)

You also need to consider whether understanding the underlying rationale, or having a framework, is important for the child.

RATIONALE OR FRAMEWORK: p 291

It may be he has a prime motivation that captures his interest and would help him learn

MOTIVATION: p 291

Build the insights gained into his *INDIVIDUAL, PERSONAL PROFILE OF DYSLEXIA.*

INDIVIDUAL, PERSONAL PROFILE OF DYSLEXIA: p 268

When such a portfolio is used to show progress and is used by all concerned with the pupil's learning, the pupil can be encouraged by seeing the progress made and will take ownership of both the progress and dealing with any problems.

Tip: Unobtrusive *OBJECTIVE OBSERVATION* of a pupil

Use games and tasks to observe a pupil objectively. Choose ones that aren't part of basic learning about words and numbers. You need to avoid any mistakes being built into a *LEARNED CONFUSION* at the early stages of important skills.

- Give a pupil tasks to do; observe how he responds.

- Get a pupil to teach you something he knows very well, or a topic that he is interested in.

- Get him to give you instructions about a game he can play.

- Get him to describe something he knows well: his room, his way to school, his computer desktop.

Analyse the way he tells you or shows you the task, or game. Use *THINKING PREFERENCES* in the analysis.

OBJECTIVE OBSERVATION:
p 288

LEARNED CONFUSION:
p 44

THINKING PREFERENCES:
p 290

The tasks used can be everyday ones as well as learning ones. Dyslexia/ SpLD are not restricted to education; they affect the whole of a pupil's life. You want to use something which is a specific task, so that you can learn from the observation how your pupil carries out the task. The explanation for using games or tasks unrelated to words or numbers is a combination of the *MAJOR PRECAUTION* and *LEARNED CONFUSION*. This approach is a deliberate, practical one. During the observation process, you are standing back from the pupil and having minimal impact on what he is doing.

MAJOR PRECAUTION: p 8

LEARNED CONFUSION:
p 44

A second approach is exploring inner thinking. Ask your pupil how he thinks his way through anything. Some children have considerable insight into how they think. Sharman Jefferies (2007- on the web, 2008) reported on her work as a psychologist assessing children. She found many of them could tell her how they solved difficulties they experienced. They were quite clear about the strategies they were using.

Jefferies
(2007- on the web,
2008)

A third approach is to consider the tasks and activities that attract the child's attention. Interpret his interests in terms of *THINKING PREFERENCES*.

The *TEMPLATE: B12 - QUESTIONS TO ASK A CHILD TO EXPLORE INNER THINKING* is designed to capture these insights. You need to probe behind the initial response, as with the student who had no problem about getting lost simply because getting lost was an adventure, *STORY BOX: CHANGED PERSPECTIVE 2: "WHAT DIFFICULTY?"*. You need to be curious as to how the pupil thinks; you need to let go of thinking your way is better.

TEMPLATES

STORY BOX: CHANGED PERSPECTIVE 2: "WHAT DIFFICULTY?": p 90

Both the unobtrusive observation and the explicit questioning are important. They will help you build an initial profile for the pupil.

Story: Drum kit in a story

One child made up a story to remember what was in his drum kit.

A Dad wearing his *high hat* took 3 children, his son *Thomas*, son's friend *Tom* and daughter *Thomasine* on a *ride* out of the city into the countryside. But on the way they came across a *snare* which tripped them up and made them *crash*. The Dad calmed them down with his deep *bass* voice.

drums: toms 1, 2 and 3, snare, bass
cymbals: hi-hat, ride, crash

The story gives you something to work with. To find out about his *THINKING PREFERENCES*, you have to explore whether he is remembering himself playing (kinaesthetic); he is seeing the drums (visual); he is remembering the story (verbal).

6.3   Build an initial profile and test it

Use the various *THINKING PREFERENCES TEMPLATES (E2, E4, E5)* to build a profile from your observations and the questioning. You start with the comments that come from observation of a pupil's behaviour and from the discussion exploring inner thinking with the pupil. You then speculate about the *THINKING PREFERENCES* that may be producing the behaviour. You involve the *THINKING PREFERENCES* in other tasks and monitor the subsequent behaviour. Progress will tell you that you are on the right track; use *TEMPLATE: B11 - MONITORING PROGRESS*.

TEMPLATES

THINKING PREFERENCES: p 290

Lack of progress will help you to change or refine your speculations and try other options. *The Template: E7 - Box 'Other'* is useful for those observations that don't seem to fit anywhere yet which you feel are significant and don't want to forget. As you explore lack of progress you are likely to be uncovering *Pitfalls*; these also need to be added to the *Individual, Personal Profile of Dyslexia/ SpLD*.

Templates

Pitfalls: p 73
*Individual, Personal
Profile of Dyslexia/
SpLD:* p 268

Example: From evidence to initial development of strategies

The primary school reports for one dyspraxic pupil with autistic elements led to the following suggested profile with ideas to test the profile comments:

School reports	Suggestions about profile
enthusiastic listener	good verbal skill
perceptive and helped by concrete purpose	MBPT Sensing type (Ⓖ p 302 MBPT)
shares ideas with others	MBPT extrovert
ideas seem to spill over	holist thinker
able to see parallel patterns	MI naturalist (Ⓖ p 302 MI)
Further comment from the Occupational Therapist was a worry that he will break things if his muscle strength is not improved.	

Ideas to test suggestions

One question: Do the autistic elements link with the dyspraxia? His body may not be co-ordinating the signals from other people about their reactions because he doesn't have a good body image of himself.

Do mnemonics help? Could they help to get a good body image?
What other verbal devices could help?
MBPT Sensing type often indicates a practical person.
Role play with others could be used to explore reactions; that would use his practical side.

Touch typing: practice that has a purpose; cover his eyes so that he thinks through his body. Get him to go slowly enough to avoid reinforcing wrong patterns. See if there is an analogy that will make sense for him to go slowly. Track changes could be used with typing, with the aim of having as few changes as possible. His practical side might engage with minimising the number of mistakes.

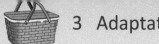

At some stage, he should recognise and enjoy the riches of holistic thinking and then develop the skill of selecting how and when to use them.

Spelling and typing: rather than tackling spelling in conventional ways, use of patterns in spelling might be more successful because it allows him to engage his observed pattern abilities.

Maths should be practical, have a purpose and involve open discussion of patterns (MI naturalist).

Lack of body awareness and breaking things might be something that always has to be accommodated. If he becomes confident about himself in other ways, he should be comfortable with the physical side of his dyspraxia and accept responsibility for it. Learning to become calm and stay calm should help minimise the effects.

To find out which suggestions will work, you need to experiment with the child and discuss progress with other teachers.

Key point: Minimal extra work for teachers

The example FROM EVIDENCE TO INITIAL DEVELOPMENT OF STRATEGIES was based on standard end of term reports from all the adults within a school about one particular boy. Some of the comments were negative in tone. Here they are used positively to reflect what they indicate about his profile. The extra time involved was less than half an hour and no extra resources.

FROM EVIDENCE TO INITIAL DEVELOPMENT OF STRATEGIES: p 169

I always tell my students that anything that doesn't work is just as important as the things that do work - both tell us about the way their minds work. You need to explore the initial profile to find out how good it is and where it needs modifying. You can continue the observation and questioning, as in FINDING OUT HOW A CHILD THINKS WELL AND WHAT MOTIVATES HIM, especially using the TEMPLATES: B3 - COMPARE EXPECTATIONS AND REALITY and B4 - ACTION, RESULT AND NEXT STEP. USING THE MIND WELL summarises a range of skills that will help your pupil to make progress.

FINDING OUT HOW A CHILD THINKS WELL AND WHAT MOTIVATES HIM: p 165
TEMPLATES

USING THE MIND WELL: p 287

As you work with your pupil, you should discover those things that stop or hinder him learning too.

Insight: Time and place

Time and place often cause difficulties for dyslexic/ SpLD pupils. Place also includes space around a person and direction. Both are discussed in *Organisation and Everyday Life with Dyslexia and other SpLDs* (Stacey, 2020).

- Sometimes, the words dealing with time and place don't easily connect with the concepts but the concepts are understood and can be used.

- Sometimes the pupil's mind does not register the concepts at all.

Problems with either can impact on learning.

Stacey (2020)

You have to find out exactly what the confusion is and develop strategies that work for the individual pupil. It may be that some part of time and place is an *OBSTACLE* that needs *ACCOMMODATION*.

OBSTACLE last bullet point in *IMPORTANT CHARACTERISTICS OF PITFALLS*: p 73

ACCOMMODATION: p 189

Exercise: Test your observations

Test your observations by using them in your instructions about tasks or in your general conversation.

- If you give him instructions or advice about a task, how does he process what you are telling him and how does he use the information?

- Which senses does he seem to use most or best?

- Does he need to understand the purpose of the task in order to do it?

- Is he being methodical and adopting a stepwise approach or is he following one random idea after another in quick succession?

- What's motivating him: Other people? Doing something for himself?

Use any other question that prompts you to watch objectively, without thinking that you already know the answers.

Use *TEMPLATES: B3 - COMPARE EXPECTATIONS AND REALITY* or *B4 - ACTION, RESULTS, NEXT STEP* to build up your understanding of what is happening for your pupil.

TEMPLATES

Modify your pupil's profile as new insights emerge. Engaging your pupil in the process will gradually teach him how to improve his learning and to take pride in his progress. It will also help him to be more at ease with the *PITFALLS*.

PITFALLS: p 73

6.4 Knowledge and skills that have to be learnt

Once you've found out how your pupil is thinking and any preferences that he uses well, you are in a better position to help him avoid the confusions of dyslexia/ SpLD as much as possible, as for the student in *STORY: BEST CASE SCENARIO, GOOD TECHNIQUES, MINIMAL DYSLEXIA*. You can then choose games about words and numbers that will help him learn.

STORY: BEST CASE SCENARIO, GOOD TECHNIQUES, MINIMAL DYSLEXIA: p 156

You should also be in a position to make sure that dyslexia/ SpLD is not being used as an excuse, either by his parents, his teachers or himself, see *STORY: A DYSLEXIC PASSENGER*. Watch for any resistance and use it to find better solutions.

STORY: A DYSLEXIC PASSENGER: p 145

Story: Pupil reluctance

Hugo was 10 years old when he started receiving support. He was new to the idea that there were other ways of learning and, initially he was suspicious of some of the techniques. The teacher didn't think that he really believed they would work.

They started with a target of learning how to spell some of the fairly short high-frequency words that cannot be taught by using phonics, e.g. said, many, piece, etc.

So, on the ground they lined up as many footballs as there were letters in the word, i.e. 4 for 'said', 5 for 'piece'. He would shout out the word and then as he kicked each football as hard as he could, he said the name of the letter; so in auditory terms, it would sound like "said, S, kick, A, kick, I, kick, D, kick".

They continued to go through this five-minute routine every day until they had covered about 10 words. At the end of the time, he was assessed and he could spell every word correctly. The teacher thought he felt that a bit of magic had happened.

Hugo is so proud and pleased with his progress that he wanted his own name used in this story.

It is possible that your pupil is too busy with other activities and not naturally ready to learn skills in the expected order. However, there are certain skills that need to be learnt while the brain is most receptive for them to develop.

The activities that are occupying children can be used to help develop the skills.   For example:

- a lad interested in cars or motor bikes could learn reading and writing using information about them (motivation)

- a practical girl would be asked to write about making cakes rather than inventing a story (kinaesthetic)

- a visual, but here-and-now pupil could be asked to describe what he can see out of the window (visual, kinaesthetic) rather than write about the holiday by the seaside, which for such a pupil could easily have moved into the realm of unreal.

The THINKING PREFERENCES in brackets are initial guesses to be explored.

If the basic elements of reading or spelling or number work are proving difficult for a pupil to learn, see whether learning more advanced ideas helps. Many of my students have told me that they never understood English language until they learnt a foreign language and the framework of language was taught, see LANGUAGE TEACHING.

LANGUAGE TEACHING: p 184

As Hugo's story shows, the approach that suits an individual learner brings pride in progress and satisfaction, 'a touch of magic'.

6.5   Keep modifying the profile

The profile may well change with time, because at different stages of growing up new tasks need new thinking skills. The point is not to determine thinking preferences for all time, but to see what the current strengths are and to use them. The same is true for interests. You test your observations by deliberately altering your approach to the next set of games and tasks that you get your pupil to engage with.

One worry about using thinking preferences, or learning styles, is that you restrict a pupil's range of options by putting them into a specific category. According to Eysenck's hypothesis, when a particular way of thinking isn't effective, the mind automatically switches to other, more efficient ways to perform a task (Stacey, 2019) and the switching is done without conscious control. If you allow your pupil to test different thinking preferences and teach him to switch deliberately between them when appropriate, you will be giving him a wider range of options to choose from, not restricting his options.

Stacey (2019)

6.6   Good performance but no learning

You need to check that tasks have actually been done in a way that will produce the desired learning. Sometimes a pupil may not even be aware that he is taking a short-cut.

Insight: A short-cut through apostrophes

The following exercise is intended for practice with apostrophes.

Example of the use of an apostrophe to show possession:
'The nest of the robin' can be written as 'The robin's nest'.

Re-write the following, using an apostrophe:
   The cap of the boy
   The basket of the woman
   The book of the girl
   The door of the house
and several other similar phrases

In doing the exercise, it is quite easy to see that you swap the second and the last words; put 's' on the last word; and miss out the words in the middle.

If words don't register easily in your pupil's mind, he can do the exercise correctly and reasonably quickly without appreciating what it is all about, i.e. the use of apostrophes to show possession.

The desired learning simply doesn't take place.

Story: Correct words but no spelling learnt

One girl was given a page of spellings to practise by writing each word out 3 times. She handed in the finished page and it was accepted as correct.

What the teacher didn't know was that her method was to write all the first letters down the page, then all the second, and third and so on going down the page each time until the words were finished. Writing the complete words was too boring.

In the insight above, the pupil doesn't realise there is anything amiss with the way he's doing the task; in the story, the girl did know she was bucking the system. In neither case was there any immediate sign that would tell the teacher no learning was taking place.

Summary: Towards an autonomous pupil

You are aiming to avoid many of the issues developing into problems for him.

- Know his *THINKING PREFERENCES*, motivations and interests and let him use them.

- Find out how he can recall anything well.

- Use mistakes positively to help probe behind difficulties to find out where the root of any problem lies.

- Find out whether he deals with time, space, place and direction well and, if not, find the source(s) of his problem(s).

- Develop his *INDIVIDUAL, PERSONAL PROFILE OF DYSLEXIA/ SPLD* and his *REGIME FOR MANAGING DYSLEXIA/ SPLD.*

THINKING PREFERENCES: p 290

INDIVIDUAL, PERSONAL PROFILE OF DYSLEXIA/ SPLD: p 268

REGIME FOR MANAGING DYSLEXIA/ SPLD: p 268

7   Whole school approach

The individual pupil is usually in a class and a school. Both should be able to support his learning needs without placing undue burdens on the teacher's resources or taking resources from the other children.

Elizabeth Henderson, a primary school teacher, decided to train to support dyslexic pupils. After her training, she made her teaching and classroom dyslexic-friendly. By the end of her career she had been headmistress of two state primary schools and in each she had introduced a regime that made the whole school dyslexic-friendly. Very few of her 'at risk' dyslexic pupils needed to be statemented before moving on to secondary school, indicating that problems were addressed as part of the overall teaching approach rather than requiring individual and much more expensive specialist tuition. The academic results for her schools were good and parents were very enthusiastic about the schools. Her final school was awarded Beacon status (Henderson, 2003) for its dyslexia-friendly regime.

statemented: the process of formally recognising that a pupil has severe special educational needs.

Henderson (2003)

Some of the practices in her schools were:

- as part of their contract, teachers spent 20 minutes a day just observing the children in their class
- the kinaesthetic route into learning was used, alongside the visual and verbal routes
- the initial stages of writing included:
    o children gaining fine motor control through making borders around their artwork
    o the first writing they did was blindfold[3] on paper stuck down to the table; the children did not have to write to fit their letters between lines and the motor movement had no interference from what their eyes saw
- the initial stages of reading were taught to all children by a variety of methods, including phonics.

I remember her telling me, "If a child is fascinated and exploring the physical world, for example a sandpit, the child may not be ready to sit down and learn. Such a child will make more progress learning in a kinaesthetic way." The time the teachers spent observing the children was used for finding out what was motivating and fascinating each child.

Henderson had realised that the early stages of writing could often be hampered by what the eyes saw.

Writing, as an end skill, needs to be:
> thought-of-the-word
>> connecting directly to
>>> the necessary movement impulse flowing down the hand to produce the written word.

The establishment of this process is not helped when the eyes are telling the brain that the hand is not doing a very good job, which is why preventing the eyes from seeing what's happening is good practice.

---

[3] Blindfolding may not be suitable for all children and some other way of preventing the eyes from seeing the movement could be used. A similar circumstance also applies to touch typing when putting card above the hands stops interference from the eyes.

Summary: Whole school catering for dyslexic/ SpLD pupils

There are many other ways in which the learning conditions that are VITAL for dyslexic/ SpLD children are GOOD practice for all. When the whole school is organised with the same ethos, there is a smooth transition between years and the dyslexic/ SpLD children can make progress with their peers.

Henderson (2003) incorporated the VITAL practices into her schools in such a way that catering for the dyslexic/ SpLD children assisted the non-dyslexic/ SpLD ones as well.

Henderson (2003)

8 Dyslexic/ SpLD friendly classroom teaching

Story: Geography by 3 methods

One geography teacher said in a workshop, "By the time I've taught a topic in 3 different ways, almost all the children have got it."

Broad strategies may go a long way towards catering for the dyslexic/ SpLD children. The ideas in *TEACHING AN INDIVIDUAL PUPIL* are also relevant to the individual pupil in the classroom. The suggestions in this section should allow you to cater for dyslexic/ SpLD children within your whole class methods.

TEACHING AN INDIVIDUAL PUPIL: p 161

8.1 Check-list for whole class teaching

Teaching that is dyslexic/ SpLD friendly would include:

1 observation and interpretation: in terms of thinking preferences and pitfalls

2 input: visual/ verbal/ kinaesthetic/ logic-framework-rationale

3   <u>checking students' understanding</u>: how complete it is; whether it is complete but very different from the intended understanding

4   <u>motivation enhancing</u>: MBPT and MI, holistic and linear variations in ways of thinking

5   <u>accepting work produced by various methods</u>: illustrations, writing/ speech, presentations/ construction, action.

In 3, be aware of your own understanding filling the gaps; it is very easy to subconsciously fill them in without realising they are gaps in your pupil's understanding.

8.2   Methods that can hinder or help dyslexic/ SpLD learners

The following are points that need to be considered, with comments about the relevance to dyslexia/ SpLD.

• Is rote learning being used? • Who is using it successfully and able to select items out of the rote learning? • Who is not able to rote learn? • Who is not able to select items from material learned by rote?	Rote learning is often impossible for dyslexic/ SpLD children; even when it's possible it may produce a long episodic memory that cannot be used a small section at a time. An example of this is the alphabet; many dyslexic children always have to start at A to find any particular letter.
• What is expected to be learnt subliminally? • Who would benefit from more explicit instruction and discussion?	Subliminal learning frequently does not take place for dyslexic/ SpLD children. They may need to recognise, for example, that they are asking a question and getting an answer. They won't necessarily realise that a useful process is happening: they won't subliminally learn the patterns of question and answer.

Ⓖ p 303
subliminal learning

• Is new technology creating new *PITFALLS* for dyslexic/ SpLD children?	'Out of sight, out of mind' is a phenomenon experienced by dyslexic/ SpLD adults (Stacey, 2020). This will affect children too. For example, when a pupil is researching on the internet, only the current screen is in sight; remembering the information on another screen could be a *PITFALL* of the obstacle variety. Possible solutions might be: • knowing how to work with two or more windows visible together • working with split screens in one file • using two monitors • printing, for example, the instructions for a piece of work. *FINDING THE ROOT CAUSE OF PROBLEM* is essential to finding the right solution (Stacey, 2020).	*PITFALLS*: p 73 Stacey (2020) Ⓖ p 303 obstacle Stacey(2020)
• Is the **kinaesthetic** sense being used equally with the **visual** and **verbal** senses?	Sometimes teaching styles are limited to **visual** and **verbal**; in some systems the **kinaesthetic** sense is also used; particularly in the early stages there should be an equal balance between these three systems. It may also be important for some children to include **smell** and **taste**. Role play can be used to engage all the 3 common senses together, see *ROLE PLAY TO EXPLORE COMPREHENSION AND THINKING PROCESSES*. It can also be used to teach several important ideas in this book.	*ROLE PLAY TO EXPLORE COMPREHENSION AND THINKING PROCESSES*: p 182
• To what extent are **frameworks**, **logic** and	For quite a few children, **rationale** and **logic** and a definite **framework** are more important than the sense being	

rationale being used in the teaching and learning environment? • The history of invasion of the English Isles can be usefully used to explain some of the variations in English spelling, for example.	used. For some children, more advanced knowledge and information may assist basic material. For example, explaining how spelling works at quite an advanced level can help with early spelling tasks.	
• Are there any individual hobbies or interests that could be used to help a pupil with a reading or writing task? • What can be gleaned about the way a pupil thinks from his comments in class and his actions? • Is this information being passed to any specialist support teacher? • Does the style of teaching include a wide range of approaches?	Use the *TEMPLATE: E1 - LIST OF OPTIONS FOR THINKING PREFERENCES* to see what could be used. *TO EXPLORE THINKING PREFERENCES THROUGH SPEECH* suggests 2 ways of listening for a pupil's thinking preferences. Sometimes a pupil's interest is sparked in one subject and he becomes a willing learner. When this interest can be incorporated into other subjects, they too can become a source of engagement. Further information can be found in *Finding Your Voice with Dyslexia and other SpLDs* (Stacey, 2019).	*TEMPLATES* @ *TO EXPLORE THINKING PREFERENCES THROUGH SPEECH*: p 184 Stacey (2019)
• How many different ways are there that children can show their understanding? • To what extent are they memorising information? • To what extent are they able to understand a topic and apply their learning in a different perspective?	Many dyslexic/ SpLD people are able to regurgitate in the short term quite accurately; repeating the process several times does not lead to more effective learning. Sometimes teachers, without realising it, use their own knowledge to make sense of what a dyslexic/ SpLD pupil says; any incompleteness in the dyslexic/ SpLD person's mind is then overlooked.	

What level of self-confidence and self-esteem do the pupils have?	High levels enable students to learn. Confident pupils who enjoy their learning are satisfying to teach.

8.3   Role play to explore comprehension and thinking preferences

Reciprocal Teaching is a teaching method based on dynamic interaction between teacher and pupils. Role play is an essential part of the method because learners take different parts in the process. You can find several systems on the web using 'reciprocal teaching' as a search string.

Reciprocal reading is part of the method. In this section I show how *Reciprocal Reading Group* work incorporates much of the practice that is VITAL for dyslexic/ SpLDs and good practice for everyone.

Reciprocal reading involves 4 different elements: summary, questions, clarity and prediction. In a system of 6 cards that can be downloaded from Fresher Schools, these elements are turned into roles for children, with a fifth role of organiser (boss): 'predictor', 'questioner', 'clarifier', 'summariser' and 'boss'.

Fresher Schools *Reciprocal Reading Group Cards* (Website Accessed 4 April 2017)

The 6 cards include one which summarises the role of each child and five relating to each role which give:

- prompts to help with the role,
- clues to help the pupil in the role
- helpful hints about working with the text.

The cards have age-appropriate cartoons on them. The layout helps the children to relate easily to different parts of the instructions.

5 children take different roles to explore a text. The boss decides who is going to take each role. The work of understanding a text takes place as the children carry out the different roles. As the discussion evolves, the boss keeps everyone on task.

As teacher, you can work with children in small groups. You can model the roles, or use others ways to demonstrate the elements during discussion.

1   The role play uses **vision**, **speech** and the **kinaesthetic** sense; so it links these three senses together. The children can experience the different roles.

2   The activity gives a **framework** for understanding through reading and discussion. The children can experience the different stages that produce understanding.

3   A teacher can teach METACOGNITION openly through discussion of what each role is asked to do and through the actual process of doing.

METACOGNITION: p 288

4   Discussion about the **framework** and METACOGNITION rule out expectation that these will be learnt subliminally.

5   Sometimes it will be a good idea to keep the text the same and ask the children to swap roles.

6   Discussion about the various ways the children approach the roles will allow them to recognise and value different ways people process information.

7   A teacher can listen to the language used and the ways in which children enact their role. The insights gained about thinking preferences can be added to profiles of the children.

8   These teaching points will meet the needs of dyslexic/ SpLD children without detracting from the progress of other children.

These points relate to important ideas in the series:

1   using all the senses, especially the **kinaesthetic** one

2   the **framework** helps those who need one in order to understand information

3   metacognition

4   subliminal learning should not be assumed to work for dyslexic/ SpLDs

5   not changing too much at one time

6   children will have confidence to use their natural way of thinking when they know differences in thinking exist and can be used well

7   objective observation and interpretation in terms of thinking preferences; the interpretations can then be tested

8   what is VITAL for dyslexic/ SpLD children is good practice for all.

8.4 To explore thinking preferences through speech

Listening to the language a pupil uses can indicate his preferred way of thinking.

1 Ask a child to explain a game or subject or event that he knows well to you, or the class.

2 With a group of children, have a collection of topics suitable to the group in a hat. The children might help to decide the choices before they are put in the hat.
Get a child to draw a topic out of the hat (no choice) and then speak for 1 minute to his peers. This exercise is primarily about speech fluency, which is gained through repeating it, but it can also be used to observe the child's thinking preferences.

In both these approaches, you are attentively listening for the underlying THINKING PREFERENCES that the pupil is using, including topics or activities that motivate him.

THINKING PREFERENCES : p 290

8.5 Language teaching

When a second language is taught, it is usually taught in a systematic way. The elements of language are built up through discussion and exercises in a way that doesn't happen for a pupil's native language. Those whose minds work with rationale and frameworks may need the systems of language and number to be taught in a systematic, obvious way.

Thinking that a pupil won't be able to cope with the more complex parts of language because he can't spell or read simple words could be ruling out the very knowledge that would help with the basics.

There are many points of confusion in language, and the way words are used is changing all the time: once you had to put a word after 'enjoy': "Enjoy yourself." "Enjoy the picnic." Now, we often just say "Enjoy."

This section contains a few of the practices that have emerged while teaching the use of the English language to dyslexic/ SpLD students. I persuaded them to engage with understanding the building blocks of language (grammar) as a skill that helps them with reading.

Language textbooks in *FURTHER READING*: Rak (1992) Gee (2004) Dykes (1992)

I offered my students various textbooks to use. I looked for books which had exercises and answers. They all had very clear layout and I ruled out any that were too wordy. Some had cartoons. The best are listed in *Further Reading*.

I tried to assess the books currently available in order to make more recent recommendations but I can't do the assessment without the needs of a particular student in mind, which is an important principle. The book that allows one student to engage with language will not necessarily work for another. You need to find the right book for each pupil.

8.5.1   The function of words

It is important to understand that words cannot simply be put into categories or classes (usually called 'parts of speech').

The following is adapted from *The Cambridge Encyclopaedia of Language* (Crystal, 1997).

Crystal (1997)

What function does 'round' have?

'You cannot tell what class a word belongs to simply by looking at it. Everything depends on how the word 'behaves' in a sentence. 'Round' is a good illustration of this principle in action, for it can belong to any of five word classes, depending on the grammatical context.' (Crystal, 1997, p 92)

In the following table, 'round' is used in 5 different ways and it is replaced in the second set of sentences to highlight the difference.

Noun	It's your round. I'll have lemonade.	It's your turn. I'll have lemonade.
Adjective	Mary bought a round table.	Mary bought a folding table.
Adverb	We walked round to the shop.	We walked back to the shop.
Verb	The yacht will round the buoy soon.	The yacht will reach the buoy soon.
Preposition	The car went round the corner.	The car went past the corner.

It doesn't help to get dyslexic/ SpLD children to learn to put words into hard and fast categories. You run the risk of the simplest ideas getting *SET IN STONE* with very little chance of later modification.

SET IN STONE : p 50

In the table about 'round', the pairs of sentences have been kept exactly the same except for the word replacing 'round'. If I had demonstrated the point with sentences that changed, the students would have been diverted by the change of topic and not seen the point I was making. The *TEMPLATE: G1 - THE FUNCTIONS OF 'ROUND' AND OTHER WORDS* has tables for making similar sentences with other words.

TEMPLATES

You need to teach the function of each category of words. I used everyday text with groups of students. It is best if the material is about something the pupils already know so that comprehension is not required at the same time as learning the patterns of language. I taught by getting the students to identify what function words had in sentences. We used colour to distinguish the various functions.

You could add shapes to colour coding for the different categories. Have enough highlighters for all the categories of words to be different.

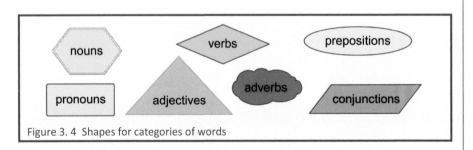

Figure 3. 4 Shapes for categories of words

I teach grammar in terms of building blocks and punctuation as gaps between the blocks. We separate complex sentences into their component parts, with minimal change to the order of the words and putting anything that has to be added in brackets, see *TEMPLATE G5 - BASIC SENTENCES FROM A COMPLEX ONE.*

TEMPLATES

8.5.2 Reading

There are many processes that need to work together for reading to be easy and to lead to understanding. Many of the adult students I have worked with have gained fluency from

- looking at the way their eyes move over the page

- preparing their minds to engage with the topic

- knowing what it is they want to gain from the material.

The eyes should move in jumps, saccades, in order to read; they should not glide smoothly over the page (Russell, 1979; Buzan, 2010). If the eyes glide, the mind is not able to pick up the fine detail of letter and word position, both of which are needed to be able to read. *Harrap's Swift Readers* (Elder, 1975) has exercises to help a pupil train his eyes to move correctly, see *TEMPLATES: G6, G7 - EYE SPAN EXERCISES*. The other training that is needed is to work with groups of words that make sense together.

Russell (1979)
Buzan (2010)
Elder (1975)

TEMPLATES

Example: Reading meaningful groups of words

If the sentence

Harry had to go to the beach shop to buy his basket ball and spades.

is read with the following groupings:

Harry had   to go   to the beach   shop to buy
his basket   ball and spades.

the initial idea, 'Harry had', is one of possession, which starts the mind with the wrong expectation.

If the child's mind is struggling to make the letters on a page into words he can sound, he won't have enough working memory to store the words long enough to change his interpretation. Gradually, the whole passage becomes meaningless.

He needs to learn to group words in a more meaningful way:

Harry had to go   to the beach shop   to buy   his basket ball   and spades.

There are a range of different reading schemes. You need to have a variety available to suit different approaches that will cater for different ways of learning to read. The material needs to be interesting to the struggling reader, as well as providing practice at the appropriate level. Some have good comprehension questions at the end of the book. A struggling reader could well benefit from *MIND SET* immediately before a reading session, so that his mind is primed to think about the topic to be read.

MIND SET: p 287

8.5.3 Spelling

As someone who to this day has problems with spelling, I think avoiding the confusions as early as possible is the best kindness to dyslexic/ SpLD children. You need to uncover misinterpretations, such as the following story.

Story: Confusion with spelling rules

As a child I learnt 'i before e except after c'. So why isn't 'acheive' correct? You've got the 2 vowels after 'c'. No-one told me that the 'h' means the rule doesn't apply.

It was years later that I worked out what was wrong and I still have to work my way slowly through the word to get it right.

You need to find out how a child learns well, spot lack of progress early and deal with it in a way that will benefit all children if possible. Hugo's story in *RELUCTANT PUPIL* is a good example of what can be done, though you probably wouldn't adopt that strategy with a whole class.

STORY: RELUCTANT PUPIL: p 172

One dyslexic teacher turned being asked for a spelling into an opportunity to teach his class to use the dictionary; his strategy was to turn finding the right spelling into a competition to see who could get there first.

If you ask adults how a word is spelt, they use different strategies to give you the answer:

- verbal: they sound out the word
- kinaesthetic: they pick up a pen, or move their hand as if holding a pen, to test the word
- visual: they think how they have seen the word
- rationale: they use spelling rules and other word formation knowledge to produce the spelling.

You should keep these different approaches to spelling in mind while teaching a dyslexic/ SpLD pupil how to spell.

Some practical suggestions about teaching spelling:

- separate the mechanics of handwriting by using the suggestions in the bullet point '*THE INITIAL STAGES OF WRITING INCLUDED*'
- teach the alphabet first; help your pupil to know the letters as individuals and not just in the complete a-z list
- use games that involve the kinaesthetic sense
- slow words down to split them into syllables or phonemes; this helps your pupil recognise what sounds are in each word
- have the alphabet visible
- use spelling dictionaries that give the suffixes
- a verbal strategy is saying a word the way it is spelt: e.g. 'Wed-nes-day' or 'Isle of Wight' as 'Is-ll of Wigit', which helped one pupil with 'isle' and to get 'g' into 'Wight'.
- mnemonics: 'There is A Rat in separate.' It is the first 'a' that is the problem, so it is no good knowing RAT is in 'separate'.
- typing using a keyboard is good in that you have to put in every letter, whereas by hand children can fudge their spelling.

Bullet point: THE INITIAL STAGES OF WRITING INCLUDED: p 177

8.6 Accommodation

Elizabeth Henderson (2003) found that changing the ethos of her schools to cater naturally for dyslexic pupils eliminated the need to make any other accommodations. The regime was good for all pupils and, once the staff saw the benefits to the children, they also felt catered for.

Henderson (2003)

The adjustments to bring this utopian state into being include:

- understanding the situations that stop dyslexic/ SpLD children being able to learn and adapting to eliminate their negative impact

- having open discussion about the different ways people learn and allowing the children to experiment with a wide range of possibilities

- letting mistakes be an opportunity for discovering how the child is doing a task

- objective observation of what each child does and why

- teaching programmes that include different approaches.

There may be accommodations that are needed for individual children, but the aim would be to show them how to learn and produce work to their best ability before discussing what pitfalls have become obstacles that need accommodations.

Summary: Inclusive classroom teaching

Inclusive teaching will include:

- observation and listening without influences from teacher's own assumptions

- wide range of ways to teach

- kinaesthetic sense included with visual and verbal

- frameworks and rationale used

- pupils' individual motivations and interests used

- in all the *IMPORTANT STAGES OF LEARNING*: attention paid to pupil's learning style

- *METACOGNITION* and active learning used instead of subliminal learning

- static material so that only one thing changes at a time

- check whether advanced knowledge and skills will help with learning basic ones

- checking whether rote learning is leading to problems.

IMPORTANT STAGES OF LEARNING: p 164

METACOGNITION: p 288

References

Augur, Jean, 1983, *This Book Doesn't make Sense,* Whurr, London
Buzan, Tony, 2010, *Use Your Head*, BBC Active, Harlow
Crystal, David, 1997, *The Cambridge Encyclopaedia of Language,* Cambridge University Press, Cambridge, 2nd ed.
Elder, T., Wood, R., 1975, *Harrap's Swift Readers, Book 5 with Teacher's Book,* Harrap, London, 7th re-print
Henderson, Elizabeth, 2003, *How to Have a Dyslexia Friendly School,* Beacon Office, Oldfield School, Maidenhead
Jefferies, Sharman, 2008, *Conference Talk,* BDA Conference 2008, Harrogate, and private communication
Russell, Peter, 1979, *The Brain Book: Know Your Own Mind and How to Use It,* Routledge, London
Stacey, Ginny, 2019, *Finding Your Voice with Dyslexia and other SpLDs,* Routledge, London
Stacey, Ginny, 2020, *Organisation and Everyday Life with Dyslexia and other SpLDs,* Routledge, London
Stacey, Ginny, 2021, *Gaining Knowledge and Skills with Dyslexia and other SpLDs,* Routledge, London

Further reading

Bell, Nanci, 2007, *Visualizing and Verbalizing: For Language Comprehension and Thinking*, Gander Publishing, San Luis Obispo, CA
Blissett, Celia, Hallgarten, Katherine, 1992, *First English Grammar*, Language Teaching Publications, Hove
Chinn, Steve, 2017, *The Trouble with Maths: A Practical Guide to Helping Learners with Numeracy Difficulties*, Routledge, Abingdon, 3rd ed.
Davis, Ronald D., 1994, *The Gift of Dyslexia*, Souvenir Press, London
Dykes, Barbara, 1992, *Grammar Made Easy: A Guide for Parents and Teachers,* Hale & Iremonger, Alexandria, New South Wales
Gee, Robyn, 2004, *The Usborne Guide to Better English,* Usborne, London
Granison, Alice, et al., (eds), 1995, *Collins Pocket English Dictionary*, Harper Collins, Glasgow
Rak, Elsie T., 1992, *The Spell of Words with Teachers' Manual,* Educators Publishing Service, Inc., Cambridge, Massachusetts
Taylor, A.J., 1991, *Chambers English Grammar*, Chambers, Edinburgh
Truss, Lynne, 2005, *Eats, Shoots and Leaves*, Profile Books, London

Wolf, Maryanne, 2008, *Proust and the Squid*, Icon Books, Cambridge

Website information

Fresher Schools, *Reciprocal Reading Group Cards,*
      http://www.fresherschools.com/index.php/15-literacy-
      resources/13-reciprocal-reading-group-cards Accessed 4 April
      2017
Jefferies, Sharman, 2007, *Education-Related Learning Difficulties and*
      Working Memory Function, https://ethos.bl.uk Accessed 19
      April 2017
Series website: www.routledge.com/cw/Stacey

4   New Paradigm

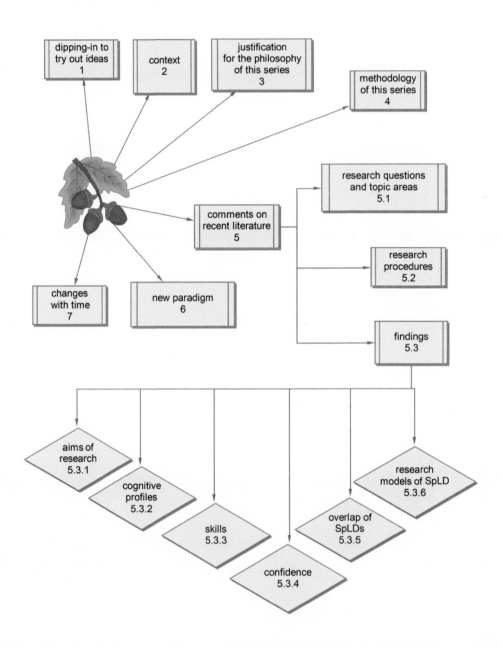

Contents

Paradigm : A conceptual or methodological model underlying the theories and practices of a science or discipline at a particular time; (hence) a generally accepted world view ('paradigm, n.4' OED Online, 2016).

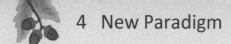

 List of key points and summaries

K = key point
S = summary

Note to academic readers:

The style of writing used in this chapter is consistent with that used in the rest of the series. It has not been made more academic or formal, i.e. into a style that researchers are more familiar with in their academic work. I hope such readers will be able to suspend their academic standards and think about the stories and insights, remembering that scientific knowledge started (millennia ago) with observations and that theoretical models gain credence when experimental results (in this case people's experience) confirm their predictions.

Working with the chapter

Make a list of the assessment tests you use or the research protocols. Summarise:

- what assumptions are made
- what your initial expectations are.

As you process the information in this chapter, reflect how you are alert to any ways different THINKING PREFERENCES and personal experience will impact on your findings. To what extent are you confident you are asking all the best questions?

THINKING PREFERENCES: p 290

Templates on the website

TEMPLATES:

Appendix 1 Resources

If you are dyslexic/ SpLD, this appendix will help you gather the information you want from this book.

APPENDIX 1: p 252

Appendix 2 Individual, Personal Profile of Dyslexia/ SpLD and Regime for Managing Dyslexia/ SpLD

APPENDIX 2: p 266

**Tip: *NEW PARADIGM* and
an *INDIVIDUAL, PERSONAL PROFILE OF DYSLEXIA/ SPLD* and
a *REGIME FOR MANAGING DYSLEXIA/ SPLD***

As you assess or do research with a dyslexic/ SpLD person, have a positive approach in your discussions. Aim to contribute to her confidence in managing dyslexia/ SpLD. Bear in mind that insights can be built into a *REGIME* and *PROFILE* which will help her to become more autonomous.

(G) p 303: autonomous

Appendix 3 Key Concepts

APPENDIX 3: p 282

APPENDIX 3: KEY CONCEPTS has a summary of the main skills and knowledge that dyslexic/ SpLD people can gain from this series of books. They fall into the categories of

THINKING CLEARLY   USEFUL APPROACHES
USING THE MIND WELL   ASPECTS OF DYSLEXIA/ SPLD
THINKING PREFERENCES

The appendix shows which of the 4 books in the series covers each idea in full.

**Tip: The skills and knowledge
dyslexic/ SpLD people can gain from this series**

When I do an audit of skills and knowledge with dyslexic/ SpLD students, I cover these key concepts. The appendix shows which of the four books covers each concept in full.

---

1   Dipping-in to try out ideas

Step 1: read CONTEXT

CONTEXT: p 199

Step 2: are you interested in:
a   the relation of this book to the general knowledge of the dyslexia/ SpLD field
b   the possible impact of the ideas in this book on research and assessment
c   the durability of the ideas in this book?

Step 3 for:
interest a): read JUSTIFICATION FOR THE PHILOSOPHY OF THIS SERIES

JUSTIFICATION FOR THE PHILOSOPHY OF THIS SERIES: p 201

interest b): skim JUSTIFICATION FOR THE PHILOSOPHY OF THIS SERIES and
          COMMENTS ON RECENT RESEARCH
          read the sections that interest you most

COMMENTS ON RECENT RESEARCH: p 208

interest c): read CHANGES WITH TIME; skim the rest of the chapter
          looking for anything of interest to you.

CHANGES WITH TIME: p 245

2 Context

One thing I learnt as an undergraduate physicist was that if you don't ask the right questions, the physical world will not give you consistent answers. My experience of working with dyslexic/ SpLD university students gives evidence that the right questions are not always asked during assessment and when exploring to find the best solutions to the related problems.

Story: Assessment test sidestepped

"Well! He (the psychologist) said I'm dyslexic. It makes sense of quite a few things and he explained some issues to me. But he said the digit span[1] showed I had a good auditory memory. And in my head, I saw my hand as I imagined writing the numbers as he said them and I read them from the picture. To read them backwards, I just read in the opposite direction. That's not verbal. I can't do it without picturing it."

This one test can be done a number of different ways: motor memory, visual memory, number relationships, verbal repetition, memory hook methods, chunking. Other tests can be approached with different thinking processes, too.

- I have heard many such stories from dyslexic/ SpLD students coming back from an assessment. They know they did a test one way and that the assessor assumed they'd done it a different, standard way. Sometimes a student is more familiar with the test material than is expected. In a series of reading tests that are designed to become progressively harder, a student may know the subject of a harder passage very well and so reading that passage is easy.

---

[1] Digit span: a test that is frequently used to assess auditory memory. You have to repeat a string of numbers after they have been read to you. The string gets longer as the test goes on. In digit span forwards, you repeat the numbers in the same direction; in digit span backwards, you reverse the order.

- The same can happen in spelling tests when 'harder' words may be quite familiar to the person being tested; they know they did well because they were familiar with the words.

The assessment and the good an assessment can do are undermined when the students don't trust the process and have questions about the outcome: "Am I really dyslexic? Aren't I just stupid?"

The THINKING PREFERENCES used to do tests are fundamental to the outcome, whether in diagnostic assessment or in research. From a professional point of view, including the research point of view, there are serious distortions, omissions and implications from the absence of qualitative data about the thinking processes used by the person being tested.

THINKING PREFERENCES: p 290

When unexpected styles of thinking are used, some of the issues raised include:

- post-testing discussion about the processes and any resultant profile is not fully informed
- some of the recommendations can be inappropriate
- the assumptions in research aren't fully tested nor shown to be systematic
- averaging research results from different people can be misleading.

For these reasons, it is important that researchers, and assessors, gather the qualitative data about the thinking processes that the participant is using. It may not be an easy task but it is a necessary one. It is central to the approach to managing dyslexia/ SpLD advocated in this book.

As a needs assessor for *Disabled Students Allowances*[2] for some years, I know it is possible to gather useful information in a two-hour appointment. I would discuss my observations with the student at the end of an assessment and write them into the notes section for the university support service.

---

[2] Disabled Students Allowances (DSAs) are government funding to support the educational needs which result from disabilities.

This chapter starts by looking at the key ideas in the *Box: Philosophy of This Series* and showing why they are part of the philosophy statement.

Methodology of the Series outlines a methodology for using the ideas in the series.

Comments on Recent Literature is based on several literature searches on the recently published work. It discusses what I found.

New Paradigm discusses a new view-point for the next phase in research and intervention. The final section *Changes with Time* discusses the ideas that are likely to remain valuable over time and those that are likely to change with time.

Summary: Experience and thinking processes

The experiences of an individual person and the thinking processes she uses need to be included in assessment and research.

---

3   Justification for the philosophy of this series

A résumé of the *Philosophy of this Series*:

1   dyslexic/ SpLD people can observe how their minds work and be effective

2   potential can be realised; dyslexic/ SpLD people can confidently contribute; dyslexia/ SpLD can be managed

3   dyslexia/ SpLD are not static; dyslexic/ SpLD neural networks can lie dormant, and be triggered into activity; the result is variations from time to time for one person

4   variation from person to person exists, even within each SpLD

5   there is an underlying constitutional cause for the different SpLDs

6   many of the problems don't have to develop when an 'at risk' child is recognised and supported early.

This section briefly gives the reasons for these principles.

1 Observing how minds work

> ### Story: Feynman on testing thinking
>
> Richard Feynman, who won the Nobel Prize in Physics in 1965, describes how he found out about his thinking in *What Do You Care What Other People Think? Further Adventures of a Curious Character* (Feynman, 1988).
>
> He wanted to know how accurately he could count 60 seconds. (He was accurate at 48 secs.) As a result of his experiments, he found out how he did the task.
>
> After he talked to colleagues about his experiments, one of them repeated the trials. They found that his colleague did the same task in a completely different way. Feynman was talking to himself; his colleague was watching a tape with numbers on it going by.
>
> Feynman wrote:
>
> 'We discovered that you can externally and objectively test how the brain works; you don't have to ask the person how he counts and rely on his own observations of himself; instead, you observe what he can and can't do while he counts. The test is absolute. There's no way to beat it; no way to fake it.'

Feynman (1988)

Feynman's method was to take a task and see which secondary tasks would have no effect on his performance, and which would impair his performance. The method suggested in this book is:

- to do a task, such as the mind exercise *KNOW YOUR OWN MIND* (Stacey, 2019)

Stacey (2019)

- the thinker reflects, possibly with help, on the processes used in the mind exercise with reference to the widest possible options for thinking, see *TEMPLATE E1 - LIST OF OPTIONS FOR THINKING PREFERENCES*

TEMPLATES:

- the indicated thinking processes are then tested in learning, memorising and recalling.

The cycle is repeated as the information about an individual's thinking processes is refined and their use is developed.

As for Feynman, comparing performance from one time to another clarifies the thinking processes used in various tasks.

Objections can be raised about finding out which thinking processes are used. Among them are that:

- it is too subjective to ask the thinker
- you can't see your thinking
- you can't tell how you are thinking.

Both the experiments of Feynman and the system put forward in *METHODOLOGY OF THE SERIES* build on the observations of the thinker and refine the understanding of what processes are used.

METHODOLOGY OF THE SERIES: p 206

Once someone knows how she thinks well, she can usually choose to use that style of thinking and so she can become effective in the tasks she undertakes.

2   Potential can be realised, confidence can be increased

One of the characteristics of dyslexia/ SpLD is that the results from different subtests[3] show considerable variation and lead to a 'spiky cognitive profile', see *COGNITIVE PROFILES*. In other words, some of the subtests indicate higher achievement than others. A misfortune of dyslexia/ SpLD has developed when the person generally achieves at the level of their lowest attainment. Quite often the person is aware that they have higher potential that they simply don't manage to use. The contrast between the higher potential and the lower achievement contributes to low self-esteem and lack of confidence.

COGNITIVE PROFILES: p 219

Much of the practical support that is given to dyslexic/ SpLD people is to find other ways of teaching them so that they can learn the skills they are lacking. Many programmes for this support show considerable success (Brooks, 2013). With success comes a growing ability to manage the dyslexia/ SpLD, so that potential is realised and confidence increases.

Brooks (2013)

---

[3] Subtests: diagnostic assessments involve a variety of different subtests each of which gives a result for the performance of the person being assessed. After statistical normalisation, the results can be combined to give a cognitive profile for the individual. That profile can be compared to the expected profile for an 'average' person.

3 Dyslexia/ SpLD is not a static state of mind:
variations from time to time for one person

Most dyslexic/ SpLD people, and those who live or work with them, know that the effects of dyslexia/ SpLD are not constant. This is an aspect of dyslexia/ SpLD that is hard to test in laboratory conditions, by its very nature. The evidence comes from case history work, such as *Dyslexia: The Pattern of Difficulties* (Miles, 1993), and *That's the Way I Think* (Grant, 2005).

Miles (1993)
Grant (2005)

A person's experience is one factor that contributes to the variations in dyslexia/ SpLD from one time to another.

Sometimes students have returned from an assessment process and told me that their reading performance during the assessment was at its best level because the content of the reading test was a subject that they knew very well.

In such a situation, reading is easy because the student will be familiar with all the words that were expected to cause problems. When given unfamiliar material, the dyslexic person's reading would show the difficulties.

There are other factors that can affect a dyslexic's reading ability, see *READING* and *Gaining Knowledge and Skills with Dyslexia and other SpLDs* (Stacey, 2021). The reading skill of a dyslexic/ SpLD individual may be very variable. Other skills may be equally variable.

READING: p 187

Stacey (2021)

4   Variations from person to person

The variations from person to person often make it very difficult to explain what dyslexia/ SpLD is about.

There isn't a unique and consistent set of behavioural patterns that you can put together and say "This is dyslexia."

The same is true for the other SpLDs. When I have run awareness workshops about dyslexia, many times dyslexic people have come to me afterwards and said, 'But you must tell them I can do…' and they name a task that is often a problem.

It is very important for dyslexic/ SpLD people to have it recognised that they do not exhibit all of the difficulties.

Sometimes I am told something is not a problem because at the time they were learning that knowledge or skill one particular person, often an adult, made sense of the task and so it never became a problem.

The experience people have growing up contributes to the variations between people with the same label.

Another complication caused by the variations is that some dyslexic/ SpLD people don't have the core problem, but do have many of the others.

For example, some dyslexic people are fluent readers and spellers, but the effects of other problems of dyslexia are significant.

It is important that dyslexia/ SpLD problems are investigated even when the core one is not in evidence.

It is important not to define dyslexia/ SpLD by a single core problem.

Labels for dyslexic/ SpLD behaviour patterns can be misleading.

A single label implies a uniformity which doesn't fit the experience of the real, live people.

Summary: Variations

Variations exist between people and from one time to another for one person. The variations are complications when trying to explain these syndromes to non-dyslexic/ SpLD people. They should be less of a problem as individual experiences and thinking processes are explored.

---

5   Underlying constitutional causes

There is a great deal of physiological research that indicates there are differences in brain organisation and structure between dyslexic brains and those of non-dyslexic people. There is research which indicates certain genes are correlated with dyslexia. This book does not discuss the underlying constitutional causes. More research has been carried out on dyslexia than any of the other SpLDs.

The underlying constitutional factors are important to dyslexic/ SpLD people because they give a cause for the difficulties experienced. In a sense, they give validity to dyslexic/ SpLD people when others don't understand what is going on. Dyslexic/ SpLD people have to get on with life and can't wait until there is agreement in the scientific world about the underlying constitutional causes.

As far as managing dyslexia/ SpLD is concerned, the nature of the underlying causes could make choosing the right approach quicker. They could inform the observations and refinement of thinking preferences and management strategies that are set out in this book.

6   'At risk' child

These SpLDs are all developmental syndromes with underpinning, constitutional causes.

A child can be born with the potential to become dyslexic/ SpLD, but isn't yet dyslexic/ SpLD because no learning has taken place.

Once the onset of dyslexia/ SpLD has been recognised, programmes are put in place so that the child learns well.

Many programmes are assessed by how quickly a dyslexic/ SpLD child can catch up with his or her chronologically matched peers.

Key point: Latent dyslexia/ SpLD

Thus, the child can be seen to be 'at risk' when born and the programmes demonstrate that the correct learning/teaching environment minimises the developing dyslexia/ SpLD.

---

4   Methodology of the series: *LIVING CONFIDENTLY WITH SPECIFIC LEARNING DIFFICULTIES*

The basic methods advocated in this series are:

to observe and listen to individual people without preconceived ideas	*FINDING OUT HOW YOUR PUPIL THINKS WELL AND WHAT MOTIVATES HIM:* p 165 or *Finding Your Voice with Dyslexia and other SpLDs* (Stacey, 2019)
to interpret the observations of thinking using all currently known patterns of thinking preferences	*THINKING PREFERENCES:* p 290 or *Finding Your Voice with Dyslexia and other SpLDs* (Stacey, 2019)

to allow anything that doesn't fit known patterns to be labelled as 'other'	use *Template E7 - The Box 'Other'* *Templates:*
to test the observations and interpretations by the individual concerned applying them to further tasks	*Chunking*, *Recall* and *Memory Consolidation* in *Using the Mind Well,* p 287, or *Finding Your Voice with Dyslexia and other SpLDs* (Stacey, 2019)
to explore anything in the 'other' category as much as possible	as previous point
to explore possible benefits from maintaining clear thinking	*Thinking Clearly*, p 285, or *Finding Your Voice with Dyslexia and other SpLDs* (Stacey, 2019)
then to refine the observations and interpretations in the light of these further tasks	using all of the above.

In this cycle you are looking for patterns of behaviour that are consistent for the individual person. These patterns will be part of a person's profile.

You are not trying to fit the person into an accepted pattern of processing.

It is important to always be ready to recognise when the person you are working with is showing you something you haven't encountered before. A prime example of work carried out with this attention to detail can be seen in *Dyslexia: The Pattern of Difficulties* by Tim Miles (1993).

Miles (1993)

The cycle may need repeating several times to develop understanding of a person's profile. It is possible that a new task or situation will require new insights about her pattern of thinking preferences and the cycle has to be repeated months or years after it is first used to good effect.

The observation by mind awareness is based on ancient yoga practice that has been established for many centuries. The processes of observing, testing interpretations and refining the interpretations have a scientific logic and can be carried out in a systematic way.

Key point: Respect the unexpected

It is good scientific practice to take particular notice of any data that does not fit the expected pattern: new discoveries can be found through such notice.

5   Comments on recent research

Before embarking on writing this series, I surveyed the materials available at the British Dyslexia Conference in Harrogate, 2008. I also attended lectures and workshops in which I might find similar ideas and I spoke to delegates. I formed the impression that writing this series would be a worthwhile contribution to the field.

An overview of the attitudes of researchers might be that they are interested in understanding what causes dyslexia/ SpLD at

> the constitutional level
>
> the cognitive level
>
> the behavioural level.

They want to know what is consistent and fundamental. They want to build models that encapsulate the key features and predict further discovery. They use standardised tests and devise new experiments to further their knowledge.

Comment for diagnostic assessors

The same, or similar, standardised tests are also used by diagnostic assessors. They want to quantify and qualify the performance of those they are assessing. They often want to recommend strategies that will be helpful. The recommendations will be based on what they have observed in the assessment process. Many of the comments in this section about research work also apply to the way observation and interpretation are carried out during assessments.

Towards the end of writing the series, I wanted to find out what significant changes there had been in the research literature.
I wanted to think about the ways in which the ideas put forward could and should inform research.

Much work has been done over the years of writing this series of books. The following story shows there is still work to do.

Story: Tears in April 2017

A 13-year-old dyslexic boy came home in tears when his school report had given him 0 for his progress.

He was attending a school with a good reputation for being dyslexic friendly. He enjoyed the 1-1 support he was getting and he was making good progress. He talks well but is still no good at writing by hand and his keyboard skills are one-fingered.

The policy of the school to monitor progress was that pupils had to write by hand. He could demonstrate none of his progress, which led to the result in his report and his tears going home.

When he was given an amanuensis[4], his ideas were fluently spoken. (I asked how much he improved but the family has other members who are dyslexic and the exact improvement is lost.)

This is not a one-off story. There has been a lot of work on educational practice, but it is still not embedded enough and putting it into practice requires trained teachers and specialists. In the era of cuts, these specialists are becoming fewer and fewer. We need an approach that caters for dyslexia/ SpLD within main-stream education at all levels.

---

[4] An amanuensis is a person who writes at dictation.

This section sets out my *Research Questions and Topic Areas*; my *Research Procedures*; and my *Findings*. As I thought through what I found in the literature survey, I formulated the structure put forward in *New Paradigm*.

Research Questions and Topic Areas: p 210
Research Procedures: p 211
Findings: p 214
New Paradigm: p 232

Story: Managing my dyslexia through this research

In doing the survey for this section, I had to manage my dyslexia:

- I needed to be very organised

- I kept a log of what I was doing

- I worked where I could ask questions immediately they arose

- I knew I was protecting my vulnerable reading abilities; I was at one point told I wanted to do something the software wasn't designed to do. I told the librarian, "That's the story of my life. I always seem to be doing something differently, I'm dyslexic." Although she didn't know the answer, attempting to explain the problem to her helped me to sort out what to do. I knew I had to work that way to protect my reading, to avoid confusion and a lot of wasted effort.

- I worked hard to keep my aims in mind.

I learnt from a fellow reader that it helps if you occasionally stand to read and work. It keeps you alert and has a good effect on your feeling of well being. One never stops learning new tactics.

I found very helpful and kind librarians in the Radcliffe Science Library, Oxford University. Their help took a lot of frustration out of the survey work.

5.1   Research questions and topic areas

My initial question was:
Question 1

Where would it make a difference if the participants had been asked
   how they processed information
   how they thought through doing a task
   how the set-up of the experiment could affect what they could
      achieve?

In searching through the methodologies, I was expecting to pay attention to the stages listed as important in the IMPORTANT STAGES OF LEARNING.

IMPORTANT STAGES OF LEARNING: p 164

A secondary question was:

Question 2

Does averaging that ignores different thinking profiles affect the interpretations?

In looking for the answers, I wanted to consider 5 topic areas:

- the use of cognitive profiles

- use of skills

- how the state of confidence was considered

- the discussion about co-occurrence of SpLDs

- the development of models.

5.2   Research procedures

I carried out a literature survey by putting several defined searches into Scopus[5], using the full library facilities of the Bodleian Library, Oxford University. (For non-academic readers: When you put a search into Scopus, you get a list of references from many published journals.) The searches for this survey were done by looking to see if the search parameters occurred in the title, the abstract or the list of key words given in each paper.

The initial search parameters were:

1   Dyslexia OR 'specific learning difficulties'
2   Dyspraxia OR DCD
3   'ADD' OR 'AD(H)D' OR 'ADHD'
4   dyscalculia

each with:

a   'cognitive profile'
b   achieve OR achievement
c   'self confidence' OR 'self worth' OR 'self concept'
d   comorbidity OR co-morbidity OR co-occurrence OR co-occurring
e   'model for' OR 'model of'

---

[5] Scopus is a database of peer-reviewed articles from research. Using its search facilities allows access to a large volume of research material.

Each of the parameter sets 1 - 4 was combined with each of the sets a - e. I restricted the searches to cover 2007 - 2013. The subject areas were Life Sciences, and Social Sciences and Humanities. The former included neuroscience, and genetics and molecular biology; the latter, psychology, social sciences, arts and humanities. Both included 'multidisciplinary' as a category.

Some searches produced only a handful of references and some nearly 2000. For the shorter search lists, I used the abstracts to assess how relevant the papers sounded; for the longer search lists, I used the titles first and then the abstracts. I developed a system for checking whether the same paper was appearing in different search lists.

Research into intervention schemes did not surface as a result of these searches. Education was not a category as such within Scopus. I have heard conference presentations on the work in the educational field and I was surprised that my research questions did not find as many references as I expected. Teachers and scheme developers are thinking about individual learning profiles but their work does not seem to be influencing the research into causes and cognitive behaviour.

I chose to start reading the full text of those papers that appeared in several of the searches and I chose to cover all four SpLDs included in the parameters. I then followed interesting lines of research, particularly in terms of models used and discussion about children who are exceptionally bright while being disabled, including dyslexic, so called 'twice-exceptional children'. For these topics, it was useful to search using the 'cited by'[6] search facility.

I hope I found a good cross-section of the literature. The searches produced over 4000 references. Selection by the titles of the papers reduced this number to 299, for which I read abstracts to select possible papers to read. I finally processed the full text of more than 30 papers. I also had a significant handout from the 2008 British Dyslexia Conference in Harrogate. My apologies to anyone whose work would have altered my impressions.

---

[6] Cited by: for a particular paper A, the 'cited by' list tells you the papers that have referred to paper A in their list of references. The more important a paper is, the more others cite it.

By the time I had found the first group of papers to read in full, I realised that the 5 topics were going to be more useful for collating information than the research questions.

Finding the right search parameters for two of them was difficult. I couldn't use 'skill' as a search parameter for the topic 'use of skills'. I wanted skill to signify what a person was good at, but too often it was used in phrases about lack, e.g. 'poor motor skills'. 'Ability' was not a helpful substitute as it too often was connected with the abilities found to be lacking, e.g. 'reading ability'.

The word 'confidence' couldn't be used as a search parameter for the topic about 'the state of confidence'; 'confidence' has a particular use in statistics.

I also realised that the aim of the work was an important piece of information.

Therefore, for reading the full texts I made 2 columns of notes for each of:

> aim
>
> cognitive profile
>
> skills
>
> confidence
>
> overlap
>
> models
>
> other

The first column was a summary of the authors' work. The second was my response to the paper.

The category 'other' was useful while doing the research. There were ideas I wanted to capture, but which weren't central to a particular paper's topic and it was easier to write about them in 'other'. When I came to put all the information together, the comments in 'other' for a given paper fitted with the work of a different paper. Hence there is no subsection in FINDINGS collating the notes accumulated in the category 'other'.

FINDINGS: p 214

5.3 Findings

This opening section of *FINDINGS* discusses:
> the answers I found to question 1
> the absence of any information about the *IMPORTANT STAGES OF*
>> *LEARNING*
> the answers I found to question 2.

IMPORTANT STAGES OF LEARNING: p 164

FINDINGS for the aims of the research is in §5.3.1, with two headings, *SURVEY FINDINGS* and *CONCLUSION*.

FINDINGS for the 5 topic areas are in subsections §5.3.2 - 5.3.6. Each subsection contains: *WHY THIS IS AN IMPORTANT TOPIC; THIS INVESTIGATION; SURVEY FINDINGS* and *CONCLUSION*.

THIS INVESTIGATION sections outline what I was looking for.
The *SURVEY FINDINGS* summarise the main points in the papers.
The *CONCLUSIONS* are the impression I formed of the perspectives for each subsection.

Answering question 1

Some of the research surveyed was conducted through questionnaires. In these papers, the way the questionnaires were worded and presented was discussed. There was evidence of putting participants at their ease (Burden and Burdett, 2007). Many questions also were designed to be open ones so that participants would feel free to contribute from their own experience (Neumeister et al., 2013; Burden and Burdett, 2007). The individual responses from experience were an integral part of the research process.

Much research is through standard procedures, either through cognitive testing or through biological, neuro-physiological experiments. New techniques, such as fMRI[7] and EEG[8], are providing data that confirms the findings of research using psychological testing (Lehongre et al., 2013).

My experience of being a participant in such experiments is that you are well looked after and comments are welcome, but they are not part of the research: you are there to go through a process and

Question 1:

Where would it make a difference if the participants had been asked
> how they processed information,
> how they thought through doing a task
> how the set-up of the experiment could have affected the outcome?

Burden and Burdett (2007)
Neumeister et al. (2013)

Lehongre et al. (2013)

---

[7] fMRI is functional magnetic resonance imaging.
[8] EEG is electroencephalogram.

produce an outcome measurement.
In neither category (psychological or biological), does the research take into account:

how you are processing the tasks,

how you process the information about the experiment and

what difference that information makes to the way you do the tasks.

It feels as if the pattern for experiments is (see *FIGURE 4.1* too):

1 task to be done
2 assumptions about task
    2.1 conditions surrounding task:
        2.1.1 controlling for extra influences
    2.2 speed and accuracy measured, as appropriate
3 results indicate level of competence on the task.

The pattern doesn't include what the participant brings:

individual thinking preferences and needs

actual processing

delivery of result.

These are ignored or controlled out of the data.

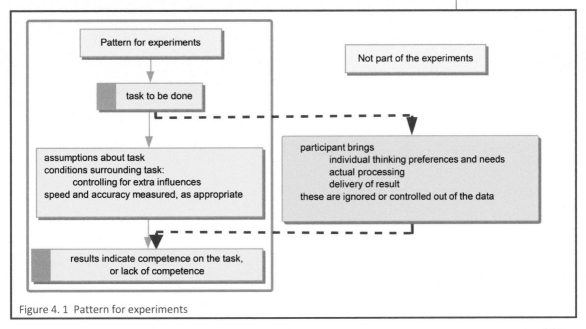

Figure 4. 1 Pattern for experiments

A direct answer to research question 1 would be:

> There would be a change in the whole design of experiments if they included what the participants bring.

The lack of any consideration as to what the participant brings by way of processing strengths contributed to the thinking that produced the structure of NEW PARADIGM.

NEW PARADIGM: p 232

Important stages of learning

Nothing about the IMPORTANT STAGES OF LEARNING caught my attention while reading the papers. These were also left out of the pattern of experiments, see the proceeding section. Even the research using questionnaires to explore participants' experience is concentrating more on the conditions surrounding the tasks rather than the thinking used to complete tasks. These stages are included in GETTING THE NEW PARADIGM ESTABLISHED and RESEARCH PROGRAMMES FOR THE PROCESS OF DISCOVERY.

IMPORTANT STAGES OF LEARNING: p 164

GETTING THE NEW PARADIGM ESTABLISHED: p 238

RESEARCH PROGRAMMES FOR THE PROCESS OF DISCOVERY: p 239

Answering question 2

As there is very little consideration given to how participants process various tasks, most of the research is indeed averaging in ways that ignores different thinking profiles. There are several ways this averaging can diminish the interpretations.

Question 2

Does averaging that ignores different thinking profiles affect the interpretations?

One body of research is using cognitive testing to distinguish between different SpLDs or subtypes of SpLD.

The patterns of results are used to draw conclusions about the extent of the OVERLAP OF SPLDS. If the different ways participants could be doing the tasks aren't taken into account, how do you know that the test results are evidence of the same cognitive functions being strong or weak in any of the research groups?

OVERLAP OF SPLDS: p 224

The conclusions might be altered when the thinking is taken into account.

One study investigating the effectiveness of learning strategies was carried out in Canada.

The participants of the study were twice-exceptional learners.

There is a good list of compensation strategies, but expressed in a very general way: e.g. 'use differentiated strategies for acquiring information through other modalities than reading'. There is no indication of discerning an individual's thinking profile that might be used for these other modalities.

The results of questionnaires are averaged to give a hierarchy of 'the very beneficial strategies' and 'strategies thought to be very beneficial, but not used'. Each individual's responses to the questionnaire is used as the basis of an interview. The thinking behind the choices doesn't feature in the interviews.

The concluding discussion starts with a quote from one participant 'Don't just assume that everyone learns in the same way.' There is a paragraph affirming this statement and its relevance to the participants in the study; there are recommendations for altering the style of projects and learning products, but no recommendations for exploring what the thinking strengths of the students are and how they can be used in learning (Neumeister et al., 2013).

Neumeister et al. (2013)

This absence of consideration of different thinking profiles could be one reason why case history and anecdotal evidence isn't translated into useful findings from larger scale research.

5.3.1 Aims of research

Survey findings

Knowledge about dyslexia/ SpLD has progressed a long way since the days when dyslexia was seen as word blindness and the other SpLDs weren't thought of. Two persistent ideas are:

We have a group of people whose minds do not function in the 'normal' way.

We want to help them become 'normal'.

Even though disability political correctness has changed the language, the underlying attitude that something is wrong with this group of people is hard to relinquish.

Research paradigms often start from what is 'normal' and explore from there. The research questions tend to be along the lines of:

How much are test scores below the normal, expected levels?

How uneven are test scores?

What skills are not being gained by children?

What can we find out about abnormal development in the brain that might be affecting the acquisition of skills?

I found at least one paper reporting research which started with a large number of children from a series of local schools (Talcott et al., 2013). Their aim was to investigate the pattern of test results without pre-selection. Thus, there was no selection of the children before the experiment.

Talcott et a.l (2013)

Other strands of research include:

recording the experiences of people with dyslexia/ SpLD (Bacon and Bennett, 2013; Neumeister et al., 2013; Burden and Burdett, 2007)

Bacon and Bennett (2013)
Neumeister et al. (2013)
Burden and Burdett, (2007)

looking for reliable early indicators of dyslexia/ SpLD so that intervention can begin early (Park and Lombardino, 2013)

Park and Lombardino (2013)

looking to see whether high achievement in one area can mask underlying dyslexia/ SpLD (Berninger and Abbott, 2013).

Berninger and Abbott (2013)

There is also a body of research which is arguing for a holistic approach. Evidence is given to show that the different specific learning difficulties have considerable overlap and trying to split them into separate syndromes is not meeting the needs of the individual people. (Nicolson and Fawcett, 2011; Kirby and Thomas, 2011; Pennington, 2006).

Nicolson and Fawcett (2011)
Kirby and Thomas (2011)
Pennington (2006).

Conclusion

The aims of research wasn't one of my original topic areas, but I found them necessary to record since they told me something about the expectations of the researchers and they seemed to influence the attitudes of the researchers.

5.3.2 Cognitive profiles

Why this is an important topic

As far as dyslexia/ SpLD assessments are concerned, cognitive profiles are obtained from the subtests used in the assessment. The profile is used to demonstrate that the tested person has weaknesses in certain areas. Thomson (1995) describes the four major functions of intelligence testing as being:

Thomson (1995)

1   "To obtain a measure of the intelligence level of the individual in order to rule out slow learning or low intelligence as a cause of written language failure.

2   To examine the interrelationship between the individual's intellectual level and written language attainments in order to describe any discrepancies between these.

3   To obtain a diagnostic profile from the intelligence test used.

4   To describe the cognitive functioning of the individual in order to identify areas of deficit and to help plan remediation."

Thus the cognitive profile is a major part of defining dyslexia/ SpLD.

In 2005, the DfES[9] working party proposed descriptions of the four major SpLDs that are widely used in the Higher Education sector, see *Glossary*.

SpLD descriptions
Ⓖ p 301

Jones (2011)

Jones (2011) affirmed that unevenness in the profile was indicative of dyslexia/ SpLD. She wrote that 'The difficult task for SpLD assessors is to construct a convincing profile of the individual ... through evaluating differences across a range of indicators [which] has the potential to expose the familiar "spiky profile" associated with SpLDs.' *Dyslexia Assessing and Reporting, The PATOSS Guide* (Jones and Kindersley, 2013) is a comprehensive guide for assessment practitioners. Under '*Diagnostic Conclusion: Dyslexia or Not?*' Jones and Kindersley suggest criteria against which assessors can test their findings.

Jones and Kindersley (2013)

One of the criteria is: 'Are cognitive processing and literacy weakness notable and unexpected in the light of an individual's wider cognitive profile and case history?'

---

[9] Department for Education and Skills

Grant (2005) has become aware of significant differences in cognitive profiles. He has listened to the people he has assessed using cognitive, psychological tests. He has explored their thinking and their experiences.

Grant (2005)

This investigation

I wanted to see how cognitive profiles are being regarded in the research literature and to what extent differences are being taken into account. I wanted to see whether a person's interests or experience were taken into account.

Survey findings

In several of the papers I read, the researchers were interested in how the cognitive profile varied between different specific learning difficulties. Among the findings and comments were:

- it is difficult to sort out what is behind a sole disability, for example, attention can impact on the development of a number of skills (Landerl et al., 2013)

Landerl et al. (2013)

- people with AD(H)D and dyspraxia were selected by non cognitive profile criteria; the cognitive profiles were then measured and compared; the results showed that the underlying deficit was not the same for the 2 specific learning difficulties (Loh et al., 2011)

Loh et al. (2011)

- that dyslexia and AD(H)D have different core causes at the cognitive level but considerable overlap at the behavioural level, and that deciding what is the same and what is different still needs to be researched (Landerl et al., 2009)

Landerl et al. (2009)

- the results of neuro-cognitive research divided a group of dyslexic participants into 3 distinct subgroups; only one of these groups was classified as having predominantly phonological difficulties; the discussion pointed out that there was little to distinguish the 3 groups at the behavioural level so that getting the right intervention needed the neuro-cognitive information as well as the cognitive (Helland, 2007).

Helland (2007)

Research on dyspraxia is growing. Kirby et al. (2011) acknowledged that dyspraxia, DCD and 'clumsy child' all refer to the same collection of difficulties.

DCD: Developmental Co-ordination Disorder.

It is gradually being acknowledged that dyspraxia has an impact into adulthood and that it has an impact on carrying out many tasks and functions, both social and work; it is not just a motor disorder.

Kirby (2011)

Kirby et al. (2011)

The researchers recognise there is a need for screening processes appropriate to adulthood; the screening needs to include both the cognitive and the motor aspects of dyspraxia (Kirby, 2011; Kirby et al., 2011; Kirby and Thomas, 2011).

Kirby and Thomas (2011)

It has also been recognised that new situations alter the balance between skills and weaknesses within the cognitive profile (Kirby et al., 2011).

Kirby et al. (2011)

Conclusion

The use of cognitive profiles still seems to be about establishing difficulties; the positive side of strengths is not usually considered alongside the problems. There is concern for the whole person, but the impact of a person's experience and interests was not taken into account in discussion of cognitive profiles.

5.3.3 Skills

Why this is an important topic

West (1991) made a strong case for the creative intelligence of dyslexic people. Research has been done to look for the creative strength of dyslexic people, but nothing very systematic has yet been discovered.

West (1991)

Sharman Jeffries at the BDA Conference in Harrogate, 2008, reported that children who she assessed were explaining to her how they solved the problems they faced. These observations were part of her doctoral thesis (Jeffries, 2007). It was quite clear to her that they were using skills in diverse, natural ways.

Jefferies (2008)

Jefferies (2007 Accessed 19 April 2017)

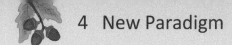

Bell (2007), among others, has investigated the difference between visualisation and verbalisation. Her work provides clear intervention strategies using these two different processes.

Bell (2007)

There are many dyslexic entrepreneurs who are held up as models of achievers. Clearly dyslexic/ SpLD people are not without skills (West 1991).

West (1991)

This investigation

I wanted to see what research has been carried out into the skills demonstrated by dyslexic people. How do researchers take into account the skills and experience of dyslexic/ SpLD people? How do these skills and experience impact on the results of any experiments?

Survey findings

Research work on skills is happening, though the focus is not yet on:

> 1) which skills are being used

> 2) how they are used to circumvent dyslexia.

- Bavelier et al. (2013) discusses how video games could be used to enhance skills; the design of the games is an important part of their effectiveness, in particular 'the processing demands inherent' in the games. I think this paper comes closest to reflecting on the processes being used.

Bavelier et al. (2013)

- Berninger and Abbott (2013) showed that exceptional verbal abilities mask dyslexia.

Berninger and Abbott (2013)

Willard-Holt, et al. (2013)

- Willard-Holt et al. (2013) worked with highly intelligent students with disabilities, so called twice-exceptional learners. The researchers investigated the perspectives that the students have about their effective learning strategies. The discussion and findings are important for development of conditions that will enable such learners. It will be very interesting when this type of research is extended to discuss internal processes as well as external ones.

- Fugate et al. (2013) investigated creativity and working-memory in people with AD(H)D. They concluded that people with AD(H)D are indeed creative and that creativity can be used for intervention purposes. However, they didn't investigate the style of the creativity.

Fugate et al. (2013)

Conclusion

Researchers want to explore the abilities of dyslexic/ SpLD people but the right questions to ask are not yet obvious. Exploring how people think, what processes they use internally, is not yet part of our cultural expectations. This is an area where the NEW PARADIGM should make a considerable difference.

NEW PARADIGM: p 232

5.3.4 Confidence

Why this is an important topic

Confidence and self-esteem are important issues for dyslexic/ SpLD people. Burden (2005) investigated dyslexia and self-concept. He concluded that dyslexia has more dimensions than simply being a reading difficulty; that these dimensions need to be included in a holistic approach to dyslexia; and that tools are available for systematic discussion and intervention. Amesbury (2008) described how she used NLP[10] work with capabilities to improve dyslexic/ SpLD students' confidence.

Burden (2005)

Amesbury (2008)

Maintaining a high level of confidence makes managing dyslexia/ SpLD very much easier. It can be difficult for specialist SpLD tutors to work on the confidence and self-esteem of their students because there is a very thin line between that area of work and the work of a counsellor.

This investigation

I wanted to see how issues of confidence and self-esteem are being regarded in the recent literature. Is any good system being put forward that is appropriate to be used by SpLD specialist tutors as opposed to counsellors? To what extent are lack of confidence and low self-esteem likely to affect performance in research tests?

---

[10] NLP: NeuroLinguistic Programming. NLP is advocated as a tool for thinking effectively in *Finding Your Voice with Dyslexia and other SpLDs* (Stacey, 2019)

Survey findings

Burden and Burdett (2007) investigated the metaphors that were used by boys in a specialist school to describe their dyslexia. They reported that the overall level of self-confidence within the school was high (which one would expect to be the case in a school specifically organised for dyslexic pupils). The metaphors that the boys used were mostly negative, showing that there is still work to do to produce neutral attitudes towards dyslexia/ SpLD.

Burden and Burdett (2007)

Daiken (2012) investigated pupils' perceptions of their elementary and secondary schooling. One of the strongest desires of these pupils was that teachers and peers would understand and would focus on the individual person and not the characteristics of the syndrome.

Daiken (2012)

Other work (Helland, 2007; Neumeister et al., 2013) showed how much the support and encouragement of people around those with dyslexia/ SpLD have an impact on their lives.

Helland (2007)
Neumeister et al. (2013)

Conclusion

This area of work seems to be increasing. It is a very important part of seeing people as whole individuals. I didn't find any research looking at the impact confidence has on measures of behaviour achievements.

5.3.5 Overlap of SpLDs (co-occurrence[11], co-existing)

Why this is an important topic

For a long time the only SpLD recognised was dyslexia. There is now a long history of research, theories and teaching programmes in relation to dyslexia. Gradually people became aware of behavioural patterns that didn't fit the theories of dyslexia, with a result that different SpLDs were discovered. It is often quite difficult to separate one SpLD from another. They do share many of the same clusters of difficulties.

---

[11] Co-occurrence: one person can have two, or more, independent SpLDs. Another term is comorbidity. Overlap seems a much better description. The way the different syndromes impact on a person can't be isolated and dealt with independently. You have to manage the lot together.

Example: The same behavioural difficulty from three SpLDs' perspectives

Take a difficulty with direction:

A dyspraxic person may have no sense of direction because their body is not giving them clear signals and there is confusion in the mind about direction.

A dyslexic person can know the directions quite clearly but not be able to verbally label them so they can still have a problem with direction and communicating direction.

A person with AD(H)D might have problems with direction because they can never pay attention for long enough to get a clear picture in their mind of where things are.

The source of the problem is quite different although to the outsider the behaviour may seem very similar.

Developmental SpLDs:
(not a complete list)

- dyslexia
- dyspraxia, developmental co-ordination disability, clumsy child
- dysgraphia
- expressive language disorder
- specific language impairment, with subtypes
- reading disabled
- maths disabled
- dyscalculia
- AD(H)D (attention deficit disorder, with or without hyperactivity)

The research into overlap of causes, cognition and behaviour is important because the real people experiencing these syndromes can by unnecessarily confused by too many descriptions that don't match their lived experience.

This investigation

I wanted to see how the overlap of SpLDs is being considered in recent research. How researchers are dividing behavioural problems between the different SpLDs? What are the criteria for doing so? To what extent are possible underlying causes being examined at the same time as investigations into behavioural achievement?

Survey findings

Kirby and Thomas (2011c) discuss the different terms used for overlap, see footnote 11, on page 203. They argue that there is sufficient shared aetiology[12] that the word 'overlap' is probably the best description.

Kirby and Thomas (2011c)

There is a significant volume of work looking at the overlap of the different specific learning difficulties.

Landerl et al. (2009)

- Some of it reports findings that show two SpLDs are distinct and are independent (Landerl et al., 2009; Loh et al., 2011).

Loh et al. (2011)

Laasonen et al. (2009)

- Other papers report that it is difficult to draw clear lines between SpLDs (Laasonen et al., 2009; Landerl et al., 2013).

Landerl et al. (2013).

Nicolson and Fawcett (2011)

- Nicolson and Fawcett (2011) uses a comparison between dyslexia and dysgraphia to argue that there should be a neural model for all developing disabilities.

- Landerl et al. (2013) argue that there is so much overlap that testing and assessment should be done for all the different specific learning difficulties together.

Pennington (2006)

- Pennington (2006) looks at the evolution of learning difficulties for individual people.

McCarney et al. (2013)

- McCarney et al. (2013) show how poor handwriting delays development of other skills and contributes to their lack of development.

Conclusion

The research is producing different conclusions still. I didn't find converging answers to my questions. This state of affairs may depend on different choices of model and definitions used in the research.

---

[12] *aetiology (Oxford English Dictionary): the causation of a disease (in this case of the developmental disabilities)

5.3.6   Research models of SpLD

Why this is an important topic

One stage of any research is to construct a model that explains observations and the results of experiments, and which predicts further interesting avenues for investigation. The model is also used to aid discussion and understanding. It can be very difficult to talk to someone without dyslexia/ SpLD and get them to understand what the effects are without a model that describes the experience and is recognised by dyslexic/ SpLD people as well as being accepted by professional people in the dyslexia/ SpLD field.

I have briefly discussed 7 models below. The first gave a general method for describing disabilities; the second does the same for working-memory. The other models were about particular factors or causes relating to dyslexia/ SpLD.

Morton and Frith (1995) proposed a model for developmental psychopathology which included the biological level, the cognitive level and the behavioural level of developmental disability. They also included 'external agent'[13]. This is effectively the *MODEL FOR SPLD* discussed in *WHAT GOES WRONG*, though that model didn't include the external agent. Morton and Frith's model has been widely used by those working in the dyslexia/ SpLD field.

Morton and Frith (1995)

MODEL FOR SPLD: p 102

Baddeley's (2007) model of working-memory is not about dyslexia/ SpLD, but it is also useful for discussing the difficulties of dyslexia/ SpLD. It is a model used in the literature to discuss research findings.

Baddeley (2007)

Nicolson and Fawcett (2011) developed a model for the cognitive and behavioural levels of specific learning difficulties. They focused particularly on commonalities and differences between dyslexia and dysgraphia. They proposed lack of automaticity at the cognitive level to be a key factor in developmental learning disabilities.

Nicolson and Fawcett (2011)

Various causes of the problems at both the cognitive and constitutional levels have been researched and reported over the years. McLoughlin et al. (2001) found inefficient working-memory to

McLoughlin et al. (2001)

---

[13] External agents examples: a virus at the biological level; negative external influence at the cognitive level (Morton and Frith, 1995)

227

be a persistent characteristic of dyslexics. The most frequent cause of dyslexia was seen to be phonological deficits (Snowling, 2006). Nicolson and Fawcett (1990) argue that an inability to automatise tasks is a key problem for dyslexics. Stein (2012) makes a case for contributions to the development of dyslexia based on imbalances in visual neural pathways.

Snowling (2006)

Nicolson and Fawcett (1990)

Stein (2012)

Many researchers and professionals in the field define dyslexia solely in terms of a phonological deficit. In their view, anyone not displaying a phonological deficit, by definition cannot be dyslexic, regardless of what other problems they have. Another camp take a wider view: they see dyslexia as a more variable syndrome in which phonological difficulties may or may not play a key role; they want the other causes to be included alongside the phonological one.

DCD in children has been seen as a motor problem. Dyspraxia only became widely recognised as a problem in adulthood when students who clearly had an SpLD were found to have no language-related difficulties.

Ⓖ p 302: DCD

AD(H)D and dyscalculia have come into prominence more recently than dyslexia and dyspraxia. AD(H)D is mainly seen as an attention difficulty; and dyscalculia is the SpLD of numbers.

I have used Morton and Frith's model in workshops about dyslexia. I frequently get people to do activities that generate dyslexic effects in their own brains, albeit temporarily. In explaining how these activities mirror the experience of dyslexia, I have used all the causes listed above for dyslexia and some of Baddeley's work on working-memory. I have wanted to help non-dyslexic/ SpLD people understand the syndromes by seeing what happens in their own heads. I have wanted to explain to dyslexic/ SpLD people the wider implications of their experience.

Morton and Frith (1995)

Baddeley (2007)

When I try to convince sceptical, non-dyslexic/ SpLD people to take these syndromes seriously it really helps to have good models and explanations of what is going on.

This investigation

I wanted to see what is included in the most recent models for dyslexia/ SpLD. What assumptions are made? How are differences between the different SpLDs treated? Whether variations from time to time or from person to person are included? Are skills and capabilities being included or is the focus still on what goes wrong?

Survey findings

The full text of Morton and Frith (1995) makes very interesting reading.

Morton and Frith (1995)

They were the first researchers to include a cognitive layer between the constitutional, biological origins and the observed behaviours in developmental disorders. They also included multiple biological causes, multiple cognitive functions and multiple behaviours.

Their model includes several different patterns. At each of the 3 levels, biological, cognitive and behavioural, there might be one, two or many components that were playing a part in the developing pathology (work on autism was particularly behind the development of this model).

One of the possibilities, but only one among many, was for there to be a single biological factor that affected a single cognitive function that in turn affected a single behavioural manifestation. This is the possibility that has been behind much of the research trying to develop a common model for dyslexia since the paper by Morton and Frith. In their paper this pattern is not given a specific name but subsequent researchers have generally called it the 'single deficit model'.

Three other possible patterns from the biological level, at the top, to the behaviour level, at the bottom, were given specific names by Morton and Frith: A, V and X. The letter shows the spatial configuration of the elements in the pattern.

The A pattern represents a single biological cause affecting more than 1 cognitive function and more than one behaviour patterns.

The V pattern represents several biological causes affecting more than 1 cognitive function but only one behaviour pattern.

The X pattern represents more than 1 biological cause disturbing 1 cognitive function which then affects more than 1 behavioural pattern.

The paper includes discussion of various other patterns between these 3 levels.

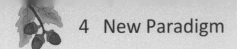

The biological level in their model can be divided into 3 levels: biological origins, abnormal brain conditions, and non-functioning brain systems. Morton and Frith also include variability. They talk about core problems, secondary ones and associated ones. Their model has considerable potential which is missed when the structure of a developing psychopathology is seen as a single deficit model.

Pennington (2006) used Morton and Frith's model when he was trying to resolve overlap issues in looking at dyslexia coupled with AD(H)D, and dyslexia coupled with speech sound disorder. He investigated the ways in which single deficit models don't work to describe developmental disorders. He argued that multiple cognitive deficit models are more consistent with observed behaviours. His paper is widely cited, showing that research is now moving in this direction.

Pennington (2006)

Nicolson and Fawcett (2011) developed 'a neural systems topography for learning difficulties'. They show how differing levels of complexity generate different groups of specific learning difficulties; their model also includes general learning difficulties. They are effectively dealing with components at the cognitive level of Morton and Frith's model.

Nicolson and Fawcett (2011)

Baddeley's model of working-memory is often used by researchers in this area. In particular, dysfunction in the executive system is thought to be the cognitive component behind AD(H)D[14] (Laasonen et al., 2009). McCarney et al. (2013) discussed working-memory while investigating handwriting; they concluded that giving children the opportunity to practice handwriting so that it becomes fluent would release working-memory and allow it to be available for other writing skills to develop, such as the skill to plan.

Laasonen et al. (2009)
McCarney et al. (2013)

De Weerdt et al. (2013) investigated working-memory in children with reading disabilities and maths disabilities. Management of working-memory is recognised as being helpful for children with these disabilities.

De Weerdt et al. (2013)

---

[14] AD(H)D: The vast majority of the work on AD(H)D is medically based and not looking at cognitive function. These papers were deselected on the basis of their titles.

McCallum et al. (2013) recognised that any model based on 'achievement discrepancy' is a 'wait to fail' model. They proposed a model for screening that looks at potential strengths as well as potential weaknesses. In their concluding discussion of test procedures available, they listed cognition, leadership and creativity as areas valued alongside literacy and maths.

McCallum et al. (2013)

Some of the research reported in the earlier sections, *§5.3.2 - 5.3.5*, uses the Morton and Frith model. Some of this work is trying to establish the single deficit model and establish clear differences between the different SpLDs.

§5.3.2: p 219 - *§5.3.5:* p 224

Talcott et al. (2013) carried out a body of research with a large sample of children from local schools. The children were not preselected for developmental problems. The research was looking at sensory processing and children's reading and cognitive skills. It showed the benefit of not being restricted to clinical groups of children. Their results are in line with multiple deficit models rather than a single deficit model.

Talcott et al. (2013)

Conclusion

It seems to me that the differences and similarities between different SpLDs are leading thinking away from a single deficit model to a more comprehensive approach. There is evidence of focus on the cognitive level and the biological core as well as on the behavioural level, and suggestions that these will be important in finding the most suitable intervention. Variations in the effects of an SpLD from time to time don't seem to be included. There isn't very much evidence of research looking at strengths in detail.

If the models used to describe dyslexia/ SpLD don't cover the complexity of each individual's experience, there will continue to be contradictory evidence from different experimental programmes.

6   New paradigm[15]

A new paradigm will emerge as a result of adding the ideas of this series to the work on dyslexia/ SpLD. The present paradigm is 'These people are not learning nor developing skills normally, we need to fix them.' The new paradigm should be 'These people learn and develop skills differently; they need to be free to learn in the way that works best for them.'

It is time to find the answer to the full question posed by Harry Chasty in 1989: 'If this child doesn't learn the way we teach, can we teach him the way he learns, and then develop and widen his competences in learning?'

Chasty (1989)

I think there are three shifts of attention that will bring about the new paradigm:

Principles[16] of the new paradigm:

- <u>the way human beings' minds are changed by any experience</u> to be at the centre of thinking about dyslexia/ SpLD

- attention to be focused on a <u>process of discovering how any individual thinks well and how that can be used in learning as well as everyday life</u>

- <u>what people can do</u> to take precedence over *what they can't do*.

In support work, the principles can be expressed as:
- You are an individual with your own history and way of doing things.
- Let's find out how you think well.
- How can you use your best thinking to help yourself?

These three principles have been fundamental in discovering the stories and experiences related in this series and, hence, the knowledge put forward in it.

---

[15] Paradigm: A conceptual or methodological model underlying the theories and practices of a science or discipline at a particular time; (hence) a generally accepted world view. ('paradigm, n.4' OED Online, 2016)

[16] Principle: a fundamental source from which something proceeds. ('principle, n.1' OED Online, 2016)

They need to be used with the widest knowledge of thinking styles
and working-memory.
They also need to be used with an open mind so that anything outside
present knowledge is recorded under the category 'other',
rather than being ignored.

FIGURE 4.2 is an elegant illustration of shifting from one paradigm to
another.

The following example shows one effect of changing the paradigm:

Example: Changing the paradigm

Observation: dyslexic/ SpLD people's minds often go
off on tangents.

Old paradigm:

Grant (2005, page 63) 'As a weak working-memory
often results in people going off on tangents, more
unusual associations of ideas tend to be formed.'
The subsequent discussion contains many
contributions from going off on tangents but always
in the context of poor working-memory and other
problems.

New paradigm:

The first reaction to students going off at tangents is
to explore whether they are holistic thinkers, see
HOLISTIC VS. LINEAR, and mostly they are. The unusual
association of ideas is part of the richness of holistic
thinking. These associations can be used to create
the links needed for chunking and expanding the
capacity of working-memory, see CHUNKING. There is
considerable potential in holistic thinking.

Figure 4. 2 Young lady or old crone?[17]

Young lady or old crone?
Can you see both?

Grant (2005)

HOLISTIC VS. LINEAR: p 291

CHUNKING: p 287

---

[17] 'My Wife and My Mother-in-Law' by W. E. Hill is used with permission from Mary Evans Picture
Library, who also supplied the picture.

Key points: Benefits from the new paradigm

- The three principles of the new paradigm should enable research and thinking to get closer to the reality of the processes involved in dyslexia/ SpLD.

- The resulting discussion should include descriptions that match the actual experiences of people with dyslexia/ SpLD.

- The positive attitude should allow a pro-active approach to develop.

- It should be cost effective to have an earlier, more general resolution of any problems caused by differences.

- The emotional baggage carried by those with dyslexia/ SpLD should be diminished.

- Non-dyslexic/ SpLD people should not be disadvantaged by any emerging, wider perspective on the diversity of thinking options available for use by anyone.

There will be new insights that emerge from the new paradigm, especially if it is used to its fullest. Eventually, it may be superseded by another paradigm. Or we may become so fluent in dealing with developmental disabilities that they become a problem of the past. However, I expect these three principles will stand the test of time beyond any further changes of paradigm. This paradigm is about opening up possibilities, it is not about categorising anyone.

This section discusses:
- minds being changed by experience
- the <u>process of discovery</u> of people's thinking preferences
- the focus on what people can do
- how the paradigm might become established
- research programmes to develop the <u>process of discovery</u> for finding out an individual person's thinking strengths
- valuing participants as part of research and assessment: some questions to bear in mind

- additions to current models of working-memory and developmental disabilities
- comments about general poor learning performance.

6.1 Minds being changed by experience: feedback systems

Minds are altered by learning and experience. How they are at any moment depends on what has happened before. In other words minds are feedback systems. You cannot reset a mind, naturally, back to the state it was in before an event took place. You cannot do experiments with people in which the starting point is the same for all the people in the experiment. Many dyslexic/ SpLD people know their experiences make a difference and that these experiences are not all the same.

With some characteristics, it is worth taking an average. If you were working out the best height for a door in a public space without spending too much on materials, averaging over people's heights would be useful. You can do the measuring several times because the height of a person is not affected by the measurement. The experiments to find out about dyslexia/ SpLD do affect the systems, the minds, being investigated. The current practice is that psychological tests should not be retaken within two years. Thus, the effect of a person having previously taken a test is minimised and not taken into consideration.

The way minds respond to learning and events needs to be at the centre of work to understand dyslexia/ SpLD. Without it, we are not looking for the real phenomena, see *STORY: SEARCHING IN THE WRONG PLACE*. We won't see the real patterns of the thinking behind the behaviour of the various SpLDs. The principle of difference behind this paragraph is demonstrated in the *EXAMPLE BOX: THE SAME BEHAVIOURAL DIFFICULTY FROM 3 SPLDS' PERSPECTIVES*

Story: Searching in the wrong place

There is a story about a man losing something in an alley-way on a dark night. A second man sees him looking on the ground and comes to help. After a while the second man asks, 'Are you sure you dropped it here?' The first replies, 'No, I dropped it over there, but this is where the light is.'

Ignoring the changes with experience is like looking for the lost object in the wrong place.

EXAMPLE BOX: THE SAME BEHAVIOURAL DIFFICULTY FROM 3 SPLDS' PERSPECTIVES: p 225

6.2 Process of discovering how an individual thinks

We have children and adults who are supposed to be learning and performing tasks. We want them to learn, and usually they do. However, they often have to struggle painfully to achieve the goals society sets for them.

What they do, their behaviour patterns, do not live up to expectations. They have different experiences; they have different emotional states of mind; they have different thinking preferences to bring to the learning process. If all they bring to the learning process has differences built into it, what can be researched to help?

The first priority of the research work should be to enable the learners. Therefore, we need a consistent process to enable the differences to flourish and the learners to be successful. This consistent process will be one of discovering how an individual thinks.

Process of discovery

Step 1: is to realise that there are a variety of ways to learn and to do any given task;

Step 2: is for people to be able to select which ways work best for them as individuals, and then to use them, see *FIGURE 4.3*.

Step 3: is to know when the selection needs changing for different tasks.

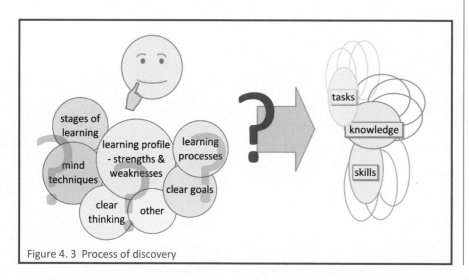

Figure 4. 3 Process of discovery

Finding and refining this process should be the main focus for research, including research to find the causes of dyslexia/ SpLD. The process needs to work with all the known differences that people bring to learning and accommodate new ones emerging.

Key points: Process of discovery

It is the process of matching the individual's capabilities to the task in hand that needs researching.

Finding someone's capabilities is not a once-and-for-all statement, but anything known is a good place to start for further development.

6.3   Focusing on what people can do

For some people, being put through a series of tasks that you can't do slowly undermines faith in yourself, and your achievement gradually declines too. You are less able to engage with the processes. Data for research obtained with such a state of mind is not going to be as helpful as data gained from someone who is achieving satisfactory results.

Other people have the opposite reaction to not doing well and the result of being faced with a series of seemingly impossible tasks is one of determination! However, this is just a different example of what someone can do: rise to the challenge of adversity.

Focusing on what people can do will not exclude the problems of dyslexia/ SpLD; they will emerge as the process of discovery is applied. If there are open discussions about people having different ways of thinking, it should be much easier for difficulties to be supported before they become problems.

6.4   Getting the new paradigm established

The new ingredient for research is focusing on the process of discovering how an individual thinks. Feynman's technique would be worth expanding, see *STORY BOX: FEYNMAN ON TESTING THINKING*. The mind exercise *KNOW YOUR OWN MIND* (Stacey, 2019) can be coupled with many of the techniques in *USING THE MIND WELL*. The various *IMPORTANT STAGES OF LEARNING* should be included in the process of discovering.

The research question is:

How good is the <u>process of discovery</u> at matching an individual's thinking preferences with the task in hand in a way that maximises progress for the individual?

Investigating the <u>process of discovery</u> could well include:

> observation - feedback - re-evaluation

> different kinds of tasks that individuals need to do.

Comments by the individuals are likely to be part of the process of discovery, as are all the differences the individual brings to any given task.

It would be interesting to study a <u>process of discovery</u> using non-essential knowledge and skills with a wide selection of children, as in Talcott et al's research (2013). The reason for using non-essential material is explained in *MAJOR PRECAUTION*.

A random selection of half the children could use the <u>process of discovery</u> to understand choices in thinking processes while the other half learn the same knowledge and skills without using the <u>process of discovery</u>. Then learning standard curriculum topics could be monitored over a period of time to see who benefitted and how from knowing more about their thinking processes.

One aspect of managing dyslexia/ SpLD that would be interesting to explore with the <u>process of discovery</u> is the effect new situations can have on the stability of managing dyslexia/ SpLD. When a new

STORY BOX: FEYNMAN ON TESTING THINKING:
p 202
Stacey (2019)

USING THE MIND WELL:
p 287
IMPORTANT STAGES OF LEARNING: p 164

Talcott et al. (2013)

MAJOR PRECAUTION: p 8

situation puts someone back into living under the influence of dyslexia/ SpLD, what is necessary to put her back into living confidently again?

Research done in this way should show various ways in which dyslexic/ SpLD people are creative and use their creativity in their approach to general living and learning.

6.5   Research programmes for the process of discovery

There are two ways I would want to research the <u>process of discovery</u>.

- One is to explore how thinking is done during some current task.
- The other is to explore the impact of thinking well through a long term project.

The former is not using the style of thinking beyond the immediate situation. The latter should cover all the *IMPORTANT STAGES OF LEARNING*.

IMPORTANT STAGES OF LEARNING: p 164

**Key points: The aim of research
into the <u>process of discovery</u>**

to find <u>systems that can be used to match</u>

a person's way of thinking or doing to:

- a task to be done
- knowledge or skills to be learnt
- knowledge or skills to be used.

For the first way, I would want to explore activities that can be used to test thinking processes in the way that Feynman used counting to 60. I would think there needs to be several primary activities and a series of interrupting activities. Using this collection should show which ways of thinking a person can use most reliably and consistently. The approach of the <u>process</u> would be more like playing games than serious learning.

For the second, the aim is to develop a <u>process of discovery</u> that involves

- building an *INDIVIDUAL, PERSONAL PROFILE OF DYSLEXIA/ SPLD* and a *REGIME FOR MANAGING DYSLEXIA/ SPLD*

- testing and evolving both
  - using learning tasks and everyday situations
  - when new situations need new processes

- matching
  - the innate capabilities of the *INDIVIDUAL, PERSONAL PROFILE*
  - resources such as teaching styles or employment habitat
  - task to be done, knowledge to be learnt and used, skills to be learnt and practised

- to allow the individual to achieve at her best level, see *FIGURE 4.4*.

INDIVIDUAL, PERSONAL PROFILE OF DYSLEXIA/ SPLD: p 268

REGIME FOR MANAGING DYSLEXIA/ SPLD: p 268

Ⓖ p 303: profile

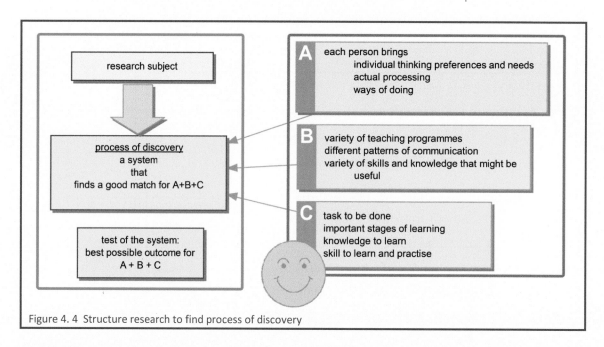

Figure 4. 4 Structure research to find process of discovery

Finding Your Voice with Dyslexia and other SpLDs has the skills and processes for building the *PROFILE* and *REGIME* (Stacey, 2019).

Stacey (2019)

Organisation and Everyday Life with Dyslexia and other SpLDs discusses ways to deal with situations that may be problematic for dyslexic/ SpLD people (Stacey, 2020).

Stacey (2020)

Gaining Knowledge and Skills with Dyslexia and other SpLDs discusses ways to deal with study and communication situations that may be problematic (Stacey, 2021).

Stacey (2021)

It may seem odd that one aim of the *NEW PARADIGM* is that many of the problems of dyslexia/ SpLD do not develop, while outcomes of the <u>process of discovery</u> are to build the *PROFILE* and *REGIME*. But the *PROFILE* and *REGIME* need to be known and used consciously in order that the problems can be minimised. Many dyslexic people are quite stubborn about the way they do tasks, see *STORY: TWO DYSLEXIC SAILORS*. The student in *STORY: BEST CASE SCENARIO: GOOD TECHNIQUES, MINIMAL DYSLEXIA* knew her strategies and the few dyslexic problems she had.

STORY: TWO DYSLEXIC SAILORS: p 4

STORY: BEST CASE SCENARIO: GOOD TECHNIQUES, MINIMAL DYSLEXIA: p 156

6.6 Valuing participants as part of research and assessment

The purpose of the <u>process of discovery</u> is to maximise progress for each individual. When people feel what they can do is important, they are more likely to feel valued.

Among the questions I think researchers and assessors should have at the fore when working are:

- Do I find out how participants do the tasks of my experiment or assessment? Do I ask for their comments and suggestions?

- To what extent am I thinking about how well the participants can do anything?

- Am I using what participants can do well?

- What do I do to enhance a participant's level of confidence? What steps do I take to raise and maintain a participant's self worth?

- Do I include spiky profiles at all levels of IQ, or am I just looking at those whose attainment has dropped?

- How are my participants directly enabled by my experiments or assessments?

6.7   Extending the models of Baddeley, and Morton and Frith

Baddeley (2007)
Morton and Frith
(1995)

The data collected to investigate the <u>process of discovery</u> will not have been gathered with respect to any particular specific learning difficulty, as was the situation in the research by Talcott et al. (2013). It is likely to be such that it can be analysed to extend the models used in discussing working-memory and specific learning difficulties.

Talcott et al. (2013)

The way in which dyslexic/ SpLD people often have individual, specific ways of learning could be an advantage in this area of research. Eysenck's *Theory of Processing Efficiency* says that minds switch their style of thinking when the current mental capacity is insufficient for the task in hand (Baddeley, 1982; Stacey, 2019). It seems as if dyslexic/ SpLD people's minds don't have the option of switching to another way of processing information. The lack of switching could add a degree of consistency to research. Non-dyslexic/ SpLD people's minds don't have this restriction. The way their minds switch between different thinking processes could show interesting contrasts.

Baddeley (1982)
Stacey (2019)

The data might show whether Baddeley's working-memory model needs extra types of short-term storage components, especially a kinaesthetic one, but possibly one for each sense.

How does the need for a framework or rationale impact on incoming information storage?

What are the characteristics that extend working-memory capacity by improving chunking?

What is the role of thinking preferences for using working-memory?

How does interest or prior knowledge affect working-memory capabilities?

The patterns of the data are likely to produce other questions. Almost every technique for *USING THE MIND WELL* raises a question about the way the mind works and therefore how the working-memory model represents what is happening in people's minds.

USING THE MIND WELL:
p 287

The role of inhibition might be found to be important. For example, holistic thinkers need to know when to rein in 'going off at a tangent' and when to encourage the richness of holistic thinking, see *EXAMPLE BOX: CHANGING THE PARADIGM*.

*EXAMPLE BOX:
CHANGING THE
PARADIGM:* p 233

Story: Inhibiting thinking

When playing the guitar using music with 'helpful fingering', I can't inhibit my mind from processing the fingering. I need my mind to process the notes. With a complex piece of music I have to resort to correction fluid to paint out the fingering instructions. If the music has fingering for the recorder, my mind is quite happy to ignore it.

Researching and developing a <u>process of discovery</u> will focus on collecting data about how an individual thinks well and in doing so will also find out which thinking processes or other functions don't work for that particular individual. The data could yield a collection of individual profiles.

Focusing on what people do well possibly adds a dimension to Morton and Frith's model: a scale from those connections that work well to those that don't. Model of SpLD - Another View, *Figure 4.5*, represents the end where connections are working well. The model of Morton and Frith represents the end where the connections don't work well.

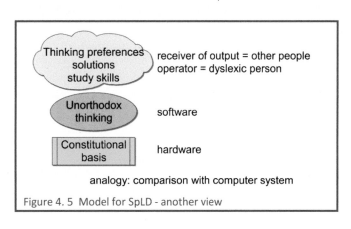

Figure 4. 5 Model for SpLD - another view

It may be that these profiles show clusters of distinct patterns. Some of the questions that could be asked are:

- What happens when thinking preferences are part of normal education?

- How often is a thinking strength or functioning behaviour used to support thinking or a behaviour that doesn't work so well? How often does this happen naturally? What happens when such an approach is taught?

- How do the patterns vary with differing levels of overall intelligence?

- Are there any consistent thinking preferences that are in parallel with particular SpLD problems?

- What consistent patterns are there between the three different levels of the Morton and Frith model? How do these vary along the suggested dimension from working well to not working?

- Are there any pure specific learning difficulties in which certain core biological causes map exclusively through cognitive function to observed behaviour?

- How many independent specific syndromes are there?

- Which levels, biological, cognitive or behavioural, will give the best indications for effective intervention?

When the process of discovery is the focus of the research, there will be no assumptions about thinking and behaviour. The patterns observed about thinking and behaviour through the research will show what the best questions are to ask people, and what needs to be thought about to avoid misinterpretation of results of tests. There may be several issues that become resolved with data that comes from those who currently experience dyslexia/ SpLD.

Key point: The process of discovery is for all

Whether patterns emerge or not, a robust process of discovery should enable anyone to find their own best way of thinking and doing, and generally living confidently.

6.8 Comment about general poor learning performance

Developing a process of discovery, especially with the intelligent dyslexic/ SpLD people, could help with understanding how the mind works and how difficulties in learning can be resolved. The process of discovery should be equally applicable to anyone, including people with general learning difficulties. They should benefit from the attention paid to specific learning difficulties; there should be no feeling that one is 'robbing Peter to pay Paul', as the saying goes.

7   Changes with time

The methodology of this series and my work is based on the scientific processes of observation, investigation and looking for goodness of fit, together with techniques of mind awareness that are ancient. All these processes are well established and unlikely to change in the future. The way people's ability to do something improves as they gain confidence and self-esteem is also unlikely to change with time.

Key point: VITAL for dyslexic/ SpLDs, GOOD practice for all

The GOOD practice in this series applies to all people; it is simply that it is VITAL for dyslexic/ SpLD people.

It is not based on a particular theory of learning, but rather it is saying that no one method is going to work for everyone in a group of learners.

This book is very much about finding what works for whom.

As the media platforms change, there will be new challenges for those whose minds do not function in predicted ways. In the future, they may have other labels than dyslexia and SpLD, but many of the techniques and processes in this book will still apply.

One benefit of using this series and its ideas will hopefully be a better understanding of dyslexia/ SpLD and a greater willingness to take action early. Early actions should be seen as benefitting society and not just the individuals with dyslexia/ SpLD.

As the research community engages with the wide range of differences to be found in the dyslexic/ SpLD group of people, they will, I hope refine their research questions. Repeating the principle I learnt as a physics undergraduate: you will not get consistent answers if you ask the physical world the questions to which it has no stable answer; you need to find the questions it can answer. Those who directly experience dyslexia/ SpLD can help find the best questions to ask.

Summary: The dyslexic/ SpLD experiences of adults can contribute

Future understanding about dyslexia/ SpLD will build on present knowledge faster when dyslexic/ SpLD people can contribute freely and widely to making comparisons between the different ways individual dyslexic/ SpLDs think and process information and to finding the best research questions.

References

Amesbury, Liz, 2008, *Information or Transformation? The Role of the Dyslexia Tutor in Higher Education,* Conference workshop, 7th BDA International Conference, Harrogate

Bacon, A.M. and Bennett, S., 2013, *Dyslexia in Higher Education: The Decision to Study Art,* European Journal of Special Needs Education, 28(1), pp 19-32

Baddeley, Alan, 1982, *Your Memory: A User's Guide,* Penguin Books, London

Baddeley, Alan, 2007, *Working Memory, Thought, and Action,* Oxford University Press, Oxford

Bavelier, D., Green, C.S. and Seidenberg, M.S., 2013, *Cognitive Development: Gaming Your Way Out of Dyslexia?* Current Biology, 23(7), pp R282-R283

Bell, Nanci, 2007, *Visualizing and Verbalizing: For Language Comprehension and Thinking,* Gander Publishing, San Luis Obispo, CA

Berninger, V.W. and Abbott, R.D., 2013, *Differences Between Children With Dyslexia Who Are and Are Not Gifted in Verbal Reasoning,* Gifted Child Quarterly, 57(4), pp 223-233

Brooks, Greg, 2013, *What Works for Children and Young People with Literacy Difficulties?,* The Dyslexia-SpLD Trust, Farnham, 4th ed.

Burden, R. and Burdett, J., 2007, *What's in a Name? Students with Dyslexia: Their Use of Metaphor in Making Sense of Their Disability,* British Journal of Special Education, 34(2), pp 77-82

Burden, Robert, 2005, *Dyslexia and Self-Concept,* Whurr, London

Chasty, Harry , 1989, *The Challenge of Specific Learning Difficulties,* in Hales, Gerald, et al., 1989, *Meeting Points in Dyslexia,* Proceedings of the 1st International Conference of the BDA, Reading

Daiken, C., 2012, *The Voices of Young Adults with Learning Disabilities: Their Perceptions of Elementary and Secondary Schooling*, Queen's University, Kingston, Ontario

De Weerdt, F., Desoete, A. and Roeyers, H., 2013, *Working Memory in Children With Reading Disabilities and/or Mathematical Disabilities,* Journal of Learning Disabilities, 46(5), pp 461-472

Feynman, Richard, 1988, *What Do You Care What Other People Think?* Penguin Books, Toronto

Fugate, C.M., Zentall, S.S. and Gentry, M., 2013, *Creativity and Working Memory in Gifted Students With and Without Characteristics of Attention Deficit Hyperactive Disorder: Lifting the Mask,* Gifted Child Quarterly, 57(4), pp 234-246

Grant, David, 2005, *That's the Way I Think,* David Fulton, London

Helland, T., 2007, *Dyslexia at a Behavioural and a Cognitive Level,* Dyslexia, 13(1), pp 25-41

Jefferies, Sharman, 2008, *Conference Talk,* 7th BDA International Conference 2008, Harrogate

Jones, Anwen and Kindersley, Katherine, 2013, *Dyslexia Assessing and Reporting 2nd ed.: The Patoss Guide,* Hodder Education, London

Jones, Anwen, 2011, *Underlying Ability – Painting a Picture,* PATOSS Bulletin: The Journal of the Professional Association of Teachers of Students with Specific Learning Difficulties, Vol. 24 (1), pp 36-41

Kirby, A., 2011, *Developmental Co-ordination Disorder and Emerging Adulthood: Not Just a Motor Disorder*, Journal of Adult Development, Vol. 18, pp 105-106

Kirby, A. and Thomas, M., 2011, *The Whole Child with Developmental Disorders,* British Journal of Hospital Medicine*,* 72(3), pp 161-167

Kirby, A., Edwards, L. and Sugden, D., 2011, *Emerging Adulthood in Developmental Co-Ordination Disorder: Parent and Young Adult Perspectives,* Research in Developmental Disabilities*,* 32(4), pp 1351-1360

Laasonen, M., Leppämäki, S., Tani, P. and Hokkanen, L., 2009, *Adult Dyslexia and Attention Deficit Disorder in Finland – Project DyAdd: WAIS-III Cognitive Profiles,* Journal of Learning Disabilities, 42(6), pp 511-527

Landerl, K., Fussenegger, B., Moll, K. and Willburger, E., 2009, *Dyslexia and Dyscalculia: Two Learning Disorders with Different Cognitive Profiles,* Journal of Experimental Child Psychology, 103(3), pp 309-324

Landerl, K., Göbel, S.M. and Moll, K., 2013, *Core Deficit and Individual Manifestations of Developmental Dyscalculia (DD): The Role Of Comorbidity,* Trends in Neuroscience and Education, 2(2), pp 38-42

Lehongre, K., Morillon, B., Giraud, A. and Ramus, F., 2013, *Impaired Auditory Sampling in Dyslexia: Further Evidence from Combined fMRI and EEG,* Frontiers in Human Neuroscience, 7, article 454

Loh, P.R., Piek, J.P. and Barrett, N.C., 2011, *Comorbid ADHD and DCD: Examining Cognitive Functions Using the WISC-IV,* Research in Developmental Disabilities, 32(4), pp 1260-1269

McCallum, R.S., Bell, S.M., Coles, J.T., Miller, K.C., Hopkins, M.B. and Hilton-Prillhart, A., 2013, *A Model for Screening Twice-Exceptional Students (Gifted With Learning Disabilities) Within a Response to Intervention Paradigm,* Gifted Child Quarterly, 57(4), pp 209-222

McCarney, D., Peters, L., Jackson, S., Thomas, M. and Kirby, A., 2013, *Does Poor Handwriting Conceal Literacy Potential in Primary School Children?* International Journal of Disability, Development and Education, 60(2), pp 105-118

McLoughlin, David, et al., 2001, *Adult Dyslexia: Assessment, Counselling and Training,* Whurr, London

Miles, Tim, 1993, *Dyslexia: the Pattern of Difficulties,* Whurr, London, 2nd ed.

Morton, J. and Frith, U., 1995, *Causal Modeling: A Structural Approach to Developmental Psychopathology,* Chapter 13 in Developmental Psychopathology, Vol 1 pp 357-390, New York; Chichester: Wiley

Neumeister, K.S., Yssel, N. and Burney, V.H., 2013, *The Influence of Primary Caregivers in Fostering Success in Twice-Exceptional Children,* Gifted Child Quarterly, 57(4), pp 263-274

Nicolson, R.I. and Fawcett, A.J., 1990, *Automaticity: A New Framework for Dyslexia Research?* Cognition, 35(2), pp 159-182

Nicolson, R.I. and Fawcett, A.J., 2011, *Dyslexia, Dysgraphia, Procedural Learning and the Cerebellum,* Cortex, 47(1), pp 117-127

Park, H. and Lombardino, L.J., 2013, *Relationships among Cognitive Deficits and Component Skills of Reading in Younger and Older Students with Developmental Dyslexia,* Research in Developmental Disabilities, 34(9), pp 2946-2958

Pennington, B.F., 2006, *From Single to Multiple Deficit Models of Developmental Disorders,* Cognition, 101(2), pp 385-413

Snowling, Margaret J., 2006, *Language Skills and Learning to Read: the Dyslexia Spectrum,* in Snowling, Margaret J., Stackhouse, Joy, (eds), 2006, *Dyslexia, Speech and Language, A Practitioner's Handbook,* Whurr, London, 2nd ed.

Stacey, Ginny, 2019, *Finding Your Voice with Dyslexia and other SpLDs,* Routledge, London

Stacey, Ginny, 2020, *Organisation and Everyday Life with Dyslexia and other SpLDs,* Routledge, London

Stacey, Ginny, 2021, *Gaining Knowledge and Skills with Dyslexia and other SpLDs,* Routledge, London

Stein, John, 2012, *Visual Contributions to Reading Difficulties: The Magnocellular Theory*, in Stein, J., Kapoula, Z. (eds), 2012, *Visual Aspects of Dyslexia*, Oxford University Press, Oxford

Talcott, J.B., Witton, C. and Stein, J.F., 2013, *Probing the Neurocognitive Trajectories of Children's Reading Skills,* Neuropsychologia, 51(3), pp 472-481

Thomson, Michael, 1995, *Developmental Dyslexia,* Whurr, London, 3rd ed.

West, Thomas, G, 1991, *In the Mind's Eye,* Prometheus Books, Buffalo, New York

Willard-Holt, C., Weber, J., Morrison, K.L. and Horgan, J., 2013, *Twice-Exceptional Learners' Perspectives on Effective Learning Strategies,* Gifted Child Quarterly, 57(4), pp 247-262

Website information

Jefferies, Sharman, 2007, *Education-Related Learning Difficulties and Working Memory Function,* https://ethos.bl.uk   Accessed 19 April 2017.

OED Online, June 2016, Oxford University Press   Accessed 29 August 2016.

Series website: www.routledge.com/cw/Stacey

Appendix 1: Resources

Contents

Series: *Living Confidently with Specific Learning Difficulties (SpLDs)*

Book 1: *Finding Your Voice with Dyslexia and other SpLDs*
Book 2: *Organisation and Everyday Life with Dyslexia and other SpLDs*
Book 3: *Gaining Knowledge and Skills with Dyslexia and other SpLDs*
Book 4: *Development of Dyslexia and other SpLDs*

Stacey (2019, 2020a, 2021, 2020b, respectively)

To Readers of Books 3 and 4

The appendices are written for dyslexic/ SpLD people.

Dyslexic/ SpLD people are the readership of books 1 and 2. They are the learners for books 3 and 4, so the appendices are written for them, even when they are not the direct readership.

Many people supporting dyslexic/ SpLD people are themselves dyslexic/ SpLD; therefore, many of the readers of books 3 and 4 may benefit by using the material in the appendices for themselves.

Templates on the website

A1   *JOTTING DOWN AS YOU SCAN*

B1   *COLLECTING IDEAS THAT RELATE TO YOU*

B3   *COMPARE EXPECTATIONS AND REALITY*

B4   *ACTION, RESULTS, NEXT STEP*

B5   *RECORDING TEMPLATE - 1 (4TH COLUMN NARROWER FOR CODING)*

B6   *RECORDING TEMPLATE - 2 (4 EQUAL COLUMNS)*

B7   *RECORDING TEMPLATE - 3 (5TH COLUMN NARROWER FOR CODING)*

B8   *RECORDING TEMPLATE - 4 (5 EQUAL COLUMNS)*

B9   *A CALENDAR MONTH FOR PRIORITISING – 5 WEEKS*

B10   *QUESTIONS TO ASK ONESELF TO HELP OBSERVATION*

B11   *MONITORING PROGRESS*

1 General resources

This is a collection of resources and ideas that will help you to capture any ideas that seem important to you. Ideas that are captured will then be available to you for use later on.

Notice anything that doesn't work for you, and use it to design your own way to capture and use information that seems relevant to you.

Tip: Margin

You can use the right hand margin to jot down your ideas as you scan or read the book.

I have used it for cross-referencing and for references to help you find these when you want them.

---

2   Collecting information together

- Create a mind map of the information; there are examples in the book. Experiment with different styles to find which work well for you. (Don't use mind maps if you don't like them.)

- Use a digital recording device; make sure you label the files so that you can remember what they are about.

- Create tables of information; this section has several suggestions for using tables.

- Use electronic note-collecting devices.

B1 - COLLECTING IDEAS THAT RELATE TO YOU

This *TEMPLATE* will help with building your *INDIVIDUAL, PERSONAL PROFILE OF DYSLEXIA/ SPLD* and your *REGIME FOR MANAGING DYSLEXIA/ SPLD*.

Column 4 allows you to reflect whether you are learning more about
1   your profile
2   your regime for managing dyslexia/ SpLD.

Column 5 allows you to note which elements are involved:

thinking preferences
pausing
pitfalls
accommodations
goals.

TEMPLATES

G p 303: profile, regime

B3 - COMPARE EXPECTATIONS AND REALITY

If you are going to observe objectively you need to keep a record of your expectations and what actually happens. The *TEMPLATE: COMPARE EXPECTATIONS AND REALITY* is one way of doing this. It can be easier to rule horizontal lines after writing in the template than forcing yourself to keep within lines already printed.

The template suggests you record the *situation* and *date*. It has 4 columns headed: *Events, Expected, Actual, Comments.*

TEMPLATES

For example:

Situation: to have everything ready for football on Saturday morning (include the date), in order to arrive on time.

Events	Expected	Actual	Comments
wash kit	Tuesday		
assemble kit	Friday		
put boots with kit	Friday		
get up	8.30 am Saturday		
breakfast	9.00		
leave house	9.45		
arrive at *venue*	10.15		

THE ACTUAL COLUMN WOULD BE FILLED IN AS CLOSE TO THE EVENT AS POSSIBLE. THE COMMENTS COULD THEN REFLECT PLEASURE AT SUCCESS OR ANY ADJUSTMENTS NEEDED TO ACHIEVE THE DESIRED RESULT.

B4 - ACTION, RESULTS, NEXT STEP

TEMPLATES

This *TEMPLATE* is very similar to *COMPARE EXPECTATIONS AND REALITY*. In *COMPARE EXPECTATIONS AND REALITY* you are planning ahead and monitoring how well the plan was executed. In *ACTION, RESULTS, NEXT STEP*, you are observing the results of actions, whether planned or not, and considering any implications for the *Next Step*, whenever that might be.

For example

Event	Action	Results	Next Step
conversation with friend	I created pictures in my mind as we talked	I remembered the details next day	try putting pictures on my lists
shopping	I drew some of the items on the list and left the list at home!	I remembered the drawings and some connected items; forgot others	see what other line drawing I can use

B5, B6 - *RECORDING TEMPLATES - 1 AND - 2*

These templates can be used for a number of different purposes.
In *B5 - RECORDING TEMPLATE - 1* the columns are uneven, which is
suitable for those times when you want to use one column for a lot of
detail while the others are only needed for brief information.
B6 - RECORDING TEMPLATE - 2 has 4 equal columns.

B7, B8 - *RECORDING TEMPLATES - 3 AND - 4*

These templates are similar to *B5, B6 - RECORDING TEMPLATES - 1* and *- 2*,
but with a 5th column. Often the fifth column is very useful for a brief
key word or symbol. It allows you to code the information you are
collecting so that you can find sections that belong together. For
instance, if you are exploring how you use different senses, you can
put visual/ oral/ smell/ taste/ kinaesthetic or V/ O/ S/ T / K in the fifth
column. Then you only have to look for the V/ visual to find all the
notes about the way you use your vision.

Useful headings for linear lists or text notes

Any of the column headings suggested for tabular forms of collecting
information could be used as headings for lists or a sentence-based
way of collecting information.

You might divide a page into spaces for different categories of
information and label the spaces.

You might write down the information you are gathering and leave
space to add in the headings later.

TEMPLATES
COMPANION @ WEBSITE

MARGIN NOTE: when
these 4 templates are
recommended,
headings are usually
suggested.

3   Prioritising

Given a collection of tasks, situations or topics (not an exhaustive list),
what are the priorities for you?

1   You might have to prioritise bearing in mind limited time and
    resources.
2   You might be trying to decide the relative importance of each of a
    set of topics.
3   You might be deciding the order in which to do a series of tasks.

You can use any form of note-taking to collect the information
together. The suggestions here use a calendar, a mind map and a
tabular form.

Step 1   With limited time or resources

First you have to establish the constraints:

- Do you have enough time or resources to do everything?
- Does anything depend on another thing being done first?

Assessing the constraints first stops you trying to do more than you possibly can.

The *TEMPLATE: B9 - A CALENDAR MONTH FOR PRIORITISING* allows you to mark deadlines and block out sections of time. You can often then decide the priority of the various tasks and the order in which to do them.

TEMPLATES

Put everything that is happening in your life onto the calendar. In particular, include time for the ordinary, everyday tasks.

It can be helpful to highlight the beginning and end of the month, whether using paper or an electronic device.

You then continue with the second stage below.

Step 2   What is involved?

A second stage is simply to brainstorm about the tasks, situations or topics under consideration. You can use any of the shapes of mind map used in the book. You could make lists of ideas.

See the *INDEX*, p 314, for a list of mind maps

In terms of reading a book, a useful set of questions might be:

       What do I know already?
       Why have I picked up this book?
       What do I think it might give me?
       What am I interested in? or Who am I interested in knowing
           more about?
       What aspect would it be interesting to know more about?
       What do I really want to know?

MARGIN NOTE: GENERATING USEFUL QUESTIONS, p 258 could help you find the right questions.

If you are prioritising actions, a set of useful questions might be:

       What do I want to achieve?
       What equipment do I need?
       Who else is involved? How? Why?
       What individual tasks are there?
       What do I need to find out?

Step 3   Deciding relative priorities

When you have decided what is involved, you can put the information together in a table and then decide the relative priorities of the tasks.

B5, B6 - RECORDING TEMPLATES - 1 AND - 2 can be adapted to gather the information.

TEMPLATES

Title = the reason for sorting out a set of priorities.

      A = the priority assigned to each task once you've assessed them all

      B = name of a task

      C = details of the task

      D = resources or time requirements.

B7, B8 - RECORDING TEMPLATES - 3 AND - 4 could be used if a 5th column is useful.

TEMPLATES

      E = Vital/ important/ non-essential.

This information would help in assigning the priorities that are written in column A.

Step 4   Plan of action

Use the priorities list in column A and the calendar to make a plan of action. Keep monitoring your progress. Adapt your plan as necessary.

4   Generating useful questions

Making a list of questions can be a very useful way to guide yourself through many different situations or tasks. The purpose of the list is to clarify what you are attempting to do, to help you be realistic and to help you achieve the end goal. Discussion around these ideas has come under: useful questions, ultimate goal, know your goal, research questions and probably a few other terms too.   It is hard to pick out any common themes that lead to a direct set of principles. However, the idea of useful questions is sufficiently important that there is an *INDEX* entry: *QUESTIONS, USEFUL, EXAMPLES*.

INDEX: p 314

TEMPLATE: B10 - QUESTIONS TO ASK ONESELF TO HELP OBSERVATION is an example of a good set of questions.

The style and wording of the questions will be slightly different depending on the circumstances, for example:

When you're organising something, you might think about how you'e going to organise it and why you're organising it in a particular way.

When you are reading something or listening, having some questions you want answered gives a structure to the material. You then understand it faster.

When you're writing an essay, doing a presentation, or communicating by some means, the purposes for your work need to be defined clearly. This approach usually gives a coherence to the work.

When you are making major decisions for your life, you can be helped by a set of questions about what you want to do, what you are most interested in, how your decisions will affect others. The list is not exhaustive.

When you need to keep your attention focused on a specific task and stop yourself getting diverted, you can use a set of questions to:

a) define the specific task

b) relate what you are doing at any moment to the specific task.

Pulling yourself back from distractions can make a task more enjoyable, or it can shorten a task you don't really want to do.

TEMPLATES

The Basic Set of
USEFUL QUESTIONS:
Why?
Who?
When?
Where?
How?
What for?

Appendix 1   Resources

Exercise: To practise generating useful **questions** 1

You are going to use *USEFUL QUESTIONS* to search the book in order to find any discussion on a specific topic:

- Think of a topic that interests you.
- What questions need answering to help you find out about the topic?
- List your questions.
- Use them as you scan the *INDEX ENTRY: QUESTIONS, USEFUL, EXAMPLES.* Then scan the rest of the *INDEX,* the *CONTENTS* and the book to find topics that are similar to the one you have in mind.
- How good were your questions? Did they help you to find the sections that deal with the topic you had in mind?
- What changes would you make to the questions for the next time?

MARGIN NOTE: this exercise could be applied to all 4 books in the series. (Stacey, 2019, 2020a, 2020b, 2021)

INDEX: p 314
CONTENTS: p xv

Exercise: To practise generating useful **questions** 2

You are going to use *USEFUL QUESTIONS* to search the book in order to find the nearest match to a specific task:

- Think of a task that needs doing.
- What questions need answering to help you find the best match, in the book, to your task?
- List your questions.
- Use them as you scan the *INDEX ENTRY: QUESTIONS, USEFUL, EXAMPLES.* Then scan the rest of the *INDEX,* the *CONTENTS* and the book to find tasks that are similar to the one you have in mind.
- How good were your questions? Did they help you to find a good match to the task you had in mind?
- What changes would you make to the questions for the next time?

MARGIN note: this exercise will work best with *Organisation and Everyday Life with Dyslexia and other SpLDs* (Stacey, 2020a) and *Gaining Knowledge and Skills with Dyslexia and other SpLDs* (Stacey, 2021)

INDEX: p 314
CONTENTS: p xv

Tip: The skill of generating useful questions

This skill is worth developing until it becomes natural. You could add the *Exercise: To Practise Generating Useful Questions 1 & 2,* above, to the card index for *Systematic Review*. It is a skill that could be usefully practised once a week until it is easy to use.

Systematic Review in *Finding Your Voice with Dyslexia and other SpLDs* (Stacey, 2019)

5 Surveying

In surveying you are looking over material to find out, in broad terms, what the material contains and where certain ideas are. As part of the process you will probably decide your priorities for exploring the ideas. 'Material' could be instruction manuals for household goods, books, articles, web pages.

Step 1 Key ideas

You need to establish a set of key ideas that you want to find out about. These will be your focus of attention as you survey any material.

Margin Note: Exercise: Initial Purpose for Reading, p 14 is a good example of surveying.

You can use one of the *Exercises: To Practise Generating Useful Questions.*
You can brainstorm around the associated topics to see if key ideas emerge.
You can look at other examples using *Questions, Useful, Examples* in the *Index*, and see if any of them help you to recognise the key ideas you want to read about.

Exercises: To Practise Generating Useful Questions: p 260

Ⓖ p 303*: brainstorm*

Index: p 314

You can discuss your interest with someone else and use ideas that come out of the conversation.

It doesn't matter how you do it, but find a set of key ideas.

The set of key ideas will still be helpful, even when they are not quite right. They will help you to focus your mind as you survey. You will be more attentive to the material than if trying to read with a wide open mind that is not looking for anything specific.

Step 2   Recording your survey

Use *B5 - RECORDING TEMPLATE - 1*.

Headings   A = key topic   B = where in the book

C = main ideas   D = order to read.

(Complete D at the end of Step 3)

TEMPLATES

Step 3   Survey (as applicable to this book)

- Use the *INDEX* and *CONTENTS* of the book to find sections of the book that cover the topics you want to find out about.
- Scan the book for useful indications of important material, such as headings, words in bold or italic; scan graphs and other visual material.
- Cover all the topics you have identified in the key ideas list.
- Have a quick look at each section to gather its main ideas.
- Write in column D the order in which you would like to read the various sections.

INDEX: p 314
CONTENTS: p xv

Surveying other books

Some books don't have an index or contents list. You can use chapter headings. You may have to use introductions and conclusions to chapters. You may have to scan the beginnings of paragraphs every few pages.

Surveying can be used with any source of information. It can be extended to work with several sources at the same time. Column B would then be headed: Source, and where in the source. Or you could use the *B7 - RECORDING TEMPLATE - 3*.

TEMPLATES

6   Recording as you scan

Scanning a section: you can randomly move through a section deciding roughly what it is about. You don't try to understand the ideas.

Several times in this book you are recommended to scan several
    sections to find material and ideas that are relevant to you.
It is frustrating to see something interesting or useful and not be able
    to find it again.

TEMPLATE: A1 - JOTTING DOWN AS YOU SCAN allows you to make brief comments as you scan.

If you want to write more, and a landscape page would suit you better, use *B5 - RECORDING TEMPLATE - 1*.

The headings would be:

A = Source and page   B = Section/ Keywords

C = What is interesting   D = Priority.

Drawing a line after each entry can help to separate the ideas that you want to record.

TEMPLATES

TEMPLATES

7 Monitoring progress

It's really useful and encouraging to see how well you are doing. It's useful to see anything that isn't working so well, because then you can do something about it.
You might want to see:

> your progress with a skill
>
> knowledge you are gaining
>
> how a situation is developing
>
> how you are managing a task
>
> other ... the list is not exhaustive.

You can collect the information by any means that suits you:

> notes   on paper or electronic device
> voice recordings   art work.

Use the ideas below, in *USING TEMPLATES ON THE WEBSITE*, to help you decide what to record and how to label or annotate your information. You want to remember the key ideas and your reflections so that you can use them again later.

You can gather the information together by category, e.g. keep all the information about situations together.

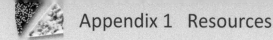

Using the templates on the website

If you collect information using the *TEMPLATES: B3 - COMPARE EXPECTATIONS AND REALITY* and *B4 - ACTION, RESULT AND NEXT STEP,* you can use the last columns, *Comment* and *Next Step* respectively, to reflect on your progress and anything you want to change.

 TEMPLATES

The *TEMPLATE: B11 - MONITORING PROGRESS* has 5 columns.

1	= date
2	= focus of interest
3	= current state of play
4	= last application
5	= reflection.

 TEMPLATES

Comments about the columns:

1. It is almost always useful to have the date recorded.
2. A few words that capture what you want to monitor.
3. Record your summary of how far you have progressed.
4. Describe what happened when you tried out your progress to date.
5. Reflect on your progress; maybe think about the next step; anyone you could usefully consult; anything that will bring further progress or satisfaction.

References

Series: *Living Confidently with Specific Learning Difficulties (SpLDs):*

Stacey, Ginny, 2019, *Finding Your Voice with Dyslexia and other SpLDs,* Routledge, London

Stacey, Ginny, 2020a, *Organisation and Everyday Life with Dyslexia and other SpLDs,* Routledge, London

Stacey, Ginny, 2021, *Gaining Knowledge and Skills with Dyslexia and other SpLDs,* Routledge, London

Stacey, Ginny, 2020b, *Development of Dyslexia and other SpLDs,* Routledge, London

Website information

Series website: www.routledge.com/cw/stacey

Appendix 2:

Individual, Personal Profile of Dyslexia/ SpLD
and
Regime for Managing Dyslexia/ SpLD

Contents

Series: *Living Confidently with Specific Learning Difficulties (SpLDs)*

Book 1: *Finding Your Voice with Dyslexia and other SpLDs*

Book 2: *Organisation and Everyday Life with Dyslexia and other SpLDs*

Book 3: *Gaining Knowledge and Skills with Dyslexia and other SpLDs*

Book 4: *Development of Dyslexia and other SpLDs*

Stacey (2019, 2020a, 2021, 2020b, respectively)

Templates on the website

A3   *BOOK MARK – PROFILE AND TECHNIQUES*

B1   *COLLECTING IDEAS THAT RELATE TO YOU*
B2   *KNOW YOUR OWN MIND*
B7   *RECORDING TEMPLATE - 3 (5 UNEQUAL COLUMNS)*
B8   *RECORDING TEMPLATE - 4 (5 EQUAL COLUMNS)*

C1   *INDIVIDUAL, PERSONAL PROFILE OF DYSLEXIA/ SPLD (SPATIAL)*
C2   *EXAMPLE INDIVIDUAL, PERSONAL PROFILE OF DYSLEXIA/ SPLD (SPATIAL)*
C3   *INDIVIDUAL, PERSONAL PROFILE OF DYSLEXIA/ SPLD (LINEAR)*
C4   *2 EXAMPLES OF AN INDIVIDUAL, PERSONAL PROFILE OF DYSLEXIA/ SPLD
        (LINEAR)*

D1   *MANAGING DYSLEXIA/ SPLD (MIND MAP)*
D2   *MANAGING DYSLEXIA/ SPLD (LINEAR)*
D3   *REGIME FOR MANAGING DYSLEXIA/ SPLD (SPATIAL)*
D4   *REGIME FOR MANAGING DYSLEXIA/ SPLD (LINEAR)*
D5   *EXPERIENCES FOR MANAGING DYSLEXIA/ SPLD (LINEAR EXAMPLE)*

E2   *TABLE OF THINKING PREFERENCES (SPATIAL)*
E3   *EXAMPLE: TABLE OF THINKING PREFERENCES (SPATIAL)*
E4   *THINKING PREFERENCES (SPATIAL)*
E5   *THINKING PREFERENCES (LINEAR)*

1   Living confidently

The aim of the whole series *LIVING CONFIDENTLY WITH SPECIFIC LEARNING DIFFICULTIES (SPLDS)* is that dyslexic/ SpLD people have ownership of their dyslexia/ SpLD; therefore this appendix is addressed to dyslexic/ SpLD people. It is essentially the same throughout the series, with the addition of the sub-sections in this section. These sub-sections are summaries of key elements about the *PROFILE* and *REGIME* covered in *Finding Your Voice with Dyslexia and other SpLDs* (Stacey, 2019).

Stacey (2019)

1.1   Individual, personal profile of dyslexia/ SpLD

A profile is a summary of information. This profile is about your dyslexia/ SpLD. It contains:

how you think best	*THINKING PREFERENCES*
how you pause well	*THINKING CLEARLY*
the pitfalls of your dyslexia/ SpLD	*PITFALLS*
any accommodations you need	*ACCOMMODATION*

THINKING PREFERENCES: p 290

THINKING CLEARLY: p 285

PITFALLS: p 73

ACCOMMODATION: p 78 and *INDEX*

Thinking well and pausing at the right times allow you to deal with any pitfalls that come your way. When you know what they are likely to be, you can recognise your pitfalls in advance. You are in a better position to arrange necessary accommodations when you are clear about your pitfalls and the strategies you have tried to use in order to deal with them.

1.2   Regime for managing dyslexia/ SpLD

Your regime is about the day to day management of dyslexia/ SpLD in the light of life's unpredictable moments. It has 3 elements in common with your profile; it has goals instead of accommodations.

In day-to-day life, you carry on assuming all's OK, then a pitfall looms. You may be able to notice it before it has become a problem. You may be into a dyslexic/ SpLD way of functioning before you notice what is happening to you. Either way, having a regime allows you options for managing the situation.

Noticing the pitfall as early as possible is the first step. The second is pausing, being able to step back and take a moment to reflect on what is happening. Your thinking preferences are valuable tools for rescuing you. If you are not clear as to what you are aiming to achieve (*YOUR GOAL*), you are likely to fall back into the pitfall even after pausing well and deciding to use your best thinking.

KNOW YOUR GOAL:
p 295

1.3   Testing and developing your profile and regime

You test your profile and regime by using them and assessing how well each section works for you. Your profile and regime are unlikely to be fixed for all time; they will develop as you use them and as you gain more insights into the way your mind best works.

1.4   Mental energy to manage dyslexia/ SpLD

(Copied from *Finding Your Voice with Dyslexia and other SpLDs*, Stacey 2019)

Stacey (2019)

Insight: Mental energy to manage dyslexia/ SpLD

By using thinking preferences and various strategies, it is possible to function at a level that is comparable to your best intelligence.

If you are a dyslexic person that means using language at a level that is much better than the dyslexic language, see *FIGURE APPENDIX 2.1.*

However, the dyslexia/ SpLD doesn't get removed. It is still there in the mind and you can be triggered into using those thought processes.

Mental energy often has to be reserved to monitor progress in order to stay out of your dyslexic/ SpLD processing.

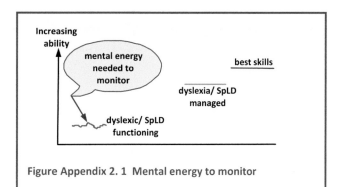

Figure Appendix 2. 1 Mental energy to monitor

2   Building up insights

The table shows the overlap between the elements of your individual profile and your regime for managing dyslexia/ SpLD. It also shows the key way for developing and testing each element.

Element	Individual, personal profile	Regime for managing dyslexia/ SpLD	For developing and testing processes	Covered in book (or see *Appendix 3* for summaries)	Page
Thinking preferences	1	3	recall & check	1	290
Pausing	2	2	practise & reflect	1	285
Pitfalls	3	1	observe & reflect	2 & 4 partly in 1	73 297
Accommodation	4		negotiate, use and reflect	2, 3 & 4 partly in 1	78 297
Goals		4	via applications	3 partly in 1	295

The aim is to build up the insights into a *TOOL BOX FOR LIVING CONFIDENTLY*. The tool box will develop and expand over time, see *UPDATING THE TOOL BOX*.

If you keep your records in a way that you can easily review, you will build on your insights in an effective way. You will be able to use them and discuss them with others.

B1 - COLLECTING IDEAS THAT RELATE TO YOU - TEMPLATE

Collect the stories, insights, examples, etc. from the book that relate to you. Collect what happens when you try any of the exercises.

To fill in the 4th column, write 'profile' or 'regime/ managing'.
Use the elements in the table above to fill in the 5th column.
It is then easy to scan these two columns to bring your insights together.

TOOL BOX FOR LIVING CONFIDENTLY: p 273

UPDATING THE TOOL BOX: p 276

TEMPLATES

Look at the layout for the summary templates:

TEMPLATES

> *D3 - REGIME FOR MANAGING DYSLEXIA/ SPLD (SPATIAL)*
> *C1 - INDIVIDUAL, PERSONAL PROFILE OF DYSLEXIA/ SPLD (SPATIAL)*
>
> *E2 - TABLE OF THINKING PREFERENCES*
>
> *D5 - REGIME FOR MANAGING DYSLEXIA/ SPLD (LINEAR EXAMPLE)*
> *C3 - INDIVIDUAL, PERSONAL PROFILE OF DYSLEXIA/ SPLD (LINEAR)*

Which do you think will suit you best?

Which do you think would be worth trying out?

You can use them as soon as you start gathering insights. They may well change as further insights are gained.

Observe and reflect

Templates that can be used for gathering insights are:

TEMPLATES

> *B2 - KNOW YOUR OWN MIND*
>
> *B7, B8 - RECORDING TEMPLATES - 3 OR - 4*
>
> *D1 - MANAGING DYSLEXIA/ SPLD (MIND MAP)*
>
> *D2 - MANAGING DYSLEXIA/ SPLD (LINEAR)*

Suggestions for headings for the *RECORDING TEMPLATES - 3 OR - 4* are:

A = date   B = situation   C = what I was trying to do

D = details, including strategies being used

E = notes on success or otherwise.

Column E could either be narrow for a single word that rated your success or it could be wider for more detailed notes. Choose the template depending on whether you want column E to be narrow or wide.

E4, E5 - THINKING PREFERENCES, one spatial, one linear, are two useful *TEMPLATES* for recording brief notes as you build your profile.

TEMPLATES

Appendix 2   Profile and Regime

Examples from a log book

A log book is another way of recording incidents and reflections. You can pull the insights together by using key words in columns down the edges of the pages. You gradually have confidence in your insights because you have experience and evidence, which you are recording in a systematic way.

These notes were taken over several weeks while observing behaviour patterns:

MARGIN NOTE:
I usually shorten my headings to fit the columns
e.g. Th-Pref for Thinking Preferences

Date	Details	Other	Pitfall	Th-Pref (Thinking Preference)
DD/ MM/ YY	Total absorption in what's current in my mind – nothing rings any bells to warn me that something else needs attention. (Example) Focusing on writing reports before a deadline meant I missed an evening class		frequent problem	
DD/ MM/ YY	Can't remember from top of stairs to bottom that I need to add something to the shopping list. Crossing my fingers at top of stairs will remind me at the bottom that I have to remember something (that's enough to remember what to add).		poor short-term memory	kinaesthetic
DD/ MM/ YY	A friend explained the mechanism of blood circulation and capillary healing; now I know how to look after my ankle injury. I had forgotten the list of instructions. When there is no logic behind information, I forget what I'm told; or I modify half-remembered instructions by trying to make sense of incomplete information.		poor short-term memory	logic needed

Date	Details	Other	Pitfall	Th-Pref (Thinking Preference)
DD/ MM/ YY	Total confusion in my paperwork. If it isn't organised and doesn't stay organised, I've had it. I won't remember where any relevant other pieces of information are; I won't remember if it exists. Not having a printer in this room is causing major problems. I can't multi-task when paper is involved.		reading problem & recall	
DD/ MM/ YY	After I've been reading black-on-white intently for a while, my vision has the black print lines across it. Bright images also leave a strong imprint.	eyes: after images		

3 The tool box for living confidently

If you consistently work through the ideas in this book and build a picture of how you think well, how you take-action well and how you manage your dyslexia/ SpLD well, you will accumulate a body of knowledge and skills. You can summarise what you learn in three templates:

Ⓖ p 303: taking-action

> D3 - REGIME FOR MANAGING DYSLEXIA/ SPLD (SPATIAL)
>
> C1 - INDIVIDUAL, PERSONAL PROFILE OF DYSLEXIA/ SPLD (SPATIAL)
>
> E2 - TABLE OF THINKING PREFERENCES

or use the linear alternative templates:

TEMPLATES

> D4 - REGIME FOR MANAGING DYSLEXIA/ SPLD (LINEAR)
>
> C3 - INDIVIDUAL, PERSONAL PROFILE OF DYSLEXIA/ SPLD (LINEAR)

If some of the insights are more important than others, add this information to the summaries.

Make cross-references to any notes you have about the insights you put on the summaries. For example, you could have a log book entry which gives a good example of you using your kinaesthetic strength. You list 'kinaesthetic' in your thinking preferences table with cross-reference '(log book, date)'.

You could also have :

> a collection of stories that reflect your experiences
>
> a log book or other systematic collection of evidence that you can easily access.

What you know about yourself will change and develop over time, which is the same for everyone. Any summary should be dated so that you know when it was the current one.

Even when nothing is causing you to update your tool box, it is worth reflecting on the whole tool box from time to time, to see whether any element needs to be developed further.

This accumulated knowledge and skills is your tool box for living confidently with your dyslexia/ SpLD.

You can use the *A3 - BOOKMARK – PROFILE AND TECHNIQUES* to record your profile and the techniques that help you. Then use the bookmark when you are reading to make sure you are doing everything possible to ease your reading.

TEMPLATES

Examples of insights of some other people are in *TEMPLATES*:

TEMPLATES

> *D5 - EXPERIENCES FOR MANAGING DYSLEXIA/ SPLD (LINEAR EXAMPLE)*
>
> *C2 - EXAMPLE: INDIVIDUAL, PERSONAL PROFILE OF DYSLEXIA/ SPLD (SPATIAL)*
>
> *C4 - 2 EXAMPLES OF INDIVIDUAL, PERSONAL PROFILES OF DYSLEXIA/ SPLD (LINEAR)*
>
> *E3 - EXAMPLE: TABLE OF THINKING PREFERENCES (SPATIAL)*

It can be useful to see what insights other people have gained.

General letter to employers

It might be possible and useful to have a general letter in your tool box from someone who has given you dyslexia/ SpLD support. These are extracts taken from a single page for a student (PG) with dyslexia. He had decided that he wanted any future employer to know he was dyslexic.

Example: Extracts from a letter to employers

To Whom it May Concern (with qualifications of author somewhere)

Re: PG and dyslexia in the workplace

Dyslexia
Short paragraph about dyslexia and giving a reference to a book that shows a positive approach to dyslexia.

Dyslexia in the workplace
Short paragraph about management rather than cure of dyslexia and that suitable environment allows dyslexic people to be as effective as any others.

PG's choice of career.
PG wants to work in pharmaceutical and medical marketing. PG has done a biology and chemistry degree at Y University. He has also discovered that he likes dealing with people and that he has appropriate, interpersonal skills. He has chosen pharmaceutical and medical marketing as a career because he will be able to use both his degree and his interpersonal skills.

Most of the time in this job, PG does not expect his dyslexia to hinder him. He may find certain electronic devices extremely useful, such as a voice recorder and an electronic organiser. The one task he may need to take extra care with is report-writing. He has found at university that he can deal with coursework assignments providing he leaves adequate time, does not work right up to the deadline and gets someone else to read his work before the final stage. He will need to use the same strategies for any report-writing at work.

Conclusion
A couple of sentences about dyslexics in general having intellectual strengths.
PG should be able to contribute his knowledge and thinking strengths to any employer provided his different ways of working are accommodated so that he can effectively manage his dyslexia.

---

4   Updating the tool box

Any time the tool box seems to be unhelpful:

- look after your confidence
- check you are pausing in ways that help you
- read (re-read) about fluctuations between the *4 LEVELS OF COMPENSATION*.

4 LEVELS OF COMPENSATION: p 60

Observe and reflect

Use any of the formats that have worked for you in building your tool box to find out what is undermining the management of your dyslexia/ SpLD and to develop any necessary new skills and knowledge.

In particular, the following could be table headings or arms of mind maps:

Date, situation	*Insights as to why the strategy didn't work
What I want to do	*What was going well
Strategy I thought would work	*Insights as to why the strategy worked
*What was going wrong	What to try next.

*In a table, I would combine these headings into one column, 'Details'. It would be wide enough to write quite a bit. I'd have a narrow column beside it which would categorise the details:

✓	or	OK
✓ ?		OK/ why?
x		not OK
x ?		not OK/ why?

Working in this way, you can find new insights about the contents of your tool box. You may simply be adding to it. You may find some of the insights you had were not as robust as you thought they were. You may be replacing them or developing them. You may find the source of your decreased management had nothing to do with the dyslexia/ SpLD. The processes set out here should help you to identify the root of the problem.

Tip: Adding new significant insights to the tool box

Whenever something significant comes to light:

- add it to the summaries

- date it.

Keep the stories that led to the new insight.
Make sure you can connect the summary to the stories.

Progress report

Progress reports can be useful.

- They can show you what you have achieved so far; they can demonstrate how those achievements have come about and what skills or capability you have.

- They can state the problems that remain.

- They can make the case for accommodations and continued support. They can contribute to updating the tool box.

- They should have a declared benefit, especially for you. The issues addressed need to be pertinent to you.

Example: Extracts from a progress report

Name XX - Progress report on dyslexia support tuition

This report outlines the progress that XX has made in study skills, and the support she is likely to need to complete her course successfully.

Five areas relevant to XX have been covered recently:

1) time management

2) organisation

3) reading and note-taking

4) essay-writing

5) exams stress control.

For example: Reading and note-taking

XX has learnt to read more effectively. She now scans contents lists and headings to get an overview and to find the sections of immediate relevance; she no longer works her way slowly through every word. She continues to have difficulty understanding some texts, and benefits from translating them with the help of pictures. For note-taking, she now uses mind maps. She still needs support to group notes by topic. She has developed various personal 'shorthand' symbols and also uses colour very effectively.

[Any significant comments about the other areas.]

General conclusion

XX has made considerable strides towards becoming a confident student, able to use appropriate strategies to overcome the range of difficulties caused by her dyslexia. She has become much more willing to try new approaches.   Her results in a number of modules show that she has the potential to achieve a good degree.

5 Negotiating accommodation

It is fairly hard to negotiate accommodation for yourself. You may need to get someone, your advocate, who has been working with you or who knows you well, to put your case.

These are suggestions as to how to make the case for accommodation. The request might be in a formal letter or in an email from your advocate.

(G) p 303: accommodation

The role and expertise of the advocate need to be stated, and the contact they have with you in relation to the case being made. If these details are already known, they could be excluded.

The advocate should:

Propose the requested accommodation directly and simply.

Explain the situation that prompts the request. Include any information about dyslexia/ SpLD that may be relevant.

Give any comparisons with the experiences of other people (if possible and useful).

Explain any solutions that you have tried in order to deal with the situation and why nothing has worked.

Give evidence of your capabilities (if not known to the person who would agree to the accommodation).

Re-state the request, possibly in greater detail.

End as fits the document being written.

Example request for accommodation

Situation: dyslexic mathematician receiving support at university, including:
notes taken by a fellow student at lectures;
a university department organising support;
a support tutor;
a system of feedback between support tutors and the university department.

It was necessary for the student to attend the lectures in order to be eligible to receive the notes from the note-taker.

Email request: with copy going to subject tutor
Dear [name of person, or person's job title],

Can XX opt out of lectures and still receive the notes from the
note-taker?

I had email contact with XX before the beginning of term and
then didn't hear from him. Last week I contacted him, asking
whether the silence meant everything was OK or whether he
was drowning. It was the latter.

He came to see me this morning. Last week he got so
demoralised that he was considering giving up the course.

He has 9 lectures a week and is getting nothing from them. He
has compared experiences with a couple of other students.
One doesn't understand the lectures either, but she gets
enough so that she is able to use the relevant sections to
help her complete the problem sheets. The other finds that
in the end everything falls into place, and that the maths
doesn't all have to make sense immediately.

XX doesn't work like this; as I mentioned in the feedback sheet
last term, he needs to understand everything as he goes, to
build up the whole subject, and he cannot make progress
when there are gaps in his knowledge. He has tried to use
the on-line handouts before lectures so that he has some
framework to listen with, but the lecturers don't follow the
handouts and XX can't work out quickly enough how the
lecture relates to the printed pages. Also, the handouts are
very wordy so trying to understand them takes XX a long
time. He records the lectures and finds that a bit useful. At
the moment XX is spending 9 hours at lectures without
understanding them, and is getting nowhere.

On Sunday he decided to go back to his preferred way of
working and he solidly worked through all the maths relating
to his problem sheets, making sure he understands
everything. He managed to get the problem sheets done,
albeit one was late.

He used the notes made by the note-taker. They are bullet points, succinct and clear. Just occasionally he has had to find extra information from the on-line lecture handouts. They are a very good resource for him.

We have worked on trying to find a solution to the problem of the lectures, but I am not very hopeful within the current situation; the lectures are really 9 hours that take time and destroy his motivation and morale.

Can XX receive the lecture notes if he doesn't go to the lectures? Is an understanding of the way he needs to work and of the problems he is having with the lectures sufficient evidence? Can receiving the notes without going to the lectures be accepted as suitable accommodation for his dyslexia?

Best wishes
Support Tutor

Result of this request

XX was allowed to have the notes from the official note-taker even though he didn't go to the lectures. He had a conversation with the subject tutor, which resulted in a radical change to the way he worked on his course. He finished his degree.

References

Stacey, Ginny, 2019, *Finding Your Voice with Dyslexia and other SpLDs*, Routledge, London

Stacey, Ginny, 2020a, *Organisation and Everyday Life with Dyslexia and other SpLDs*, Routledge, London

Stacey, Ginny, 2020b, *Development of Dyslexia and other SpLDs,* Routledge, London

Stacey, Ginny, 2021, *Gaining Knowledge and Skills with Dyslexia and other SpLDs*, Routledge, London

Website information

Series website: www.routledge.com/cw/Stacey

Appendix 3:   Key Concepts

Contents

Book 1		*Finding Your Voice with Dyslexia and other SpLDs* (Stacey 2019)

Book 2		*Organisation and Everyday Life with Dyslexia and other SpLDs* (Stacey 2020a)

Book 3		*Gaining Knowledge and Skills with Dyslexia and other SpLDs* (Stacey 2021)

Book 4		*Development of Dyslexia and other SpLDs* (Stacey 2020b)

Useful Template on the website:

B1   Collecting Ideas that Relate to You

TEMPLATES

To Readers of Books 3 and 4

The appendices are written for dyslexic/ SpLD people.

Dyslexic/ SpLD people are the readership of books 1 and 2. They are the learners for books 3 and 4, so the appendices are written for them, even when they are not the direct readership.

Many people supporting dyslexic/ SpLD people are themselves dyslexic/ SpLD; therefore, many of the readers of books 3 and 4 may benefit by using the material in the appendices for themselves.

Templates on the website

B1 COLLECTING IDEAS THAT RELATE TO YOU
E1 LIST OF OPTIONS FOR THINKING PREFERENCES

Context

The books in this series are written to be used individually, but people's lives can't be separated quite so neatly. In any situation, you may need information from more than one book.

THINKING PREFERENCES are highlighted in orange in this appendix.

This appendix has summaries of many of the skills and knowledge that I cover when going over all that is useful in managing dyslexia/ SpLD. It has been included to allow the books to be used individually.

The book that covers each key concept is indicated by the icons and the coloured lines in the CONTENTS, and the coloured lines on the left hand side of the text.

1   Thinking clearly (pausing)

Pausing is the second element in both your *INDIVIDUAL, PERSONAL PROFILE OF DYSLEXIA/ SPLD* and your *REGIME FOR MANAGING DYSLEXIA/ SPLD. Finding Your Voice with Dyslexia and other SpLDs* (Stacey, 2019) discusses the benefits of thinking clearly and gives you several different methods for doing so.

Thinking Clearly in *Finding Your Voice with Dyslexia and other SpLDs* also discusses confidence and self-esteem. Maintaining good levels in these two states of being is important.

You need to practise some of the methods for pausing in order to experience the benefits. As you work with the ideas in this series of books, you will be able to reflect on what is happening for you. You can add your insights to your *PROFILE* and *REGIME*.

This section repeats 2 of the exercises from *Finding Your Voice with Dyslexia and other SpLDs*.

1.1   Breathing

If you switch on good breathing, you switch off panic, anxiety and many other unhelpful emotional states.   Focusing on your breathing allows you mental space to stop and step back from the immediate situation.

Tip: CAUTION

If you feel dizzy, get up and walk about, or hold your breath for a count of 10. Dizziness, from poor breathing, is caused by too much oxygen and you need to use it up by walking about or to retain CO_2 by holding your breath a while.

INDIVIDUAL, PERSONAL PROFILE OF DYSLEXIA/ SPLD: p 268

REGIME FOR MANAGING DYSLEXIA/ SPLD: p 268

Stacey (2019)

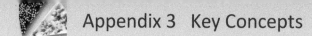

If you carry a lot of tension in your body, you may find it more useful to work through the relaxation *EXERCISE: PHYSICAL RELAXATION* before attempting the following exercise.

EXERCISE: PHYSICAL RELAXATION: p 287

Exercise: Breathing

First, see the *TIP: CAUTION* above.

During the exercise, as you breathe in you feel the sensations in different parts of your body; as you breathe out you let go of the sensations. You can imagine the out-breath flowing easily into each part of the body.

Sit comfortably and close your eyes.
     Breathe naturally while doing the exercise.
As you breathe in[1],

    feel the sensations in your:

face	and let go
neck and shoulders	and let go
arms and chest	and let go
stomach	and let go
buttocks and legs	and let go
whole body	and let it relax further

Repeat the cycle several times.

1.2 Relaxation

Being able to deliberately stop and relax is another way to give yourself the opportunity to pause well. Relaxation, however you do it, allows you to focus on the here and now and to step back from any situation that requires you to manage your dyslexia/ SpLD.

---

[1] When I lead this exercise, I usually say "As you breathe in" just once.
I say "feel the sensations in your (*name the part of the body*)" for at least the first cycle.
When it feels right, I just say the part of the body and "and let go".

Exercise: Physical Relaxation

Sit comfortably and close your eyes.

Tighten the muscles	of your face	and let go
"	of your neck and shoulders	"
"	of your arms, clench your hands	"
"	of your chest	"
"	of your stomach	"
"	of your buttocks and legs	"

Tighten your whole body and let go.

Repeat this cycle several times.

2   Using the mind well

Using the Mind Well is a chapter in *Finding Your Voice with Dyslexia and other SpLDs* (Stacey, 2019) which discusses many techniques and skills for thinking. A selection of the techniques is summarised here.

Stacey (2019)

2.1   Mind set

If your mind is expecting a particular subject, it is able to handle relevant information more effectively.
Take about 5 minutes to switch your brain onto the subject you are about to deal with. Recall to mind what you already know or what your most pressing questions are.

2.2   Chunking

Working-memory stores information more effectively when it is linked together in some way that makes sense to you. The packages of linked information are known as 'chunks'.
Deliberately notice the links between pieces of information, or create your own links if necessary, or if you prefer. The process of making links is known as 'chunking'.

Ⓖ p 303: chunking, working memory

2.3   Recall and check

You strengthen your memory of information, knowledge or skills by recalling what you know and then checking against a reliable source. Re-reading material is not nearly as effective.

2.4   Memory consolidation

Your memories of knowledge are made much more permanent by having a pattern of repeated recall and check. You start by recalling your knowledge the next day, then after a week, then after a month, then after 6 months.

Done efficiently, memory consolidation is an extremely effective strategy.

The same memory consolidation is required for memories of skills. 'Little and often' is a better time scale for skills.

2.5   Concentration

Concentration is often a problem for dyslexic/ SpLD people. As you observe the way you do things more precisely, you should look out for those places, times and conditions when you can concentrate easily. Gradually build up your knowledge of the things that help you and see how you can use them when you find concentration difficult.

2.6   Metacognition

Metacognition is the awareness of the fact that you are doing or thinking something; it is not awareness of how or why. Just by noticing what is happening as you manage your dyslexia/ SpLD you will be developing the skill of metacognition. Be positive about the things you notice: enjoy those things you do well; find ways that enable you to be positive about anything you don't do so well.

2.7   Objective observation

Ⓖ p 303: objective

Observation is most effective when it is objective. If you keep factual records and reduce any emotional aspect to a minimum, the way forward with anything you want to change will be clearer.

2.8   Reflection

Once you have collected some observations on a common theme, you can look at them all together and see what sense to make of the whole group together. This is the skill of reflection, which is helpful in making decisions.

2.9   Prioritising

PRIORITISING: p 256

PRIORITISING is also a skill for using the mind well. It is a section in APPENDIX 1.

2.10   A model of learning

There are various stages in learning when you need to pay attention to how you are processing information, these are:

Input: any time new information is given.

Immediate use: very shortly after input.

Feedback loop: when what is being learnt is checked against what is intended to be learnt.

Recall: information is brought back from memory some time after input.

Direct use: information and skills are used exactly as they were given.

Developed use: knowledge and skills are modified in some way.

Long-term memory: knowledge and skills are established in long-term memory, and can be recalled.

Understanding: an appreciation of significant concepts has taken place.

You might use different ways of thinking:

* for each stage of a task
* for different tasks
* at different times for any particular task.

You need to experiment to find out what works for you. You will often have to be quite determined about what's right for you, and not let others persuade you to adopt ways that you know don't suit you so well.

289

3 Thinking preferences

THINKING PREFERENCES are part of both the PROFILE and REGIME (Stacey, 2019). They are often key to a dyslexic/ SpLD person being able to function well. Often in this series there is a section on THINKING PREFERENCES.

Stacey (2019)

INDIVIDUAL, PERSONAL PROFILE OF DYSLEXIA/ SPLD: p 268

REGIME FOR MANAGING DYSLEXIA/ SPLD: p 268

It is unusual for people to pay attention to how they think, so the usual – orthodox – approach is to ignore how anyone is thinking. These thinking preferences can be seen as unorthodox simply because they are outside the orthodox approach.

The TEMPLATE: E1 - LIST OF OPTIONS FOR THINKING PREFERENCES has suggestions for using the different preferences.

TEMPLATES

One way to find out about your THINKING PREFERENCES is to use RECALL AND CHECK, together with MEMORY CONSOLIDATION; then to reflect on your ways of thinking.

RECALL AND CHECK: p 288

MEMORY CONSOLIDATION: p 288

Make sure you know what your preferences are and that you have the confidence to use them.

Attention is often given to visual and verbal aspects of communication and education. The same attention should be given to the kinaesthetic sense and to the RATIONALE OR FRAMEWORK. If the kinaesthetic sense and the need for a framework are part of your thinking preferences, do find ways to make sure these needs are met.

RATIONALE OR FRAMEWORK: p 291

3.1 The senses: visual, verbal and kinaesthetic

(taken from the GLOSSARY, ^G, p 303)
The five physical senses are vision, hearing, taste, smell, and kinaesthetic which is made up of touch, position and movement. The use of taste and smell to help use information is not covered in this series, although they are important for some people.

ⓖ p 303:
kinaesthetic sense, rationale, framework

See INDEX for examples in this book.

Words used in this series for acquiring and applying knowledge and skills through the different senses are:

Sense	Acquiring	Applying
Visual	Reading	Writing
Oral/ aural/ verbal	Listening	Speaking
Kinaesthetic	Doing	Taking-action

ⓖ p 303:
taking-action

'Kinaesthetic' is used as an umbrella term for the physical senses, by comparison with the visual sense or the verbal senses, aural or oral. The term also includes experiences that are primarily remembered through a connection with the physical part of the experience.

3.2   Rationale or framework

Some dyslexic/ SpLD people do not keep hold of information or understanding if they don't know what the overall rationale or framework is. Their minds don't retain the seemingly random information long enough for the framework to emerge; it has to be given in advance.

Ⓖ p 303: rationale, framework

3.3   Holistic vs. linear

'Holistic thinking is happening when a large area of a topic is held in the mind and processed simultaneously. An example is when you look at a scene in front of you, you see that scene as a whole. This type of thinking doesn't involve words, but you are definitely thinking.' (Stacey, 2019)

Stacey (2019)

'Linear thinking involves analysing and breaking topics into their component parts. Linear thinking is thought to be localised to definite areas for specific tasks, whereas holistic thinking is diffused over larger areas.' (Stacey, 2019)

3.4   Motivation

Two schemes for looking at individual differences between people are used in *Finding Your Voice with Dyslexia and other SpLDs* (Stacey, 2019):

Stacey (2019)

     Myers-Briggs Personality Type

     Multiple Intelligences.

In the context of this appendix, the most interesting characteristics from both schemes are the motivations that people have, and which some dyslexic/ SpLD people can use to help themselves think well.

3.4.1 Myers-Briggs Personality Type (MBPT)

The Myers-Briggs scheme is based on 4 mental functions and 4 attitudes. The scheme characterises people as:

4 mental functions:	4 attitudes:
sensing	extroverted
intuiting	introverted
thinking	perceiving
feeling	judging (deciding).

MARGIN NOTE:
Judging is used in the sense of being able to make decisions, not in judging right or wrong.

The motivations of the different types come from their approach to the world around them.

Mental functions

- **Sensing** people are practical, pay attention to the here-and-now, like practical skills and learning with their hands.
- **Intuiting** people focus on concepts, ideas and plans.
- **Thinking** people tend to be logical, to like structures and organisation.
- **Feeling** people engage with people dynamics and feelings.

Attitudes

- **Extroverted** people sort out their ideas with the people and environment around them.
- **Introverted** people sort out most of their ideas on their own, before engaging with anyone else.
- **Perceiving** people like to carry on gathering information.
- **Judging** people like to come to a decision.

3.4.2 Multiple Intelligences (MI)

The Multiple Intelligences scheme includes 8 different, independent intelligences. Most of the intelligences have overlap with the Myers-Briggs system, as far as motivation is concerned, so I don't use them. However there is one intelligence that is distinct and worth noting.

The **Naturalist Intelligence** involves accurate observation of the world around. People skilled with this intelligence are able to see parallels between topics or within a group of objects. They are able to classify ideas or objects and they instinctively sort information into categories.

3.5 'Other'

The list of thinking preferences has grown as I have worked with dyslexic/ SpLD people and tried to make sense of what happens to or for them. There was no point in trying to make them fit already known patterns, so I have always worked with a category titled 'Other'.

'Other' is a holding category that allows you to keep hold of experiences that don't fit any category you already know.

4   Useful approaches

You will be managing your dyslexia/ SpLD during everyday events and while you tackle tasks. *Organisation and Everyday Life with Dyslexia and other SpLDs* and *Gaining Knowledge and Skills with Dyslexia and other SpLDs* deal with the practical application of using your *PROFILE* and *REGIME*. The approaches summarised here are those that help you make a good start with most tasks.

Stacey (2020a, b)

4.1 Materials and methods

For many situations or tasks, you will want to collect information together. You should find out your best way of doing it. The options depend on how you think best.

Materials include: paper, recording device, computer; using colour; using pen or pencil with a suitable grip. You need to think how you manage your materials, e.g. being able to spread out can make a significant difference.

Methods include: making lists (linear thinkers); mind maps (holistic thinkers); doing for yourself (kinaesthetic learners); bouncing ideas off other people (Myers-Briggs feeling, extroverted people).

When something is working well for you, notice what you are using and how you are doing it.

4.2   Model for developing organisation

The model puts forward 5 steps that need attention in organisation:

Step 1	gather strengths
Step 2	assess hazards
Step 3	describe what needs organising
Step 4	recognise insuperable obstacles
Step 5	develop constructive ways forward.

Ⓖ p 303:
hazard, obstacle

By changing the text at step 3, this model can be adapted to work with different situations or tasks when no organisation is required.

As you work with the tasks and situations, record what happens for you. Have a system so that you can see what is working for you and you can deliberately make the progress you want.

4.3   Comprehension

To comprehend something is to have a mental grasp of it.

You need your mind to hold information together and for long enough so that you can understand, comprehend, what it is all about.

All the skills in this appendix will help with comprehension. Observe how you comprehend anything. Keep records so that you can reflect on your experience over time. Explore different approaches until you find the ones that work best for you.

4.4   Key words

Key words are the words that hold the essence of
an idea, a paragraph, a subject ...

Take something that you are very familiar with. Jot down some words that are most important for describing it. Cut the number of words down and find the fewest words that you feel comfortable with. These words should be the keywords of your chosen topic. Repeat the exercise over time, until you are good at producing a minimum collection of words to hold the essence of a subject.

When you can work well with key words, you can use them to give an overview of something or to help you sort out a main theme from minor details.

4.5   Know your goal

Knowing your goal is the 4th element of your *REGIME FOR MANAGING DYSLEXIA/ SPLD*. Quite often, when you are using *MENTAL ENERGY TO MANAGE DYSLEXIA/ SPLD*, you can do all the right things:

- observing what is happening
- pausing well
- deciding how to use your thinking preferences

but you still can't get matters under control and you still find yourself
        struggling in a circle.
Knowing what you want to achieve can help you to see the way out,
        or the way to resolve the situation.

Key words can help with knowing your goal. Learning how to hold your goal in a few keywords means it is much easier to stay focused and not get lost in a maze of ideas.

4.6   Planning

Planning is when you consider all the steps necessary to achieve a given outcome.

Almost all dyslexic/ SpLD people need to plan their work in order to minimise problems; for example, dyslexic people often write well when they have a good plan, but without a plan their writing will rarely reflect their ideas.

You need to find the level of detail that yields the result you want.

A big project can be broken down into smaller sections and separate plans constructed to achieve each section. This process makes the big plan less daunting and allows you to tackle it more readily.

REGIME FOR MANAGING DYSLEXIA/ SPLD: p 268

MENTAL ENERGY TO MANAGE DYSLEXIA/ SPLD: p 269

5   Aspects of dyslexia/ SpLD

You need to stay confident and positive in order to manage dyslexia/ SpLD. The aspects summarised here help you to know more about the characteristics of dyslexia/ SpLD so you are prepared for the inevitable fluctuations; the full discussions are in *Development of Dyslexia/ SpLD* (Stacey, 2020b).

Stacey (2020b)

5.1   Learned confusion

As a dyslexic/ SpLD person develops, certain patterns of confusion tend to become established in your brain, see *USEFUL PREFACE CONTEXT*. When you are older, you probably learn in better ways but you don't erase the original confused ways; they remain in your brain. They are there for your brain to activate.

USEFUL PREFACE CONTEXT: p 4

5.2   Oldest memory trace

When you unexpectedly need to think of something it is often the oldest memory trace that is used, not a later one. For example, you have learnt correct spellings, but when you use the words the older incorrect versions spring to mind.

5.3   Attention to learning

Most dyslexic/ SpLD people have to pay attention to all levels of a task; they do not learn subliminally. Reading a large number of books does not teach spelling.

Ⓖ p 303: subliminal learning

5.4   Average level of language skills a disadvantage

Intelligent students are often first recognised as being dyslexic/ SpLD at college or university, when they can no longer find ways round underlying problems. They have language skills that lift them above the group who are recognised as being in need of extra help at school, but those skills are not at the level of overall intelligence and the difference makes its mark in Higher Education.

5.5   4 levels of compensation

As you work on managing dyslexia/ SpLD, you gain skills and you become a 'compensated' dyslexic/ SpLD (McLoughlin et al., 2001).

McLoughlin et al. (2001)

There are different levels of compensation:

1   'People at level 1 are not aware of their weaknesses and have developed no strategies to overcome them.

2   'Those at level 2 are aware of their weaknesses but have not developed strategies to overcome them.

3   'People at level 3 are aware of their weaknesses and have developed compensatory strategies, but have developed them unconsciously.

4   'Finally, people at level 4 are aware of their weaknesses and they have consciously developed strategies to overcome them.'

The most important aspect is to realise that you do not remain consistently on any particular level. Even when you mostly operate as a 'compensated' dyslexic/ SpLD, i.e. on level 4, you may find you have dropped back into one of the less compensated ways of managing.

5.6   Pitfalls

Gradually, as you learn to manage your dyslexia/ SpLD, you will recognise certain things that often tip you into dyslexic/ SpLD functioning: these things are called pitfalls in the context of these books.

A pitfall is defined as 'a hidden or unsuspected danger, drawback, difficulty or opportunity for error' (OED Online, 2016).

('pitfall, n.'
OED Online, 2016)

I've divided pitfalls into 'hazards' and 'obstacles'. I've used the term 'glitch' for those moments when you notice a potential pitfall and deal with it immediately.

Ⓖ p 303: hazard, obstacle, glitch

5.7   Accommodation

Accommodations are adaptations put in place to address or reduce the problems caused by dyslexia/ SpLD; sometimes called 'reasonable adjustments' or 'provisions'.

There are certain situations in which a PITFALL of your dyslexia/ SpLD is very likely to be a significant issue, and it is known in advance. For some of these situations, e.g. exams and tests, accommodations are well established. Other situations may be specific to your circumstances.

5.8   Degrees of severity

Dyslexia/ SpLD is not like short- or long-sightedness: there is no equivalent pair of glasses that you can put on and find that the problems are reliably sorted. Learning 'coping strategies' gives you ways of dealing with issues, but you will constantly have to be putting effort into doing so.

I argue that 'degrees of severity' is not a useful concept. The statements usually used are that someone is 'mildly dyslexic/ SpLD' or 'severely dyslexic/ SpLD' as if this describes a static level of being dyslexic/ SpLD. The lived experience of dyslexia/ SpLD is that how you will be is variable and unpredictable.

It would be more useful to talk in terms of McLoughlin's 4 compensation levels (McLoughlin et al., 2001). For each person:

4 LEVELS OF COMPENSATION: p 60

McLoughlin et al. (2001)

What does level 4 consist of?

How well can the person maintain level 4?

How often does the person get triggered out of level 4?

How much time and effort are required to get back to level 4?

5.9   Stress

Stress usually makes the problems of dyslexia/ SpLD worse. You and those around you need to recognise this.

5.10   Benefits of recognising the problems

It is very difficult to do anything about problems that are not being recognised. When you know what your strengths are, and you realise you can make useful contributions, it is easier to acknowledge the problems and discuss them fruitfully with those around you.

References

McLoughlin, David, et al., 2001, *Adult Dyslexia: Assessment, Counselling and Training,* Whurr, London, 6th re-print

Series: *Living Confidently with Specific Learning Difficulties (SpLDs):*

Stacey, Ginny, 2019, *Finding Your Voice with Dyslexia and other SpLDs*, Routledge, London

Stacey, Ginny, 2020a, *Organisation and Everyday Life with Dyslexia and other SpLDs*, Routledge, London

Stacey, Ginny, 2020b, *Development of Dyslexia and other SpLDs*, Routledge, London

Stacey, Ginny, 2021, *Gaining Knowledge and Skills with Dyslexia and other SpLDs*, Routledge, London

Website information

OED Online, June 2016, Oxford University Press Accessed 29-30 August 2016.

Series website: www.routledge.com/cw/Stacey

Glossary

Contents

1 Table: Symbols

Symbol	Explanation
§	Symbol used to denote a section.
Ⓖ	Symbol used to indicate an entry in the GLOSSARY. The page number is to the beginning of the appropriate section of the glossary.
@ COMPANION WEBSITE	The symbol signifies material on the companion website, www.routledge.com/cw/stacey. The section of the website is indicated.
Book icon and blue line	Used in USEFUL PREFACE to show text that is significantly different from one book to another.
Peach strip inside the margin	Sections of the book in which 'you' specifically addresses a dyslexic/SpLD person.

2 Table: Specific Learning Difficulties (SpLDs) descriptions

Dyslexia/ SpLD is used in most of this book because dyslexia is the most researched and recognised form of SpLD and because the dual term keeps the variations in mind.

SpLD	Definitions from DfES Report (2005)
Dyslexia	'Dyslexia is a combination of abilities and difficulties; the difficulties affect the learning process in aspects of literacy and sometimes numeracy. Coping with required reading is generally seen as the biggest challenge at Higher Education level due in part to difficulty in skimming and scanning written material. A student may also have an inability to express his/her ideas clearly in written form and in a style appropriate to the level of study. Marked and persistent weaknesses may be identified in working memory, speed of processing, sequencing skills, auditory and/or visual perception, spoken language and motor skills. Visuo-spatial skills, creative thinking and intuitive understanding are less likely to be impaired and indeed may be outstanding. Enabling or assistive technology is often found to be very beneficial.'
Dyspraxia / Developmental Co-ordination Disorder (DCD)	'A student with dyspraxia/DCD may have an impairment or immaturity in the organisation of movement, often appearing clumsy. Gross motor skills (related to balance and co-ordination) and fine motor skills (relating to manipulation of objects) are hard to learn and difficult to retain and generalise. Writing is particularly laborious and keyboard skills difficult to acquire. Individuals may have difficulty organising ideas and concepts. Pronunciation may also be affected and people with dyspraxia/DCD may be over/under sensitive to noise, light and touch. They may have poor awareness of body position and misread social cues in addition to those shared characteristics common to many SpLDs.'
Dyscalculia	'Dyscalculia is a learning difficulty involving the most basic aspect of arithmetical skills. The difficulty lies in the reception, comprehension, or production of quantitative and spatial information. Students with dyscalculia may have difficulty in understanding simple number concepts, lack an intuitive grasp of numbers and have problems learning number facts and procedures. These can relate to basic concepts such as telling the time, calculating prices, handling change.'

Attention Deficit Disorder ADD AD(H)D indicates ADD with or without hyperactivity	'Attention Deficit Disorder (ADD) exists with or without hyperactivity. In most cases people with this disorder are often 'off task', have particular difficulty commencing and switching tasks, together with a very short attention span and high levels of distractibility. They may fail to make effective use of the feedback they receive and have weak listening skills. Those with hyperactivity may act impulsively and erratically, have difficulty foreseeing outcomes, fail to plan ahead and be noticeably restless and fidgety. Those without the hyperactive trait tend to daydream excessively, lose track of what they are doing and fail to engage in their studies unless they are highly motivated. The behaviour of people with ADD can be inappropriate and unpredictable; this, together with the characteristics common to many SpLDs, can present a further barrier to learning.'

3 Table: Acronyms

Acronym	Explanation
ADD, ADHD, AD(H)D	Attention Deficit Disorder with or without Hyperactivity
DCD	Developmental Co-ordination Disorder
DfES	Department for Education and Skills
HE	Higher education
MBPT	Myers-Briggs Personality Type
MI	Multiple Intelligences
NLP	Neuro-Linguistic Programming
OED	Oxford English Dictionary
SENCO	Special Educational Needs Co-ordinator
SLI	Specific Language Impairment
SpLD	Specific Learning Difficulty
STM	Short-term memory

4 Table: Words and phrases, alphabetical list

Entry	Explanation
Accommodation	Accommodation refers to adaptations put in place to address or reduce the problems caused by dyslexia/ SpLD; sometimes called 'reasonable adjustments' or 'provisions'.
Autonomy autonomous	Control over your life by self-determination: acting and thinking for yourself; independent; free; self-governing. An autonomous person has autonomy.
Brainstorm	Collect all your ideas or thoughts about something; collect them in a concrete way, either on paper or on a white board, etc, straight into a computer or using a recording device; the collection of ideas is then available for further processing. The initial stages of brainstorming are often not selective; all ideas are captured even if they don't seem very relevant.
Chaotic chaos theory	Chaos theory is a field of mathematics. 'Behaviour of a system which is governed by deterministic laws but is so unpredictable as to appear random owing to its extreme sensitivity to initial conditions'. (draft addition for 'chaos, n.' OED Online, 2016)
Chunk	A chunk is 'a package of information bound by strong associative links within a chunk, and relatively weak links between chunks' (Baddeley, 2007). The capacity of working-memory is discussed in terms of chunks that can be stored.
Chunking	The process of making strong links between pieces of information so that more can be stored in chunks in working-memory (Baddeley, 2007).
Confidence	Assurance arising from reliance on oneself (OED, 1993).
Doing See also KINAESTHETIC and SENSES	In this series of books, 'doing' is used to refer to acquiring knowledge and skills using the kinaesthetic sense.

Glossary

Entry	Explanation
Framework	A structure made of parts joined to form a frame; especially one designed to enclose or support; a frame; a skeleton ('framework, n.' OED Online, 2016).
Glitch	A sudden short-lived irregularity in behaviour (glitch, n.' OED Online, 2016). A glitch is a time when dyslexia/ SpLD has an effect on your behaviour, but you see it immediately and correct it. Any error is short-lived and there is no impact to prolong dyslexic/ SpLD functioning.
Goal	The end result of a task or activity. Knowing the goal of anything is often an important element in managing dyslexia/ SpLD.
Hazard	A hazard is a danger or a risk which you can take steps to deal with. 'Hazard' is used to describe one category of the pitfalls of dyslexia/ SpLD.
Innate	Existing in a person (or organism) from birth; belonging to the original or essential constitution (of body or mind); inborn, native, natural. ('innate adj. 1' OED Online, 2016)
Intelligence	'The faculty of understanding; intellect. Also as a count noun: a mental manifestation of this faculty, a capacity to understand.' ('intelligence n. 1' OED Online, 2016) A 'count noun' refers to something that can be counted. From this definition there is more than one intelligence.
Kinaesthetic See also PROPRIOCEPTION and TAKING-ACTION.	Used as an umbrella term for the physical senses, by comparison with the visual sense or the verbal senses, aural or oral. The term also includes experiences that are primarily remembered through a connection with the physical part of the experience.
Mind map	To map ideas in an organised, spatial way, with relationships shown by linking lines or branch structures. Sometimes called a spider diagram.

Entry	Explanation
Mind set	A process of switching your mind on to the topic you are about to work on: for study, for a meeting, for planning a project, etc. It is the equivalent of warm-up exercises before vigorous exercise. (Mindset as one word is something quite different.)
Neural networks	Neural networks are established when neurons repeatedly fire in set patterns. These set patterns are related to learning.
Neuro-Linguistic Programming (NLP)	NLP is about the mind and how we organise our mental life; about language, how we use it and how it affects us; about repetitive sequences of behaviour and how to act with intention. Some of the ideas from NLP are used in THINKING CLEARLY (Stacey, 2019). For further information, see O'Connor and McDermott (1996).
Neuron	A basic cell of the nervous system.
Neuron firing	A neuron fires a signal along its axon when the conditions in the neuron rise above a certain threshold; the conditions depend on all the many other neurons that input to that neuron.
Objective vs. subjective	Objective: existing as an object of consciousness, as opposed to being part of the conscious [person]. (OED, 1993) Subjective: of or belonging to the thinking [person]; proceeding from or taking place within the individual's consciousness.
Obstacle	An obstacle is something that blocks your way or prevents progress; you have to go round it, or avoid it. 'Obstacle' is used to describe one category of the pitfalls of dyslexia/ SpLD.
'Other'	'Other' is a useful category. Whenever I'm sorting something out, for myself or a student, I keep the category 'other' in mind or give it space on the sheet of paper I'm working on. I use it for anything that I don't want to forget and that doesn't fit into the categories I already have.

Glossary

Entry	Explanation
Paradigm	A conceptual or methodological model underlying the theories and practices of a science or discipline at a particular time; (hence) a generally accepted world view ('paradigm, n.' OED Online, 2016).
Pitfall	A hidden or unsuspected danger, drawback, difficulty or opportunity for error ('pitfall, n.' OED Online, 2016). Used as part of an individual's profile with respect to dyslexia/ SpLD.
Profile: Individual or personal	A representation of a structured set of characteristics of someone or something. A description of a person, organisation, product, etc.('profile, n.II.10' OED Online, 2016). The dyslexia/ SpLD profile used in this book is an outline of: 1 the thinking preferences 2 the dyslexia/ SpLD pitfalls 3 strategies for pausing 4 accommodations that need to be made. The profile is highly personalised and is the foundation for managing the dyslexia/ SpLD.
Proprioception	The reception of information by sensors which receive signals relating to position and movement ('proprioception, n.' OED Online, 2016); part of the kinaesthetic senses.
Pruning	Has been proposed as an idea to account for the reduction in synaptic connections that occurs during normal development (Kolb, 1995, p154).
Rationale	1 A reasoned exposition of principles; an explanation or statement of reasons 2 The fundamental or underlying reason for or basis of a thing; a justification ('rationale, n.2' OED Online, 2016).

Entry	Explanation
Regime	A way of doing things, esp. one having widespread influence or prevalence ('regime, n.2a' OED Online, 2016). The regime for managing dyslexia/ SpLD profile used in this book includes: 1 recognising the pitfalls 2 pausing 3 using best thinking preferences 4 knowing the relevant goal. The regime is highly personalised.
Schema	An (unconscious) organised mental model of something in terms of which new information can be interpreted or an appropriate response made (OED, 1993).
Self-esteem	Esteem: value, worth, favourable opinion (OED, 1993); hence self-esteem is valuing oneself.
Senses	The five physical senses are vision, hearing, taste, smell, and kinaesthetic, which is made up of touch, position and movement. The use of taste and smell to help use information is not covered in this book, although they are important for some people. Words used in this book for acquiring and applying knowledge and skills through the different senses are: *Sense* / *Acquiring* / *Applying* table below

Sense	Acquiring	Applying
Visual	Reading	Writing
Oral/ aural/ verbal	Listening	Speaking
Kinaesthetic	Doing	Taking-action

Entry	Explanation
Subliminal Subliminal learning	Subliminal: below the level of consciousness. Subliminal learning is learning which happens without conscious effort or attention; it simply happens alongside other learning or through everyday life.

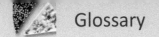

Glossary

Entry	Explanation
Taking-action	Used in this book to mean: 'applying knowledge and skills in a practical way through the kinaesthetic sense'. The hyphen is deliberate. See SENSES for the words used for acquiring and applying knowledge and skills via the different senses.
Thinking preferences	A major component of dealing with your dyslexia/ SpLD is to know how you think best (Stacey, 2019).
Working memory	Part of the mind/ brain which has the capacity for complex thought; it has temporary storage and its workings can be monitored and directed by conscious attention.

References

Baddeley, Alan, 2007, *Working Memory, Thought, and Action,* Oxford University Press, Oxford

Kolb, Bryan, 1995, *Brain Plasticity and Behaviour,* Lawrence Erlbaum Associates, Mahwah, NJ

OED[1], Brown, Lesley Ed in Chief, 1993, *The New Shorter Oxford English Dictionary on Historical Principles*, Clarendon Press, Oxford

O'Connor, Joseph, McDermott, Ian, 1996, *Principles of NLP,* Thorsons, London

Stacey, Ginny, 2019, *Finding Your Voice with Dyslexic and other SpLD,* Routledge, London

Website information

DfES Report, 2005, https://www.patoss-dyslexia.org/Resources/DSA-Working-Guidelines Accessed 10 June 2020

OED Online, June 2016, Oxford University Press   Accessed 29-30 August 2016.

---

[1] The online OED has been consulted every time, and the meanings are consistent. Sometimes the words used in the hard copy of OED (1993) are clearer, or more to the point in the context of this book; in which case the reference is to the hard copy edition that I have consulted.

List of Templates
on the Website

This table lists the *TEMPLATES* on the companion *WEBSITE* that are recommended in each chapter.

The sections on the *WEBSITE* are:

A: Aids for Reading

B: Gathering Insights

C : Individual, Personal Profile of Dyslexia/ SpLD

D: Regime for Managing Dyslexia/ SpLD

E: Thinking Preferences

G Developing skills

There is no significant difference between ✓ and ◊; having 2 symbols just makes tracking easier.

Website information

Series website: www.routledge.com/cw/stacey

Name of Template U-P is Useful Preface A1 – A3 are Appendices 1 – 3			✓ U-P	◊ 1	✓ 2	◊ 3	✓ 4	◊ A1	✓ A2	◊ A3
Jotting down as you scan	A	1	✓	◊	✓	◊	✓	◊		
Book mark – purpose	A	2	✓	◊	✓	◊	✓			
Book mark – profile & techniques	A	3							✓	
Jotting down as you read, with a few guiding questions	A	4	✓	◊	✓	◊	✓			
Collecting ideas that interest you	A	5	✓	◊	✓	◊	✓			
Collecting ideas that relate to you	B	1	✓	◊	✓	◊	✓	◊	✓	◊
Know your own mind	B	2							✓	
Compare expectations and reality	B	3				◊		◊		
Action, results, next step	B	4				◊		◊		
Recording template - 1 (4th column narrower for coding)	B	5						◊		
Recording template - 2 (4 equal columns)	B	6						◊		
Recording template - 3 (5th column narrower for coding)	B	7						◊	✓	
Recording template - 4 (5 equal columns)	B	8		◊		◊		◊	✓	
A calendar month for prioritising – 5 weeks	B	9						◊		
Questions to ask oneself to help observation	B	10						◊		
Monitoring progress	B	11				◊		◊		
Questions to ask a child to explore inner thinking	B	12				◊				

Name of Template
   U-P is Useful Preface
   A1 – A3 are Appendices 1 – 3
			✓
			U-P
				◊
				1
					✓
					2
						◊
						3
							✓
							4
								◊
								A1
									✓
									A2
										◊
										A3

Individual, personal profile of dyslexia/ SpLD (spatial)	C	1							✓	
Example individual, personal profile of dyslexia/ SpLD (spatial)	C	2							✓	
Individual, personal profile of dyslexia/ SpLD (linear)	C	3							✓	
2 Examples of an individual, personal profile of dyslexia/ SpLD (linear)	C	4							✓	
Managing dyslexia/ SpLD (mind map)	D	1							✓	
Managing dyslexia/ SpLD (linear)	D	2							✓	
Regime for managing dyslexia /SpLD (spatial)	D	3							✓	
Regime for managing dyslexia /SpLD (linear)	D	4							✓	
Experiences for managing dyslexia/ SpLD (linear example)	D	5							✓	

Name of Template U-P is Useful Preface A1 – A3 are Appendices 1 – 3			✓ U-P	◊ 1	✓ 2	◊ 3	✓ 4	◊ A1	✓ A2	◊ A3
List of options for thinking preference	E	1				◊	✓			◊
Table of thinking preferences (spatial)	E	2				◊			✓	
Example: Table of thinking preferences (spatial)	E	3							✓	
Thinking preferences (spatial)	E	4				◊			✓	
Thinking preferences (linear)	E	5				◊			✓	
The box 'Other'	E	7				◊	✓			
The function of 'round'	G	1				◊	✓			
Basic sentences from a complex one	G	5				◊	✓			
Eye span exercises 1&2	G	10				◊				
Eye span exercises 3	G	11				◊				
Check-list for researchers and assessors	H	1					✓			

Index

*in front of an entry marks a word or phrase that is in the *Glossary*, Ⓖ , p 303

The following may be useful *Index* entries:
(sub-entries are shown in brackets)

Reason	Entries	
to understand SpLD issues	manifest behaviour of SpLDs stories, key elements of experiences and examples new situations causing problems mind (SpLD experience)	compensation, levels of severity of SpLD, degrees of learning (learned confusion) persistence of SpLDs pitfall stress
to teach reading	reading recall from memory, remember scanning	motivation from thinking preferences learning (attention to) monitoring progress
to enhance learning	teacher (good enough) neurons (firing and wiring together) learning (important stages of) chunking observation, objective	techniques for using the mind well questions, generating useful thinking preferences language, teaching maths
to minimise problems in learning	whole school approach learning (attention to) new situations causing problems	place (a factor of learning) learning (subliminal) learning (rote) stress
to build the new paradigm	paradigm, new observation, objective learning (important stages of)	techniques for using the mind well thinking preferences feedback

Tip: To find a word in the text

If the word you are looking for doesn't show quickly, try running a ruler or envelope or other straight edge down the page. Doing this makes your eyes look at each line and you are more likely to find the word.

Occasionally, the entry refers to the context and not a specific word; so sometimes you need to read the text.

B B C SOUNDS

BRITISH LIBRARY

The BBC Listening Project records conversations between different people about many different kinds of experiences between people with a wide range of relationships.

Ginny and Sally — A Dyslexic Brain

Sally and I have enjoyed our journey working together on these four books and we recorded our thoughts about the experience for The Listening Project in April 2018. Though we are both dyslexic, our experience of dyslexia is quite different; we have different processing strengths and different ranges of problems. We are both positive about dealing with any problems and we both enjoy our various strengths. It has been huge fun working together, as we hope you can hear from our conversation.

An extract from our conversation is available on the BBC website at
https://www.bbc.co.uk/sounds/play/b0b1tmbl

The whole conversation is archived at the British Library and will be made available later this year (2020) at https://sounds.bl.uk

Full details of the recording can be found on the British Library's Sound and Moving Image catalogue at http://sami.bl.uk (search for C1442/1554).

Ginny Stacey and Sally Fowler
Photo by Louise Pepper for the BBC Listening Project

T - #0084 - 231020 - C348 - 246/189/15 - PB - 9781138207813 - Gloss Lamination